This Is My Life

Mary Byrne
with Eddie Rowley

THE O'BRIEN PRESS
DUBLIN

First published 2011 by The O'Brien Press Ltd
12 Terenure Road East, Rathgar, Dublin 6
Tel: +353 1 4923333; Fax: +353 1 4922777
E-mail: books@obrien.ie
Website: www.obrien.ie

ISBN: 978-1-84717-310-2

Text © copyright Mary Byrne with Eddie Rowley 2011

Typesetting, editing, layout, design © copyright
The O'Brien Press Ltd

British Library Cataloguing-in-Publication Data
A catalogue reference for this title is available from the British Library.

1 2 3 4 5
11 12 13 14

Editing, typesetting and design: The O'Brien Press Ltd
Printed and bound by CPI Group (UK) Ltd, Croydon CR0 4YY
The paper used in this book is produced using pulp from managed forests

The publisher would like to thank Mary Byrne, her family and her management team for permission to
include images in the picture sections. Other images courtesy of: Georgie Gibbon, picture section 2, page
1 (top); Getty Images, picture section 2, page 1 (bottom); Ken McKay/TalkbackThames/Rex Features,
picture section 2, page 2 (both); Maureen Grant, picture section 2, page 3 (bottom); Press Association
Images, picture section 2, pages 4 and 6 (both); Will Talbot, picture section 2, page 5 (bottom), picture
section 2, page 8 (top).

Dedication

To my daughter, Deborah

Acknowledgements

From the bottom of my heart, I want to thank all my family, friends and colleagues for their love and support through the decades. You have helped to make me the person I am today. I will never forget all the kindness I experienced during the low times in my life. And I have so many cherished memories of the good times, too. So thank you, everyone, you know who you are and many of you pop up in this book.

My thanks to all associated with 'The X Factor', from the judges to the staff working so hard behind the scenes to make me look good and to pick me up whenever I fell. Thank you all so much. It was a crazy, wonderful time in my life and it has opened up incredible opportunities for me.

Special thanks to my manager, Will Talbot, and all at Modest Management, including Richard and Harry, who keep me on the right path in my new career. I just couldn't do it without all you guys.

Finally, I never imagined that one day I would have my life story published as a book. I'm thrilled. I've laughed and I've cried as I relived my life while working on the book. I couldn't have done it without the help of my co-author, Eddie Rowley, and editor, Rachel Pierce. I'd also like to thank my cousin, Maureen, Uncle Jim's daughter, who helped me with some of my early family history.

Finally, thanks to all at The O'Brien Press for a lovely book.

Contents

Will the real Mary Byrne please stand up...

Sometimes it can feel like I'm leading a double life. There's Mary Byrne – Diva, who can scrub up and look glamorous and in control, but then there's Mary Byrne – Normal Woman, and that's the Mary who was born in a working-class suburb of Dublin, who was brought up by loving but broke parents, who got pregnant when she was young and dangerously in love with the wrong man, who suffers from depression and arthritis and who worked on a shop till for eleven long years while dreaming all the while about having the guts to be a singer. It seems crazy, even to me, that these two women are in the same body, but they are, and together they make life very interesting and, sometimes, a bit of a challenge.

I haven't really had time to digest all that has happened to me in the last two years, but one thing I'm grateful for is that 'The X Factor' and all the wonderful opportunities it has given me isn't what shaped my life. I was fifty years old when I entered the first public audition, so I was already a whole person with a whole life. When I looked at my young fellow contestants, I was very aware that this *was* them. But for me, standing up on that stage in front of the judges and viewing public, there was decades of a life lived feeding into that moment and making me who I was. That's what I put into my singing, that's where my voice came from – not from a desire for fame and fortune, but from a well deep inside me that had been sealed shut for many years while I struggled to find my own path and also to put food on the table for me and my daughter. When that spotlight turned to me and it was my turn, what people saw was me blasting the lid off that well and letting all of that emotion and dreaming and hoping and waiting flood out. Those performances, in fact every performance I do, is the merging of Diva me and Normal me. I'm fully myself up there and that's why I love it so much.

I've been asked to do lots of things since 'X Factor', so I suppose it was inevitable someone would suggest a book. When it did finally come up, I really had to sit down and think about it. I could have written an 'X Factor' book – a story of the dream being realised. That would have been easy, but it would have shown only one Mary to the world. If I'm going to do this right, I have to go back to the start and explain it all. There's fifty-one years of living going into every song I sing, and that's what I want this book to be, too – the story of the real Mary Byrne.

1. Officially, I was never born

Long before I got caught up in the whirlwind of 'The X Factor', there was always some kind of drama in my family. We're the kind of family where people make mistakes, take wrong turns and end up in places they never expected. It makes for some great stories and for some sad endings.

My father's mother, Mary Catherine Dunne, came from a rich farming family in the midlands of Ireland. She grew up an only child in Cloghan House, a big house on the Laois–Offaly border, near Portarlington. As the family had money, she got a decent education and qualified as a nurse. Her life was running smoothly until love intervened at the age of nineteen, when my grandad, James Byrne, then aged twenty-two, caught her eye. A handsome devil, he too came from farming stock, from a place called Ballyadams in County Kildare. Even though James was born and reared on a thriving farm, his family weren't as well-off as Mary Dunne's, so her parents felt that she was going out with someone beneath her and hoped it would end quickly. Of course, passion, lust and love are powerful forces in a person's life and my Granny Mary was so caught up in her great romance, there was no way she was going to be swayed by her mother and father, or by anybody else for that matter. Realising that she was never going to melt her parents' hearts towards the man of her dreams, Mary took a very brave stand: she turned her back on her family and eloped with Grandad Byrne.

After their marriage, they lived for a time on Grandad's family farm in

THIS IS MY LIFE

Ballyadams, with his widowed mother, before moving to Dublin. In the city, Grandad got a job driving the old trams while Granny worked in a hospital, making full use of her nursing skills. As life moved on, they established a newsagents and sweet shop in the Dublin southside suburb of Harold's Cross and were soon surrounded by a big Catholic family of seven boys – John, Eddie, Paddy, Dinny, Jim, Thomas and Tony – and two girls – Annie and Mamie.

Grandad Byrne's whole world collapsed when Granny died while having gallstone surgery in her early forties. Their second youngest child, Thomas, who would go on to become my father, was just five years old at the time. Amidst this terrible upheaval and trauma in the family, the eldest daughter, Mamie, stepped in to run the home and help raise her younger siblings. By all accounts, my Granny had been a beautiful human being. I can't even imagine the heartache my poor grandfather must have endured in the aftermath of her passing. It was obviously a desperate struggle for them all, losing the rock in their lives. They all had to pitch in to keep the family going. My Dad used to tell stories of how he'd get up at four in the morning to deliver newspapers and then back home for breakfast before going off to school. He also admitted to not going to school very often after that. People survive terrible things that come to test them in life and eventually my father's family came out the other end of that dark period.

My mother was born Elizabeth White, later shortened to Lily, and she was reared with her four siblings in Corporation Buildings, located in the heart of what was once Dublin's notorious red-light district, known as Monto. (Montgomery Street, which is near Talbot Street, is now called Foley Street.) They grew up dirt poor in very harsh times among salt-of-the-earth people. Grandad White was in the army and Nanny White also helped to make ends meet by working on a fruit-and-vegetable stall in the city. My sister, Betty, remembers her wearing an apron with a money bag around her waist, but I have no memory of her.

When my mother was twelve years old, the family moved out of Corporation Buildings and into a new home in Kimmage, on Dublin's southside.

My mother never learned to read or write, but she had an adventurous spirit and was keen on seeing what existed outside her little world in Dublin. She was small in stature, but had a lovely shape – she was 36-26-36. She had a fine bust and was very good-looking, with big brown eyes and gorgeous dark hair. There is an old photo of her in my home, which was taken when she was about seventeen. In it, she looks like a young Queen Elizabeth, the current Queen of England. She has that beautiful look of a film star.

In her teens, my mother and her friends used to go to the picture house (cinema) in Harold's Cross, and it was there that my father first spotted her. I don't know if it was love at first sight for him, but he certainly fancied her straight away because he made his move and asked her out on a date. My mother accepted and they started going out together, but the story didn't end there. There was another determined suitor on the scene … my father's brother, Tony. She started seeing Tony as well and was soon two-timing the pair of them. My mother would later claim that she didn't know they were brothers, as if that took the harm out of it.

She told me one story of how she had arranged to meet my dad, but then bumped into Tony in the park across from where she lived and he persuaded her to go to the pictures with him. The arrangement with my dad was that they would meet at the shops and go for a walk. She hadn't cancelled this arrangement, so my dad was still waiting for her at the corner, outside the shops, when he copped her and Tony leaving the cinema together and followed them back to my mother's family home. This led to a huge bust-up between the two brothers outside my mother's house in Kimmage. There was murder in the garden, with the two of them punching each other senseless. Grandad White had to come out and break it up, and then he sent the two of them on their way. After this, my mother had to make her choice: which one was she going to marry?

In the middle of all this great commotion in her life, Mam decided to emigrate to England. At this stage, she was only seventeen and still going out with my dad … and still seeing Tony, too! She headed off to Manchester, over to her brother who lived there, my Uncle Jimmy. He helped her get a job working in a local pub called The Hillman. She was employed there as a waitress, but somewhere along the line her talent as a singer emerged. At the end of the night the staff and customers would encourage her to stand up on a table and sing the Vera Lynn songs that were popular at the time. This was during the war and by all accounts my mother was a big hit with the customers, and they would throw money at her. She was delighted with her new life, but back home my father wasn't a very happy man.

By now, Tony had lost interest in her, but my dad, who was four years older than my mother, just couldn't get her out of his mind. From what I learned, he was finding it very hard to cope with the separation during that first year my mother spent in England. He would send her the odd letter, but he never got a reply because, as I mentioned, my mother couldn't read or write. He obviously wasn't aware of that, though, and must have thought she'd lost interest in him. She was in England a year when he decided to go over and see her in person. There was another shock in store for my poor father. He turned up in Manchester to find that she was going out with an American soldier called Andrew Gill. Still the little two-timer! I remember my mother saying one time that Andrew Gill was from Montana and that his mother had sent her a box of chocolates from America. During the war the American soldiers could get stuff through from the States. Mam later admitted that she wasn't mad about Gill; she just thought he was nice. He was young and very affectionate, by her account.

Dad was obviously completely mad about Mam because even after discovering her relationship with Andrew Gill, he was still determined to win her over. He went to my Uncle Jimmy's house and had a long talk with her. At the end, he insisted: 'You're coming home with me and we're going to get married.' She said, 'No, I'm not!' He said, 'Yes, you are!' Eventually, he persuaded her to come home and when they got off the boat, he ripped up her passport and told her she wasn't going away ever again. She was married at nineteen.

My Grandad Byrne wasn't very happy about his son marrying Lily White. It was history repeating itself: just as Granny's family had been opposed to her marrying him because they felt he was of a lower status, Grandad Byrne took the same view of my mother because she came from Corporation Buildings. Even though her family had got a house when those buildings were torn down, she was still a Corporation person and the prejudice remained. My grandfather was great with money and always had it, whereas Mam's family always struggled to get by. I suppose my grandfather was also a bit miffed that his two sons had been fighting over this two-timing lass, but it didn't matter – my Dad was determined to be with her. He loved her and he didn't care what anybody else thought. He would be crazy about her until the day he died. My father was a very good-looking man, nearly 6 ft tall with broad shoulders and a lovely warm smile. You knew you were welcomed when my Dad smiled, he just had it, whatever that is. He had a Mediterranean look and people would say he reminded them of the Hollywood actor Anthony Quinn. While most of my father's family, including his own father, had weight issues – and unfortunately passed them on to me! – he wasn't a fat man. He was lean and muscular and he had huge hands, like shovels. I remember looking at his hands and feeling safe. Even as an adult, I felt safe knowing that my Dad was there to protect me. I was very, very close to him. My Dad was a gentleman, and that's not just me saying that as his daughter. Anyone who met him and all his old workmates loved and cared for him. Everyone respected him because he was such a good man.

After they wed in 1945, Mam and Dad went to live with her mother in Kimmage. Children came along fairly quickly, and I'm sure the pair of them were shocked by the first arrivals – a set of twins, my brother and sister, Jimmy and Betty, who are twelve years older than me. Mam was very sick throughout that pregnancy; she was only a little woman and very thin. Next came another boy, in 1949, but this was a time of terrible heartache for my parents because he didn't survive. Then came my brother, Tomo, who is eight years older than me.

At that point my parents were able to move out of my grandmother's house because the Corporation gave them their own house at Kylemore Drive, in Ballyfermot. It was there that my brother, Willie, was born in the front bedroom in 1952. Seven years later, on 3 November 1959, I came into the world in that same bedroom.

My mother took very bad after I was born. She had a hard birth on me because I was a big baby. I was taken away from her that evening because she was haemorrhaging badly, and I was brought to the Coombe maternity hospital. But the next day she said to Dad, 'Go and get my baby.' My Dad came in on 4 November and took me home to Ballyfermot, and I was christened in a church on Francis Street on 6 November. Those events took place very quickly because Mam was so afraid that something was going to happen to me, or to her seeing as she was so ill. We both thrived, of course, and I recall how over the years, whenever I was bold, Mam would say to my Dad, 'Are you sure you took the right child out of that hospital?' Parents can unwittingly cause damage to their children and that expression of my mother's cut deep. It gave me a bit of a complex because I can remember thinking as a child, 'I don't think my Mammy wants me.' It created an emotional upheaval in my head, even though she wouldn't have meant it and was only joking.

I think I was born into this world to cause trouble. There is no official record of me having been born, for a start, because amid all the toing and froing after my birth, no one remembered to register me. My mother presumed that the doctors in the hospital had done it. So, officially, I was never born. To this day, I have never yet had myself registered. I got my passport by using my baptismal certificate. In my early adult years, one of the companies I worked for, CB Packaging in Clondalkin, sorted out my passport for a business trip to Germany and France. If it wasn't for that company, I wouldn't have got a passport at all. They made a huge search in the Customs House in Dublin, but there was no record of me. I was then issued with a passport based on my baptismal certificate and a letter from the Customs House, which I still carry around with me. For years, I've been threatening to go and register my own birth; I was told that my sister or brother could come in as a witness. The other witnesses are all dead and buried – my parents and the doctor who delivered me. It's now on my top priority To Do list, which means I should get to it by 2020, if I'm lucky! You know, with old age looming, you have to get yourself registered as actually being alive.

2. From Manchester to Ballyfermot

Before I was born, when Mam was pregnant with me, she used to pray to Our Lady and say: 'If it's a little girl with brown eyes, I'll call her Mary.' I don't have brown eyes, mine are hazel-green, but she called me Mary anyway. She was thirty-five when she had me and she went through menopause soon after. She wasn't a very well woman when I was little. When she was forty, she was in the change of life big time. I remember how, as I got older, I used to probe her about personal things and ask her all kinds of intimate questions that my sister, Betty, who was twelve years older than me, would never have asked. Although it made my Mam very uncomfortable, she would eventually open up to me in a way that not many of her generation would have, I think. She appreciated the fact that I would wait until Dad had gone to bed before I asked her about certain things.

During one such conversation, my mother confessed that she felt sorry for Daddy. I asked her why and she said, 'Because I took it away from him at a very young age.' At the time I didn't know what she meant, but later I realised she was talking about sex. She had taken those privileges away from him because she had gotten to the change of life and didn't like having sexual relations with him anymore. That would have been when she was around the age of forty and as my father was only four years older, he was still a young man. I remember her telling me that, and it had obviously haunted her; she couldn't understand why he stayed with her. Remembering those conversations today, I feel that my mother was quite lost in herself and that I probably inherited my low self-esteem and insecurity from her.

People who knew her or met her would always say, 'Ah, Lily is a great woman, the heart and soul of a party.' But she was very lost, very lonely. I know that after they passed away, she missed her parents terribly, despite not having got the emotional love from them that she needed, as I discovered from our conversations. I never met my maternal grandparents. My sister Betty had known them and I believe that they were lovely, though apparently Grandfather White was quite strict. My Nanny was a soft woman, but she could be quite stern as well – not like my mother, who was a big softie through and through. Nanny was more like my Aunt Mary, my mother's older sister, who was a divil in her heart. She was one of those women who didn't care how she got something, as long as she got it. Nanny would possibly have been like her, but not to the same extent.

Aunt Mary was seven years older than my mother and she had her way of doing things. Her brother, my Uncle Willie, lived with Aunt Mary for years, and he used to have one of those televisions that you rented, which were common at the time. Uncle Willie worked for the Department of Posts & Telegraphs (P&T) and wasn't there in the daytime when the television man would come to collect the rent, so he'd leave money with Aunt Mary. Whatever money was left over went straight into Aunt Mary's purse. She'd never pass on the change to Uncle Willie. And she used to rob money out of his trouser pockets, too. Oh, she was a demon! I loved her, though.

Aunt Mary was one of those independent women who went out and had four children before she got married … by four different men! I don't think she was a bad person for having all those different relationships. I'd say she was just looking for love, but the men she chose let her down. I knew her very well and she could be quite cunning, but I suppose she had to be to survive. We lived in the Crescent in Ballyfermot, and she lived just around the corner from us. While she could take the shirt off your back, she could also be very generous. I remember how Mam and Dad and all of us children moved in with her for a short time while we were waiting for our Corporation house. We had come back to Ireland after spending some time in Manchester and we all moved into her parlour, the room at the front of her tiny house that was kept 'for best'. The whole seven of us – and our big Alsatian, called Rex – were cooped up together in that room. To me, it was an adventure, but it must have been a very difficult time for my parents.

The reason we had gone over to England was because Dad had no work and Mam had run up debts. My mother was a terrible woman for buying things on the 'Never Never'. She ended up owing a lot of money for furniture and stuff like that. With no work going at home, my father decided to head off to England and try his luck there. He said to my mother, 'Look, I'll have to do something because we can't pay for this.' He went ahead of us, just taking my brother, Tomo, with him on the cattle boat from the docks in Dublin to Liverpool. Even though he was only a young child at the time, Tomo remembers the cattle boat and describes the stink of the animals and the smell of sweat and vomit from the humans. But he said it was a great adventure all the same. When they reached England, they went straight to Uncle Jimmy, my mother's brother, in Manchester.

Dad quickly got a job doing a bit of labouring and he sent over for Mammy and the rest of us. I was just six weeks old at the time and Grandad White was devastated to lose his baby granddaughter. I remember Mam telling me that he cried to her, 'You're taking that little baby away from me. I won't be here when you get back.' She said, 'Of course you will, don't be silly. I'm only going over because we need to get some work.'

In Manchester, we lived above a butcher's shop for a long time. I remember Betty, Jimmy, Willie and Tomo telling me the things they used to get up to there. Even though Dad was working, he wasn't earning a great deal and sometimes Mam wouldn't have milk for me. There was a little shop on the corner and my sister and three brothers would rob milk from it. Betty was sent in as the decoy and she'd go and chat to the shopkeeper and keep him distracted while the rest of the gang put their plan into action. The three boys would sneak in behind her and rob bread, milk and eggs. They got away with it for months, but one day the shopkeeper spotted what was going on and nabbed Betty. The three boys scarpered, leaving their sister to face the music. The shopkeeper roared, 'I'm going to see your mother and father! You better get back home now and tell them what you've been up to.' Betty remembers weeing herself with the fright. At least they weren't robbing for themselves or for plain badness. They were robbing for the family and they brought home the milk for me. They didn't want Mam worrying about having to provide bread and eggs. She knew where they were getting it from and used to give out yards to them when they came home with their loot, but they still went out and did it again.

There was a major family drama in Manchester, when I was about six months old. Jimmy, my eldest brother, was left minding me while Mam hung out the washing. Apparently, Jimmy put me up on the table to amuse me, and the next thing my mother heard a bang. When she ran inside, Jimmy was gone and I was lying on the floor. My mother started screaming, 'The baby is dead! The baby is dead!' I obviously have a hard head because there wasn't a bother on me, but as far as poor Jimmy knew, he had killed me. He disappeared out of sight in a flash. After my mother got over the shock of finding me on the floor and realised that I was alright, she went searching for Jimmy. He was nowhere to be found in the house and there wasn't a sign of him on the streets either. When several hours passed and Jimmy still hadn't been found, Mam became frantic and alerted the police.

Although at first they treated it as a minor incident, Jimmy's disappearance became a major police matter when they failed to trace him overnight. By now everybody, including my distraught parents, had begun to fear the worst when two days passed and the police were still no nearer to finding any clue as to what had happened to young Jimmy Byrne. He seemed to have disappeared off the face of the Earth. It wasn't until the third day that the mystery was finally solved, when he suddenly turned up in the house. He had been hiding, like a fugitive, in the attic all along! He only came down after finding a big jar of pennies that some previous tenant had stored there and obviously forgotten about it, so that was Jimmy's peace-offering. He thought that Mam would be so delighted with all the money, she'd forgive him for killing me. Jimmy says he remembers coming down and giving the jar to my mother and then Dad getting him by the ear and telling him off for putting everybody through that ordeal.

Betty has a store of memories about Manchester and describes how she used to drive our brothers mad in the house by constantly singing. They were always screaming at her to 'Shut up!' but Betty would ignore them and continue singing to her heart's content. They warned her that they would get their revenge, but she turned a deaf ear to their threats. The toilets were outside the house, but a bucket was used indoors in case someone needed to go during the night. On this particular night, Betty was in the bedroom, singing away as usual, and the brothers had had enough. They went out and got the wee-wee bucket and filled it with water and put it at the end of the stairs when they knew that Betty was on her way down to the living room. There wasn't much light in the house and, of course, Betty walked straight into the bucket and collapsed on the floor with water spewing out all over her. She says she'll never forget the fright she got, thinking it was wee. Betty discovered the hard way that it wasn't a good idea to mess with the brothers!

During our time in Manchester we moved from one house to another. The places we stayed in, I'm told, were all old buildings that needed a lot of work, but nobody bothered to do them up. In one house where we lived there was an old marble fireplace that had come loose from its sockets. Mam said that when she would light the fire, she had to put up poles against it, to make sure it didn't fall. One day Uncle Willie, who by then had come over and was living with us, was sitting reading the newspaper. I was around three years old and I was running around the place like a wild animal. All the floorboards were loose and creaking. Uncle Willie described how he glanced away from the paper just in time to see the heavy marble fireplace falling away from the wall and heading towards me. As they told the story years later, Mam remembered Willie screaming, 'Oh my God! The child will be killed.' The fireplace struck me, knocking out my shoulder, but Willie had sprung out of his chair like lightning, and with the weight of his body he prevented it from crushing me to death.

After three years in Manchester, we moved home to Dublin. My parents had given our old house back to the Corporation when they left for England, so that was when we moved into Aunt Mary's parlour, where we all slept together on a big mattress on the floor. This was the good side of my Aunt Mary, putting us up like that, but there would be always a darker tale, too. One of the family later told me that when we went to Manchester, Mam arranged for Aunt Mary to collect the children's allowance and hold onto it for her. But Aunt Mary was spending it while we were away. So the money that should have been saved over the three years we were in England was gone. Mam still forgave her, though, crazy as that seems. No matter what Aunt Mary did, my mother didn't have the heart to fall out with her. I mean, Aunt Mary's own kids would say she was a demon in disguise, but no matter what she did, we all loved her.

Those early days back in Dublin were hard. We lived on beans on toast because my Dad had no work. Even though we were struggling, Dad still kept his sunny side out and he'd entertain us on winter nights in front of a big fire in the parlour by telling us stories. Those memories have never left me and they're part of the reason why I think that, despite the hardship, my childhood was primarily a happy one.

Dad finally got a job with a building firm called McLaughlin & Harvey and he would go on to spend nearly forty years with them. He was a bricklayer, a scaffolder and a Jack-of-all-trades – he could turn his hand to anything. The day he got the job, you'd think he had won the Lottery. He was thrilled because he was finally providing for his family again. He was a real family man. I remember watching out for him coming home from his first day on the new job and running out Aunt Mary's gate to greet him when I spotted him cycling up the street. I ran up to him and he put me up on the crossbar. He was full of the joys of life.

Mam went to the Corporation to look for a house of our own, but there were no houses available in Ballyfermot. Before we got the house that would become our final family home, the Corporation gave us temporary accommodation in Keogh Square, Inchicore. We all went down to have a look at it the first time, and everyone was bitterly disappointed. It was a very dismal place, they all agreed. Even though I was very young, it even looked creepy to me. At the time, Keogh Square was an old English barracks and it was grey, damp and full of mice and, for all I know, the odd rat or two.

My parents' bed was in the sitting-room and one night as I was sleeping between them, shortly after we'd moved in, I woke up to hear scratching sounds. Then I noticed that my Dad was getting his torch from beside the bed – this must have disturbed me – and when he pointed it towards the kitchen, I could see what to me looked like millions of mice running along the top of the cooker. Dad said, 'Don't be frightened.' He got up and grabbed a sweeping brush to swish them away and they scattered all over the place. I'm sure they all came back when we were asleep again. Maybe it happened every night, but I remember that one night so well.

My sister had a bedroom to herself and the three boys were in the second bedroom. Betty's bed was one of those old metal ones with a big metal headboard. She had pictures of Elvis Presley on the wall and she wore her hair in a big beehive. I really looked up to her. Willie, Tomo and Jimmy used to hang around with Johnny Doran, whose family lived a few doors down from us. There was an archway in our block where it was said you could hear a ghostly woman screaming in the depth of night. According to local legend, she had been murdered in the archway by her own son. I remember one night pleading to sleep in Betty's bed and she didn't want me to be there because I was just a nuisance to her. 'You're going to be frightened out of your life, I'm telling you now,' she declared, trying to put me off. But I didn't care, I just wanted to be with my big sister. Johnny Doran was staying in the house that night and the boys decided to play a trick on him. 'We'll go around to the archway to listen to the screaming lady and you'll see the son coming at you with a hatchet,' they told him. Willie and Tomo stayed behind in the house and the plan was that they would pretend to be the ghosts and frighten Johnny. On the way, however, Jimmy told Johnny what the two boys were up to and they decided to turn the tables by banging on the bedroom window to terrify Willie and Tomo. Somehow they lost their bearings out in the dark and rapped on the wrong window. It was Betty's room. She leapt from the bed screaming, and so did I. My father ran out to see who was being murdered and when he found out the divilment the boys had been up to, he battered the whole lot of them. Then he barred Johnny Doran from staying in the house. I was still crying from the fright and I remember my father carrying me down the dark corridor and telling me, 'You're alright, you're alright,' as he tried to calm me down.

I started school in Inchicore, when I was four years old. The school was situated at the back of our house and I used to climb through a hole in the wall every morning to get into the schoolyard. I had been there for about a year-and-a-half when we got offered what was to become our final family home, in Ballyfermot Crescent. I vividly remember the day I first saw our new house on the Crescent. Willie, Mam and myself went up to look at the new place and I was dancing with excitement. It was a modest two-bed house, but it looked really modern and compared to the dingy place in Keogh Square, it was palatial. Only one other family had lived there before us, so it was practically new, too. The front door was lime-green with lots of glass. Mam opened it and my first memory is of the bare floorboards stretching off through the house. I remember racing through the rooms and darting upstairs to see the bedrooms. My biggest thrill was discovering a bathroom upstairs – this was the first time we had an indoor toilet. Willie and myself kept pulling the chain and flushing it until Mam shouted, 'Stop! Stop! You'll break the chain.'

There was a tiny fireplace in the front room, with two rings on the side for cooking over the hot coals. They slid back and forth, over the fire. When we moved in we had no electricity as it hadn't been switched on yet. We had very few possessions to bring with us, and I remember the first thing Mam did was to scrub the floors until they were gleaming. On our first night Mam cooked sausages and rashers in the frying pan in the fireplace, as there was no cooker. Many a time in the years that followed we would cook on that open fire when the electricity had been cut off because we couldn't afford to pay the bills. Mam had the fire blazing the night we moved in. The frying pan was sizzling on the ring that was directly over the fire and there was a can of beans in a saucepan, ready to go on. A big pot of tea sat brewing beside it. We were all served sausages, rashers and beans on two large slices of bread, with the butter oozing across it. It was lovely because we didn't get that treat very often, and I sat there lapping it up. I preferred that kind of food to the dinners we normally ate, like healthy stews. That house, small and all as it was, became our mansion. We all knew this was home, this is where we would settle. I don't know how we knew it, but we did. The Byrnes had found their place in the world.

3. A very Dublin childhood

I was never going to be a star pupil in school, but I always had a good brain and I copped on to things very quickly. Maybe I could have been an achiever academically if I'd applied myself better, but as it happened I got my education from life more so than from school. That was just the type of child I was. I knew from an early age that I was advanced for my years and had a more open mind than the majority of children I hung around with. I'd say it probably came from having a sister twelve years older than me who I looked up to – I was always trying to be like Betty and having older siblings meant I heard more than the average young kid would have been exposed to. I was sensitive and prone to having my feelings hurt easily, but I wasn't as vulnerable or as gullible as most children of my age, and that's what saved me one day when I was seven years old and I was confronted by evil.

My mother had a little routine whenever she had to do grocery shopping: she'd drop into Hardy's pub, in Ballyfermot, with Aunt Mary, for a tipple, usually a glass of Guinness, as they sauntered home with their groceries. It was summertime and I was off school. Kids were playing in the playground as I headed down to the shops to meet Mam and Aunt Mary. They had been gone from early morning and it was now one o'clock in the afternoon, so I knew they were probably in Hardy's with their shopping before they continued on their way home to make the dinner.

Shortly after leaving my house, as I made my way along the street, a car pulled up suddenly right in front of me. The driver rolled down his window and said, 'Hello, Mary' – he must've heard someone say my name. I just said hello back, but I knew that I didn't know him. He asked me where I was going and I told him I was going up to my Mammy. He said, 'Where's your Mammy?' I said, 'She's up in Hardy's.' 'Get in,' he said pleasantly, 'I know your Mammy. Your Mammy's name is ...' and of course, I said stupidly, 'Lily.' Then I added, 'No, you're alright. I'll walk up.' But he kept saying, 'No, come on. Get in.' I started backing away from the car. All around me everybody was just going about their business, but at that moment the world to me seemed to be moving in slow-motion. 'Come on!' the car driver said again, 'I have sweets here as well.' Those were the exact words he said. I remember what he looked like: he had very dark hair, piercing blue eyes and a bit of a beard. He had an off-white shirt with short sleeves and a grey, V-necked tank top over it and a loosened tie. I probably thought of him as an old man back then, but now I'd say he was in his late twenties/early thirties. I still remember it all so well. It was a big black car. It probably wasn't that big, but to me it was huge. I stepped back from the road, and with that I took off like a feckin' greyhound back to my house. He revved up the car and shot off down the road.

The keys of our house used to hang down the back of the letterbox and I grabbed them and burst through the door. Betty was in the house and as I stood there, with my heart beating like mad against my chest, she asked me, 'What are you doing back?' I just said, 'Oh, I forgot something,' and ran up the stairs. I never told her or any member of the family about that incident. I didn't know what he was planning to do, but instinct told me that I was in danger. Some time later I heard either on the radio or from my mother that a young girl had gone missing from around the Ballyfermot area. I don't know what happened to her, maybe she had just got lost, but I remember saying to myself, 'Oh that could have been me!'

Afterwards, I pushed the whole thing out of my head and 'forgot' about it, but that incident has been stored away in the back of my mind since then. That whole day is gone except for that specific moment – kids playing on the swings and in the sandpit in the playground, mothers talking at doors and this guy stopping in front of me. Incredibly, nobody around me copped on to the stranger trying to get me into his car. We had been taught in school to stay away from cars. If somebody calls you over, we were told, stand way back and run away if you feel you're in danger. Each time he spoke to me, I moved my feet backwards another bit. He saw I was doing it because I could see him getting anxious. That's when he mentioned the sweets. I could see them on the seat beside him, the sweets in a bag. 'Just jump in,' he kept saying. Real nice. I ran and I didn't look back. I'll never forget it as long as I live.

I buried that for a long time. It's another of the reasons I became insecure in myself, because I always wondered why he picked on me that day. Why me? Today, I realise he wanted to do something horrible to me, but at the time I just knew that I wanted to get away from this man. I don't think I went outside my front door for about three days after that. I wouldn't go up towards the playground. I just stood on my garden gate and swung back and forth. I hung around the house. I wouldn't leave the safety of it unless I was with my Mam or Dad. It put a fear in me. And I still have that fear sometimes when a car comes up behind me, even though I'm now an adult. If a car comes behind me without me hearing it, I get a fright and tell myself, 'Just keep walking, Mary.' I still get that horrible sensation that there's something sinister about to happen. It's amazing how big an effect things that happen in childhood can have on you and for how long. I didn't realise how much that incident had affected me until I got older.

That was one bad experience, but for the most part my childhood was a great one. Like all kids, I remember Christmas being particularly magical.

At Christmastime, I still love going to the Midnight Mass because that was the tradition in our family when I was growing up. Mammy always had a big red candle in the parlour, which she'd light after Midnight Mass down at our local church. Then I'd kneel down with her and say a few prayers. The idea behind the lighting of the candle at that early hour of Christmas morning was that you were bringing the light of Christ into the world because it's his birthday, the day he was born – that's what we were taught. And then on Christmas morning, when we got up, the candle was lit again because we were welcoming his birth into the world, and I still do that to this day. On Stephen's Day it's lit once more, but then it's not lit again until New Year's Eve, when you're saying goodbye to the old year and welcoming in the New Year and hoping that Christ is staying with you. That's the tradition I was brought up with and I observe it still.

Christmas Eve was very exciting as Mam and Dad prepared for the festivities the following day. Dad would clean the turkey and cut off its head and legs – the butchers didn't do that for you back then – and then he'd chase us around the house with the bird's claws. After he'd prepared the turkey for the oven, Dad would go up to the County Bar for a pint. My Mam would then tie rags around her feet and polish the whole linoleum floor. She was very house-proud when she was younger. We'd slide all over the floor and polish it at the same time. It was great craic. The radio would be playing American country singer Jim Reeve's Christmas songs and we'd be skidding all over the place, laughing our heads off.

After all that we'd go to Midnight Mass and upon our return home, the red candle was lit. Mam then knelt down to pray and myself and Willie would stand behind her, with Willie making faces while I was trying to look angelic. We'd be hyper with excitement, but sent off to bed anyway. Most kids we knew were in bed early, but my Mam was different. She'd say, 'Well, Santa will come when you're asleep.' It didn't matter if we went to bed early or late, so we'd go to bed about half-past twelve and be asleep in seconds because we'd be so exhausted by then. I know it's a late time for children to go to bed, but it was Christmas. Next morning we'd be up at 8.00am for our presents.

My earliest memory of Santa Claus is from our first Christmas in our new home at Ballyfermot Crescent. I was five-and-a-half. I used to sleep between my Mam and Dad and I remember waking up with my arm around Daddy's neck. I looked across the room and my eyes jumped out of my head when I saw a pram and a huge white-haired doll that was too big to fit into it. The doll was wearing a nappy and the pram was made of tin, with transfer stickers on it. Daddy took my hand and said, 'See what Santa brought you, Mary!' I jumped out of bed and ran over. The doll was nearly as big as me and I loved her like no other, but right then I was really, really excited about the pram. It was old-fashioned, like a Victorian pram. Since the doll was so big, I had to put her sitting in the pram as she was too long to lie down in it. I remember standing with the toys and looking back to the bed, and there were Mammy and Daddy, smiling at me. Willie was there, too, in his bed. There were only two bedrooms and he wouldn't sleep with the boys. He was a real Mammy's boy, and he loved my Dad to bits as well. Willie looked up and called out, 'What did you get?' I almost shouted, from the excitement, 'I got a pram and doll!' He got up and shot downstairs, where his stuff was waiting for him under the Christmas tree. Other presents I remember getting included a little cookery set, which I adored. Another year, Willie and I got a table-tennis set. We battered each other over that. We also got the same duffel coats, which were mauve in colour. We wore them for Christmas and then we never saw them again – they probably went to the pawn shop.

My fondest memories are of the Christmas dinners and the parties in our home. It was the only day we all sat around together to eat – me, my Mam, Betty, the boys, Uncle Willie and Daddy. We'd have our dinner and the radio would be on. Even if we did have a television, the programmes didn't start until six in the evening; until then all you'd be looking at was a test card. The red candle would be lit in the middle of the table. We had the traditional dinner: turkey, ham, roast potatoes … and cabbage cooked in the bacon water. Dad loved pigs' trotters, so Mam would have to buy two or three of them. We'd all have one of the trotter bones to suck on at some stage and I loved them as well. My Dad would also have a pig's tail with his turkey and ham.

The house party would start about five o'clock in the evening. As my brothers got older, they would pool their money together to buy two kegs of Guinness, with taps. Then they'd put up a sign saying, 'Jimmy and Tomo's Bar'. It was mostly family at the party, though a couple of friends might drop in now and then. Aunt Mary would come and a few of the other aunts and uncles who lived near us. The party started early and finished before midnight. It would continue again on St Stephen's Day, then the barrels of Guinness wouldn't be touched until New Year's Eve.

The sing-songs in our home at Christmas are what I remember with great fondness, and the warm atmosphere of the family being together. I loved it; it was just brilliant. I'm not saying everything was perfect, we had our arguments of course, but Mammy was great at defusing rows. If there was trouble looming over someone breaking something or somebody getting aggressive, she would start a sing-song to calm things down. It always worked. We weren't the Waltons, but I'm sure plenty of families had rows over Christmas.

Apart from Christmas, my other very happy memory of that time is the annual trip to Wicklow. Although born and bred in the city suburbs of Dublin and being a complete townie, I did get a taste of country life as a school child when the St Vincent de Paul Society (SVP) took us children on trips to the hills and countryside in County Wicklow, which is also known as the 'Garden of Ireland' because of its scenic beauty. As I recall, we stayed on a farm called Oakwood and it was beautiful. I remember there was a big lake near a bridge and they told us that a 'White Lady' could be seen sitting there at night. We'd all be taken on a 'Ghost Walk', under the stars at midnight on a summer's night, and trek down to this bridge to see the ghost of the 'White Lady'. We were supervised by the adults from the SVP, but of course the boys would be jumping out of the bushes to frighten the life out of us girls. We never did see the ghost, but we all believed that she was there. We'd be brought on walks in the lashing rain to see a haunted house – it was just a barn that had burnt down, but to us it was a haunted house – and we'd hear a story that never happened, but we'd believe it. We even believed there was a handprint of the ghost who'd returned, and when it was pointed out to us, we'd gasp, 'Oh my God!'

Oakwood was a working farm and it had pigs. Whenever we went back, there were new little pigs. You knew what had happened to the old ones, but you pretended that you didn't. The girls stayed on one side of the house and the boys on the other and we slept in bunk-beds. It was a lovely time. The kitchen of the farmhouse was huge, with a big long table for everyone to sit around at mealtimes, for breakfast and dinner. There was a big fireplace and I remember many a night sitting around it learning songs. Every year we went down we had a new song to learn. The SVP was a religious society, but they never made a big deal out of that – they were just there to help us and our parents when help was needed. I respected that about the Society – they focused on their own beliefs rather than trying to form ours. I was very lucky, in fact, in that religion was never beaten into me when I was growing up, like so many others of my generation, and because of that I developed a great love for the Church. When Mam was going to Mass on a Sunday, she'd ask if any of us wanted to go with her. If we didn't want to go, we weren't forced into it. Later on in life we asked her why she had done that, and she said, 'I told you about God and about how I felt about Him and religion, but it was up to each of you to decide how you felt about it.' I loved her for that.

After moving to our home in Ballyfermot, I went to the local Dominican Convent school. It was run by the nuns, but there were also some lay teachers. At this stage, I was five-and-a-half years old and had already been to school in Inchicore, when we lived in the dingy place in Keogh Square. At the convent school my desk was next to a window and I spent most of my days gazing out at the sky and daydreaming. Through the years, teachers would tell my mother that I was an intelligent young lady, but that I didn't concentrate on my work. 'She's a daydreamer,' they would tell her again and again. And they were right. I do remember loving the religion classes in school, though. We had a Catechism filled with pictures and wonderful stories about Jesus. I was fascinated by those pictures and stories as a child.

Apart from religion, history was the other subject that captured my imagination, and still does to this day. I think it's fascinating to go right back and see how people lived and nations developed. I was also quite good at picking up the Irish language in school, but I don't have a word of it now. I found an old school report recently as I was sifting through my bits and pieces, and everything was either 'Good' or 'Fair'. The exceptions were music, religion and history, which were 'Very Good'. I was a disaster at geography and maths.

I got off to a good start in the Dominican Convent because my first teacher there was a lovely lady called Mrs Doherty. She was a small woman with jet-black hair and lots of freckles. I fell in love with her; I think I was fascinated by her. She was a very gentle woman and she never lifted the ruler to us. Whenever she was out sick, we had one of the nuns sitting in with us, whose name I don't remember. What I do remember is that I didn't like her because there was always the threat that she'd give you a slap. She had a long, pointed stick that she used to demonstrate things on the blackboard, but it was also her weapon to rap you across the knuckles if you weren't paying attention or you caused some kind of trouble during class. That nun never hit me, but the fear was always there. I did get my hands slapped by another nun, called Sr McCormack. She was a nice nun and never ill-treated us, but when she did what she had to do, by God you felt the sting!

Every Friday, Mam would buy me treats for school off a local guy called Charlie, who sold the goodies on a street corner in front of Ballyfermot church. It was usually crisps and packets of Rolo and Smarties. They were my Friday treat and in those days if you had sweets in the schoolyard, everyone wanted to be your friend. I learned from an early age about fair-weather friends. The first Friday I got my sweets I shared them, but the moment they were gone, my 'friends' disappeared, too. When I copped on to this and stopped sharing, it led to me being bullied. 'Don't play with her,' they'd say. I ended up being stuck in a corner of the yard by myself. It was just kids being kids, but I remember being very hurt by it. You always remember the hurt that other children inflict, for some reason. I have memories of being teased about my weight, which would go up and down. I was never huge, but whenever I put on some weight I got called names, and that humiliation has stuck with me. Sometimes I was a skinny child and other times I could be a little frumpish, depending on whether Mam had money or not. But most of the time I was a normal-sized kid.

Two of the big events in a child's life during the primary school years are religious ones: First Holy Communion and Holy Confirmation. Before you reached those heights, though, you had to get through your First Holy Confession. I was absolutely petrified going to church the day I made my own first confession. I was afraid I'd forget the words, afraid I wouldn't be able to see where I was going in the darkness of the confession box and fall over and embarrass myself. When I stepped into the confession box and closed the door behind me, it was pitch black and scary. I was all alone, waiting to talk to this strange man on the other side of a little window, which had a shutter. There was a step to kneel on in the box and because I was only a little kid, my head barely reached the window. Then there was the shock of the shutter suddenly sliding back with a bang and the priest talking in a deep voice, 'What do you have to tell me, my child?' I was thinking, 'Holy Shit! What's happening here?' I then raced off into a rigmarole of 'sins' that I had rehearsed. 'Bless me Father for I have sinned ... This is my first confession.' Pause. The deep voice on the other side said, 'And?' Panic. I said in a rush, 'Em ... em, I cursed, I was bold to my Mammy ...' I said stupid things that wouldn't be a sin and some of which I hadn't even done. That first confession frightened the life out of me, but then there was a great feeling of relief when the priest finally said, 'Say an Our Father and three Hail Marys', which was my penance for the sins. Once you'd reached the penance bit, you knew confession was over. Then there was another bang of the shutter and I was out the door and back out into the light again.

I knelt down at a pew to say my penance, but Lolo Hannon, my school friend, was immediately in my ear, making me laugh. I'm sure if the teacher had caught us, we'd have been sent straight back in for another confession. As I knelt there, trying to ignore the persistent Lolo, I began to feel quite odd. The next thing I knew, there was a bang to my head. When I woke up I was outside, propped up on the church step, with my mother holding me. I had fainted because I'd been forced to fast for twelve hours before making my confession. Normally you only fasted before receiving Holy Communion, but they had made us fast as a practice run for the main event. I hadn't eaten since the night before and this was now the afternoon. After collapsing, I ended up with a lump on my head the size of a golf ball. Luckily, I had a week to recover before the First Communion Day. Lolo, of course, thought it was hilarious.

Lolo Hannon was a character who I really looked up to and loved in school. She was the person I wanted to be because she stood up to everyone. She wasn't a nasty person, but she wasn't afraid of anyone and no one talked back to her. Most of the girls in my class were good girls. There were a couple of them who came from families that had a lot more than we had. I wouldn't say they were wealthy, but they were always in different dresses and had beautiful combs and brand new ribbons in their hair. They would look down on those of us who didn't have nice things. Even though she was only a kid, Lolo would stare over at those well-off girls and say with buckets of attitude, 'We're as good as they are, Mary. Who do they think they are?' I admired her manner and the way she went on and was delighted when we became friends. Of course, being her friend meant you got into trouble, as well as having lots of laughs. I'd be reading aloud in class and she'd pinch me on the sly and I'd let out a yelp, then be chastised by the teacher for messing. I'd glance furiously at Lolo and she'd be in stitches laughing.

The trouble didn't really matter so much, because I loved Lolo and she was my ally in school. She stood up for me because I was a bit of a wimp. I didn't like fights or arguments, but it was Lolo who taught me that sometimes you had to fight in order to stand up for yourself. Up until about the age of eleven, I would just back away from trouble. Then being friends with Lolo started to have an effect on me and once I turned eleven, if you called me a name, you got your hair pulled. Lolo probably wasn't even all that brave herself, but she refused to let her side down. I now know that she is a big softie underneath it all, but back then I used to envy her and wished I was more like her. She had this 'get up and go' attitude that might have been what helped me to do that for myself. She was a great role model. I think a lot of quiet girls in the class would have been afraid of her, but for the wrong reasons because she wasn't a bully. They would have been afraid of her because she was loud and they knew you didn't mess with her.

A week after the Communion, we got ready to make our First Holy Communion. I remember the morning of my Communion. Mammy gave me a bath, put on my dress and fixed up my hair. My brother, Tomo, said, 'Jaysus, I've never seen Mary's knees so clean.' Later, I recall being in the church and the excitement of all the girls around me. I remember my dress and the colour of my coat, which was unusual: it was cherry purple with white glass buttons. The material was bubbly and it looked knitted, but it wasn't. To top it all off, I had a little veil and a tiara.

Mam had bought herself a new coat for the day, but would later pawn it for cash. It was a big heavy coat with a wide collar, deep pockets and massive buttons. She loved that coat so much that she got it back from the pawnshop and wore it for years afterwards. She completed her look with a scarf and a pair of second-hand shoes she had gotten in the Iveagh Market in Francis Street. Maybe my dress was second-hand as well, I don't know, but I thought it was gorgeous. I felt like a little princess. Dad wasn't there for my big day because he was working and couldn't get the time off, so Tomo came with us instead. The following day, Sunday, Dad proudly took me over to his two sisters, Aunt Mamie and Aunt Annie, on the crossbar of his bike, all decked out in my communion gear, to show me off.

In terms of the religious aspect of the Communion, I had read my Catechism and I knew I was going to get a bit of God's body inside me that day. Then, the nuns warned us, God would be able to watch me all the time, so I couldn't ever do anything bold. I wasn't too happy about that, to be honest, because I was afraid I'd do something bad and God would take me with him. But at the same time I was looking forward to receiving Holy Communion because I felt very close to my Catechism and the stories I was learning about Christ. They were read in a childish way to us, not like how they are in the Bible. I loved hearing them because I loved stories being told to me.

When the moment arrived for me to go up to the altar to receive Communion, I thought I was going to feel God going into me ... but I didn't. It was a big anti-climax. I just felt what tasted like a lump of cardboard in my mouth. It was the host – a dry, hard wafer that immediately stuck fast to the roof of my mouth. I was swirling my tongue around in desperation, trying to dislodge it, but there was no budging the Body of Christ from the roof of my mouth. I walked back to my seat and my mother, who spotted what I was doing, kept saying, 'Don't touch it with your hands.' You weren't allowed to touch it with your hands or teeth because the body of Christ was sacred. After a few minutes I had a pain in my jaw from trying to unstick it and on top of all that I was starving because I'd had to fast in order to receive Communion, and now I felt sick. Then I remembered what happened to me on the day I made my Confession and I began praying, 'Oh my God, please don't let me faint again or I'll die of embarrassment.' I felt weak because they kept us kneeling for ages, but thank God I didn't collapse as I would have been utterly mortified if my tiara had fallen off.

So there I was, rooting around with my tongue to dislodge the Body of Christ and sending up desperate prayers to preserve me from fainting, when the next thing I spotted Lolo Hannon, in stitches laughing. I was immediately distracted from my own problems, wondering what she could be laughing about on this holiest of holy days. I couldn't look at her because I knew I'd only get a fit of the giggles, too, and I didn't want to upset our nice teacher. Eventually, though, curiosity got the better of me and I managed to ask Lolo, in a tiny whisper, what she was laughing at. Out of the side of her mouth she said the most stupid thing, as only a child would say, 'The priest is in a dress!' Now we both knew they were robes and we were used to seeing the priests in them, but Lolo had a way of turning things into a comedy. So, of course, I started laughing then and the laughter went down the line of girls as the joke was passed on. We all got into trouble when we went outside because you could hear us tittering away during the Mass. Plus, we were sitting in the front row, which made it worse.

I remember coming out of the church after the Mass and getting photographs taken with the nuns. They look really angelic in the photo, but I didn't like the photo when it was developed because it looked like I had no teeth. I remember standing on the path, with the old Ballyfermot church and a statue of Our Lady of the Assumption behind me, as Tomo took my photograph. My father's brother, Uncle Jim, who was then a bus conductor on the number 79 buses in Dublin city, was also there to mark the day and there was another photograph taken with me standing beside him. It looks funny: I'm in my Communion finery and he's in his bus conductor's gear, smiling widely.

One of the great traditions of First Communion is that you get lots of money from family, friends and neighbours on your big day. I got the money alright, not that I saw much of it. In those days the mothers would take the Communion money off the kids because they needed it themselves. Aunt Mary gave me a half-crown and that evening, as a treat, Daddy went up on his bike to The Lido, our local chipper. It was half-crown for a batter burger and a single of chips, so he brought that back to me out of my first half-crown, and I never saw another penny after that.

Looking back, it was a great day. After the church we went to Hardy's pub, where I got loads of money, crisps and orangeade. Then we went to 'The Diddy Room' in the County Bar, to get money off Mammy's other friends. It was called 'The Diddy Room' because that's where all the women drank. There were two sections in the County Bar: a huge bar/lounge where the men drank and a little room where all the women met up on a Friday night to have their glass of Guinness and a sing-song. It was the men, naturally, who named it The Diddy (titty) Room. The

County Bar was Mam and Dad's local pub. They were even there the day it first opened. There's a photograph of them sitting on the stairs and they both look so young and handsome. It was one of the biggest pubs in Ballyfermot at the time and it became a local to the lot of us as we grew up. I think everyone ended up in the pub the day of my Communion. After the pub I went to my Aunt Ellen's and she gave me another half-crown. The money was rolling in, but, as I said, I wouldn't be seeing any of it.

The next day, Sunday afternoon, I went to see my father's sisters, aunts Mamie and Annie. It was still raining, so Daddy put a big cover over me to keep my dress from getting soaked as he booted along on his bicycle, with me on the crossbar. When I got home again it had stopped raining and I wanted to go outside and play with the other kids on the road. Mam warned me, 'Don't get that dress dirty! Come inside in ten minutes and take it off.' The kids were playing kiss-chasing, where the boys ran after the girls, grabbed them and kissed them on the cheek – and the girls pretended they didn't want to be caught. Our young neighbour, Pat Doyle, was chasing us and I remember running and my foot slipping off the side of the path. Pat came up behind me just as I went face-down into the muck. My Communion dress was destroyed, as was the coat over it, and I was covered in muck from head to toe. I was really upset, thinking, 'I can't go home, my mother will kill me.' I even thought about running away, but I knew there was nothing for it but to go and face the consequences. Dragging my feet, head down, I went in the door of our house and Mam let such a scream at the sight of me! Of course, she knew she'd have to get the coat cleaned before it could go to the pawn shop. She kept me inside the house as punishment and made me sit in silence on a chair. It felt like a century to me, but it was probably more like an hour.

Mind you, Mam shouting at me wasn't as bad as Dad shouting at me. If that had happened, I really would have been upset. When Daddy roared at me, I went to pieces, because he rarely roared. It was like thunder in the house when he shouted; the whole place shook. Neither of them ever raised their hand to me, though. Mam cleaned down the dress and coat and they went back to the pawn shop. I didn't mind the dress going, but I was very sad to lose the coat; I never saw it again. I was allowed to keep my black patent shoes for two weeks, but when Mam noticed them getting scruffy, she took them off me and I never saw them again either. I guess they ended up in the pawn shop as well.

No doubt it will sound strange to young people of today, but back then the pawn shop was a very normal part of our lives – it kept the family finances ticking over for the majority of people. You went in on a Monday with all the good things you owned, like clothes, shoes, suits and jewellery, sometimes even heavy pots and pans, which could be worth something. The guy in the pawn shop would look at all your worldly goods and put a value on them. He'd give you money in exchange and a ticket to redeem them when you could afford to. When you were reclaiming them, he'd charge you a little extra on top of what he had originally given you. I guess it was a sort of money-lending operation, but more polite. If you couldn't afford to take your items back the following week, you had to pay some money off them to keep them from being sold. You had a limited time to reclaim them, around six months. After that, the broker would sell them off to recoup his money – it was all in the pawn shop's favour, of course.

I can remember going to the pawn shop with my mother, which to me was just another grand adventure. My Mam would go there on a Monday with Aunt Mary, and afterwards they'd end up in a little pub on the corner of Queen Street, where the pawn shop was situated. In fact, if you go to Queen Street today, you can still see the three brass balls that hung over the shop back in those days, which marked it as a pawnbrokers. For me, it was just an exciting place to go to because I didn't know what we were in there for. All I knew, or cared about, was that Mam was going to get money and then I would get lemonade and crisps.

The pawn shop was a small place, with a counter and two hatches. One of the displays was a jewellery case full of rings that had never been collected by their owners, so they were now for sale. There were some beautiful pieces and God knows what story they'd have had to tell about their previous owners if they could speak. The clothes brought in to be pawned had to be in a brown paper bag and once in the shop, you put them through the hatch. I remember watching Mam wrapping up clothes in a brown paper bag in our house and tying it up with string, and not understanding what she was doing. When I went to the pawn shop, the mystery of that was solved. Everyone at home noticed that their stuff was gone – Daddy's suits and Jimmy's shoes would disappear regularly – but they never mentioned it. Mam would collect them again on Friday, unwrap them and put them back into their wardrobes, ready for the weekend.

On our trips to the pawn shop, I always looked forward to a glass of red lemonade and a packet of Tayto crisps in the little Queen Street pub. We didn't go into the main part of the bar, of course, because that was for the men; there was a little cubby section with a long seat where the women went. Mam and Aunt Mary would have two glasses of stout before we headed off to catch the bus home. I remember there was a little shop beside the pub that sold doll sets and if I was really lucky, my mother would go in and buy me the tiny plastic furniture for the dolls' house that Daddy had made for me out of cardboard. I played with it for hours in the parlour, using the names of the neighbours for my characters. 'Hello, Mrs Gibbons!' I'd say grandly, completely engrossed in this little doll world where everyone was lovely and polite and no one had to pawn their stuff on Mondays.

I'm sure the pawn shop did good business from my Confirmation as well. I don't remember an awful lot about that special day, except that I wore a straight cream dress with a slip that was too long and hung down below it. I had a jockey's hat and a cream and brown coat. I look at the photo from that day now and I just think I was horribly turned out. I even had a stupid smile on my face. The only redeeming feature is the lovely black patent shoulder bag I wore. My mother had told me that the day I made my Confirmation was the day I would become a lady. It was part of the rite of passage and meant that I was going to step into my religion and move into my teenage years, with the life of an adult just around the corner. I found the notion of that quite frightening because at the time, I was still very much attached to both my parents. In fact, I lived with a paranoid dread of anything happening to them. My mother told me once how around this time, she came running out of her bedroom at six o'clock one morning to find me clutching a photo of her and Daddy and sobbing my heart out. 'What's wrong, what's wrong?' she gasped. 'I don't want yous to die,' I wailed. I must have had a bad dream or something, I suppose. I might have been more independent and wily than other kids my age, but I was still absolutely terrified of losing my parents. I think underneath that fear was a fear of growing up. I wanted to be Mammy and Daddy's baby forever. Like everything in life, that would soon change.

4. Boys and bailiffs come calling

My eldest brother, Jimmy, was the first to leave home. He joined the army in 1963 and was sent off to Cyprus on a peace-keeping mission. With him on that tour was his friend, Liam Donovan, who fancied my sister, Betty – or 'Betty Boob', as she was called by friends because she had a fine bust. Jimmy was a couple of months shy of his sixteenth birthday when he joined the army, so he was underage, but he got in somehow.

Liam was a good bit older than my brother and he had just returned from England, where he had been with the British Army. The two lads hit it off the first time they met, the day they signed up for the Irish Army in Dublin, at Cathal Brugha Barracks, which we also called Portobello Barracks. After they joined up, Liam gave Jimmy a lift home on his Honda 50. Betty and I were peering out our window, to see who was coming up on the motorbike with her twin, Jimmy, perched on the back of it. When she laid eyes on Liam, Betty fancied him immediately. I remember her saying, 'Who is that fella Jimmy is with?' Then she added, 'Oh God, he's gorgeous! He looks like Rock Hudson.' When Liam came through the door and caught sight of Betty, he was smitten too.

At that time we were still living at Keogh Square in Inchicore, so I was very young, which means I've known my brother-in-law Liam since I was a child. I grew up with him, so he's like my own brother. Liam is one of the greatest human beings you could ever hope to meet in the world, but he had a terrible childhood. When he was young, Liam's mother went out to buy sausages one day and never came back. She abandoned her family, leaving Liam and his young brother and sister with their father. His father wasn't able to cope with the children, so they were put into care. Liam and his brother, the poor souls, were sent into the city's notorious Artane Industrial School, while their sister went to another religious-run institution, in Islandbridge. Even in those days Artane was known as a terrifying place; parents would threaten their children with it when they were bold. In recent years, the full horror of the physical and sexual abuse suffered by innocent young boys at the hands of depraved Christian Brothers in Artane has come to light. Liam has described some of it to us, how he was beaten and abused, but I can't even begin to imagine the nightmare he endured there as a child. Some of the stories he told me would make you throw up. When Liam's brother left Artane in his teens, he drowned himself. He just couldn't mentally cope with what had happened to him in that institution. Liam finally got out of that hellish place and returned to his father's home, where he found his father in a relationship with another woman. Liam wasn't happy in the house, so as soon as he was able, he left home and took the boat to England, where he joined the army.

After meeting Betty in our house, Liam pursued her and their relationship developed into a full-blown romance. Betty, who is small, dark and looks a lot like me, although she's a lot slimmer, the cow (but I love her!), married him when she was almost nineteen and he was twenty-six years old. They went to live in the married quarters of the army barracks in Portobello. Liam became a part of our family very quickly and I don't think any of us regard him as a brother-in-law; we look upon him as a brother. He has always said that the only real mother and father he knew were our mam and dad.

Tomo, who had gone to work as a manual labourer with my father, was the second to get married, to his girlfriend, Geraldine. They went to live with her mother. Seven months later, Jimmy tied the knot with Kathleen, the love of his life, and he also went to live with his mother-in-law. With everyone being so poor, it was quite common for young married couples to move in with their in-laws in those times, until they got their own home from the Corporation. We lost the two boys in one year, leaving me and Willie at home with Mam and Dad, just the four of us. It was very sad to see the family breaking up and moving on in life. In fact, I screamed when Tomo left because he was the heart and soul of the family. He was very funny and was the one who made everyone laugh, and still does to this day. It broke my mother's heart when he left – I'd say she felt like screaming, too.

Mam had cried when Jimmy left because he was her first son. She really went to pieces when he left our house. I don't think Jimmy realised how much she felt for him. The rest of us could see that she idolised him. We all did, to be honest, even me. If I smoked, I'd hide it from Jimmy. Daddy was the head of the house, but Jimmy had a presence about him that he carries to this day. He has an air of authority that makes you want to get his approval. He used to call me, 'My little Mary'. We were very close. The house was awfully quiet with just the four of us, but slowly we adapted to it.

You might think that with only Willie and me to concentrate on, my mother would have been into every aspect of my life. She wasn't, though – she continued to give us leeway in our choices. Neither Mam nor Dad ever put pressure on me to focus on getting a good education, with the result that during my school days I knew I could get away with doing as little as possible. My mother was such a softie, I was often able to persuade her to let me skip school altogether. 'I'll clean the stairs for you if you let me stay home today,' I'd offer with a big smile. She'd eventually give in to my pleading and then I'd be home for the day, washing, scrubbing and polishing. Given her relaxed approach to my education, it was no surprise that I was able to persuade her, when I was just thirteen and only three months into sixth class, to let me quit school.

At the time, Liam was away on a tour of duty, either in Cyprus or in Lebanon, so Betty was living on her own at the barracks with her little daughter, Diana, who was just two years old. I asked Mammy if she'd let me go and stay with Betty for a while, to help her out. Mam agreed because she felt sorry for Betty being on her own in the barracks with a little child. So I hopped on the number 18 bus to Rathmines and on to Portobello and I lived with Betty and my niece Diana for three weeks. When I came home, I announced that I wanted to leave school for good and get a job. My mother kicked up a bit of a fuss at first, but she needed the money I could earn so she agreed that I could leave school for good. That was the end of my education, and off I went looking for a job.

As a child, just turned thirteen, my chances of getting employment with a local factory wouldn't have been good. But my Aunt Mary, being the crafty person that she was, forged a baptismal certificate and turned me into a fifteen-year-old. Good old Aunt Mary, you just had to love her! That certificate was my passport into a factory called Belinda's on the Kylemore Road in Ballyfermot, where I began my working life making plastic knickers for babies! These were essential at the time because the only nappies available were terry-cloth nappies, so the plastic overlayer was a staple for mothers. It meant Belinda's was kept busy.

I worked there for a year. I started off as a packer: you'd roll the knickers around in your hand, put them into a plastic bag and place them in a box, twelve to a box, and then someone would come along and take the boxes away, and you'd start again. There were eight to ten of us doing the packing, lined up in two rows, all women. I worked from eight in the morning until five in the evening, which was a long day for a young girl, but I loved it. I have to admit that I did miss school for a while. For a good time after I left I kept all my books in a leather bag that Jimmy had brought me home from Cyprus. Some evenings I'd go home from work and take out the schoolbooks and read them – although that didn't last very long. I did keep up my reading, though, through the *Bunty* and *Judy* comics that I loved.

When I left school I was able to read and write, but I have a problem with spelling to this day. It's partly in my head and as a result of trauma, I believe. I remember missing a long stretch at school one time due to illness, and when I returned, I thought that I had escaped all the tests because they were finished. The teacher had other ideas. She put me in a corner of the classroom, with two other girls, and made us take the tests. She left us there, with no time limit, and she continued to teach the class while we tried to ignore her and concentrate on the exams. I think that's where my trouble started. I remember the fear of not being able to spell for those tests. I was sweating and felt sick, like an anxiety attack. Somehow I did pass the tests, but that fear never left me. Even now, if I have to spell a word in front of people I get very nervous and start to shake. If I'm asked for an autograph and I ask for the person's name, I'll know how to spell it but I won't dare write it down without checking it with them first. There are two things that happen when I try to write: I either get a mental block or I spell the word as it sounds to me and know it doesn't look right on the page. Sometimes I wonder if I'm dyslexic, but then, I do know how to read and I don't see the words back-to-front, so maybe not. I had a young man tutor me one time and he couldn't believe that I could read so well, but was unable to put pen to paper.

After leaving school, I missed my friends, too, but it wasn't much of a hardship because I had never been a 'hanging around the streets' kind of girl. It made me the odd-one-out, I can tell you, because all my friends from school were into that: they'd spending hours just hanging around in little groups, looking at fellas. I was never interested in that either. I was a late-starter when it came to the opposite sex. Nowadays, I'm struck by how much kids know about sex, and from a very young age. You could argue that they know too much, too young. It was very different in my day. There was no sex education in the school for starters, and you wouldn't have seen anything even a bit naughty on television. As for Mam, well, she was never going to tell me anything about it. There was definitely no touchy-feely culture of sharing and caring when I was growing up – the birds and the bees were strictly on a need-to-know basis, and my mother wasn't ever going to get to thinking that I needed to know. I remember when I was about twelve, hearing Mam, Aunt Mary and my cousin, Bridget, chatting in the kitchen after a few drinks. Mam was saying, 'No, you tell her.' Aunt Mary said, 'No, you!' Eventually I was called down to the kitchen and Bridget, who was about two sheets to the wind at that stage, says to me, 'Mary, you know the way you're nearly twelve? Well, Our Lady is going to send you a gift.' I was so excited. 'Is she?' I asked, wondering what this 'gift' was going to be. It was quite a shock when it arrived. 'I don't want it, Our Lady, you can have it back,' I thought to myself. So, that's how I learned about my period.

As for the rest, I think I was thirteen when I had my first real kiss, with tongues. I nearly got sick. I ran home to my mother, asked her to put pigtails in my hair and told her that I never wanted to grow up. The whole thing had frightened the life out of me. The Casanova in question hung out with a big gang around the corner from my house. He had fancied me for ages and kept asking my friend if I would meet him and go for a walk. Eventually I gave in and said I'd go for a walk with him, as long as my friend came with me. I was still very childish. When he leaned in to kiss me, I was just kissing with my mouth, but he slipped the tongue and I thought it was disgusting, but I carried on with the kiss. As soon as he finished I said, 'I have to go, I'll see you tomorrow night.' But I never had anything to do with him again, even though he followed me around like a love-sick puppy for weeks afterwards.

I have to be honest, though, that was the first and last time I was shy with a boy. I think he kind of opened me up to the kissing game and the groping hand. You didn't tell your friends what you did, but it was harmless enough: if you really liked him, you might let the fella rest his hand on your breast outside your clothes, but it wouldn't go any further than that. I became a bit wild then and I started fancying every fella that I saw, but all they ever got was the hand on the fully clothed breast. They got nothing else because I refused to do 'the deed'.

I had a fine chest as a young girl, like my sister, 'Betty Boob'. I was well stacked up top and I soon became aware of it when I noticed the attention I was getting from the boys. I remember the first time I became conscious of it. It was in the summertime and I was walking down the street with my friends, wearing a new bra that Mam had bought me and a yellow Mickey-Mouse T-shirt. The guys were all openly staring, and it was in that moment that I realised I had something that I could use to my advantage. So, I did. Of course, I quickly got a name for myself because all the other girls were jealous of the reaction I was getting from the boys. They would say, 'She's a slapper!' But I wasn't doing anything even approaching full sex. Yes, I got more kisses than they did and I loved kissing by now, tongues and all, but that was only ever as far as I went. The fellas probably thought they'd get a lot more from me and because they didn't, they moved on quickly to the next girl and I'd have to find a new one. I didn't mind because I was enjoying it anyway.

I knew my shapely figure was a weapon I held and my attitude was, 'If you've got it, flaunt it.' It frightened me at first that I could have such an effect on the boys, but at that age you believe you're always in control. Of course, I was playing with fire, and it was inevitable I'd get burnt one day. There was one particular time I was with a guy who I fancied like mad. He was a bit older than me. At this stage I still didn't know anything about the actual act of sex. We were up a laneway in Ballyfermot and while he was kissing me, he got very carried away. The next thing I knew he had unzipped himself, taken his manhood out of his pants and was trying to do something to me. I was horrified and instantly tried to push him away, but he was strong and had me pinned up against the wall. Eventually I managed to escape from him without being harmed and I raced to the security of my home. I didn't go out for weeks afterwards and I never went near that guy again. I would have been just going on fifteen at the time and I was confused and upset by it. It put me off boys for a while, but that could never last long.

I was at an age where I was learning lots of things that would have been hidden from me before. Like all teenagers, I was finding out more and more about the adult world, and I didn't always like what I discovered. One day, while I was at work in Belinda's, Dad arrived in looking very stressed. 'What's up?' I asked. He glanced at the ground and then looked up again. 'Now, I don't want you to panic or get upset, but the bailiffs are at the door,' he said, almost in a whisper. I hadn't a clue what a bailiff was, but I was about to find out. He had come to tell me like this because I would have turned up at home for lunch within the hour, so he knew I'd walk in on the scene unprepared otherwise. I was given permission to finish early for lunch and we went home. There was a line of cars parked outside our door. I thought there must be a party underway, such was the commotion on the street. All the neighbours were out, standing around in little bunches, but I didn't know what they were talking about as I walked by. I certainly didn't know that they were talking about my mother. Dad just kept telling me to keep going; he never looked at any of them. It wasn't that they weren't good neighbours, because they were, but everyone loves a drama, so they were out for a look and a gossip and Daddy hated that. I don't think they would have been judging us too harshly, though – I'm sure most of them had had the bailiff at their doors at some stage. It happened a lot in those times because a lot of people lived in debt. Then again, many people seemed to handle their financial affairs just fine. Mrs Gibbons, who lived two doors down from us, had a houseful of children and she managed. My mother, on the other hand, just couldn't.

When I reached my house Mam was crying and I couldn't understand why she was so upset. There were big black plastic bags all tied up neatly in the parlour. It turned out that all our clothes and bits and pieces were in them. I asked her why she was crying and she sniffed, 'We're going to have to move house.' Mam had got herself into debt and hadn't paid the rent for months – unfortunately, that was pretty typical of her. Dad had been blissfully unaware of this situation until the bailiffs arrived to throw us out of our home. 'We'll manage,' I said to Mam. I don't know why I said that because I hadn't a clue what was going on or what it all meant. What I remember most is my father watching my mother, and I could see the pity in his face ... and also the annoyance because he was earning enough money to keep our heads above water. I'm sure he was sitting there wondering, How the hell did this happen? I'm bringing in a wage. I'm working every hour God sends. She wants for nothing. So, why is she in debt?

I don't know how long we all sat in the parlour together, watching the bailiffs outside. They hadn't knocked on the door yet. Then this big old car pulled up and a tall, thin man wearing glasses got out, and my mother said, 'There's Tomás Mac Giolla.' Now, I didn't know who Tomás Mac Giolla was at the time, but I now know him to have been a very good politician and a member of the Worker's Party. All I knew then was that he was a saviour. He went to the bailiff in the first car and said something to him, and the chap he spoke to roared down to the others, 'Wrong house! Let's go!'

Tomás came into my mother then and she broke down in his arms, while my father just sat there, looking relieved and hurt at the same time. It was the first time I had seen my father look hurt. I could see it in his face. There was no row, though; Dad wouldn't row. All he said was, 'How did you do this?' All she said was, 'I don't know, Tommy, I don't know.' The matter was cleared up that day, somehow, but there would be problems with Mam and debts over the next few years, again and again. I don't think it got as bad as that time, though, because that was the only time the bailiffs came out to the house.

Personally, I never felt any shame over that incident. I wasn't angry at my mother for bringing the bailiffs to our door. That was nothing to do with my age because I never felt ashamed as I got older and the debtors continued arriving at our house, shouting their demands. What I did do, when I could, was contribute money to help to get rid of some of the debts, and Betty and the boys did the same, so eventually there were no more debt-collectors turning up on the doorstep. Mam wasn't really reckless, but when she had money, she was a generous soul. If I asked her for £50, which was a huge amount back then, she'd give me whatever she had in her purse and she never ask for it back. I think in her heart she felt, 'Well, if you have respect for me, you'll give it back,' and so we did. But a lot of other people she lent money to didn't pay her back. Her money went out the door and it was never returned. To be fair to her, she was often a victim of her own kindness.

I was getting used to having a bit of cash myself now, thanks to working full-time, but after a year in Belinda's I got itchy feet. I wanted to work in the factory next door, Leemarks, because they made jeans, which was much cooler than plastic knickers. I applied and got a job there without much bother. It was the 1970s after all, a time when you could just walk from one job to another because Ireland was experiencing a boom. My work in Leemarks involved putting in the 'eyes' and the buttons on the jeans, and a bit of overlock stitching. I worked there for eight months and

I loved it. But the itchy feet hit again and I left Leemarks and went to work as a packer in the factory producing Ritchie's Milky Mints. I went back to work at Belinda's two or three times, just for short periods before I'd leave again. The final time I went back, I was there for six months. It was the end of the boom by then, so they had to let people go and because I was the last one in, I was the first one out. I remember crying because I knew I could never go back there again, so it was the end of an era for me. We were all sad leaving Belinda's. Once the option was taken from me, I really wanted to stay. But sure, I probably would have left after another six months anyway. That was just the way I was.

I was still living at home, of course, and my only social activity at that time was two-timing one fella at one end of the street and then doing the same to another fella at the other end. Like mother, like daughter! We were all doing it and it was just seen as harmless fun. That was my entire social life, sad to say: I'd meet the guy on the corner and get a kiss and say, 'See you later,' and off I'd go, to get a kiss from the other fella on the next corner. About four of us girls were doing this and having a great giggle, but we all got caught in the end and were left with nobody. There's a moral in there somewhere! It was all innocent fun, though, just kissing, no sex. The guys would tell me they loved me, so it was very good for the ego.

The post-boom period was tough, so I was very lucky to land a good job at CB Packaging in Clondalkin, when I was fifteen. I loved it and spent the next five years there. The work was easy – I fed bags into a big machine – and the money was great. The factory made cement and powdered milk bags. Two years after I joined, I became shop steward for the women. That was when I finally got a passport and developed a travel bug because I was invited to go to Germany and France with the company.

As shop steward I generally felt I hadn't a clue what I talking about, but someone there seemed to think that I was making sense. I couldn't put pen to paper, but I used the little brain power that I had and somehow, for some strange reason, the words came out right most of the time. It's not that I had to deal with heavy issues, but if the girls had any kind of problem or grievance they would come to me, and I'd take it up with my superior. A meeting would be called, and I'd present the worker's case to the management. I would have enjoyed it a lot more if the women I was representing had had the guts to see the process through to the end, but more often than not they'd back down when the heat was on. What usually happened was that I'd call the meeting and during it I'd repeat something the girl had told me and wait for her to back me up, but she wouldn't. I found that really frustrating. I didn't last long in that role because that inconsistency drove me mad. I wanted to get people their rights, but after listening to these people moaning and then going into a meeting and standing up for them, stating their case as they asked me to state it, and then them standing behind me but not opening their mouths to back me up, well, that pissed me off. After a year of listening to people moan without purpose, I decided I'd had enough.

The very best thing that happened during the year I was shop steward was the trip to Germany and France. It was my first time to travel outside of Ireland and it really made up for all the moaners. A small group of us went to Düsseldorf and Nice, to look at state-of-the-art machinery because ours was outdated and required a lot more labour. Off we went to look at these new, all singing, all dancing machines and we thought they were brilliant – not realising that they were going to do away with some people's jobs. There were redundancies offered as a result and some people took them. For those of us left, it actually worked in our favour. The machines were fantastic for productivity and as we were on a productivity deal, our wages went up. At that time, in 1977, I would have been coming home with £400 a week. There was shift-work as well, so I could double the money if I wished. I was earning a fortune by anyone's standards.

As I was earning so much money and loved the job, I soon got itchy feet of a different kind – I decided it was time to move into a place of my own. I was almost seventeen by now, so felt I was well old enough to live independently. I never consulted my parents about this or gave them any hint about what I was planning. I found a flat in Tallaght and took it. The night before I left home, I packed a few things in a bag, went to work the next day and never came home. I went to my new home and that was that. It was a cruel thing to do and my poor parents didn't deserve it, but I knew that Mam wouldn't have let me go. The next day, she sent Dad up to try to persuade me to come back home. I was in the office in CB Packaging when Dad arrived in, and he started crying. It broke my heart to see him that upset. He said, 'Your mammy is very upset. Why did you leave?' 'There's no specific reason,' I replied, 'I just want to live on my own.' He said, 'All I want is for you to be happy, but I'd feel you'd be safer if you were at home with me.' As hard as it was, I stood firm and gently told him, 'Dad, I'm okay. I'm well able to look after myself. I still have my job and you know where I work.' Dad nodded. Then he gave me a big hug and a kiss, and he walked out the door with tears in his eyes.

It was one of the hardest things I ever had to do, not to give in to Dad in that moment. It killed me to see a grown man cry, especially my poor Dad, who I absolutely adored. But at the same time, I always knew he was a very emotional man, it was something I loved about him. For me, I just wanted my independence. I can't really say why I wanted it so much, given that I was happy at home, even if Willie and I were constantly fighting. The two of us couldn't seem to help clashing and would blame each other for everything. We're very close now, live very near each other and laugh to think about our young years when we fought like cat and dog. Whatever it was that drove me to find my own place, it certainly wasn't my family, that's for sure. I was happy and loved and supported, but in those unpredictable teenage years, that was no longer enough. I wanted freedom.

Six months after I moved out, everyone had more or less got used to it, though Mam was still upset. At work one day there was a phone call for me from an alleged nun, who Mam had persuaded to ring me. Now, whether it was a real nun or not, I don't know for sure, but I suspect it was a well-meaning neighbour. Whoever the 'nun' was, she was adamant that I should come home and make amends for the hurt I had caused my parents. I told her that I had never meant to hurt them and that they knew I was safe and where I was. I said, 'This is something I just want to try and if it doesn't work out, I'll come home.' The 'nun' kept on and on and in the end I had to say, 'Look, I've to go back to work, I'm working on a machine,' which I was.

I put down the phone and about thirty minutes later there was another phone call for me. My boss came down to tell me and said, 'On the phone again, Byrne? Now, come on, get off it!' It was my mother this time. I said, 'Was that you just now on the phone?' And she said, 'No! Who rang you?' I think Mam realised then that all the pressure she was trying to pile on me was falling on deaf ears and that she would have to accept the fact that I needed to assert my independence and stand on my own two feet. At the same time, my parents knew they could contact me whenever they wanted to. I stood my ground. I knew if I went back to the house then, I'd never leave again. Plus, I had a new reason for wanting my own space – the new man in my life.

5. The Love of a Good Man

I kept my chastity belt on, so to speak, until I was seventeen years old – that was a lot longer than many of my friends, I can tell you. Even in those days, kids were 'doing it' at a far younger age than their parents imagined. For me, though, it was kisses and hand-holding ... until I met Brian. Then after all that waiting and anticipating, I ended up losing my virginity on the spur of the moment and in the most unromantic setting my little world had to offer ... a deserted graveyard in Tallaght!

Brian was tall, dark and handsome and worked with me in CB Packaging. I started seeing him when I was sixteen-and-a-half, eighteen months after I joined the company. Brian was my first serious boyfriend. He had a little beard and moustache, was seven years older than me, and I vividly remember him saying to me, when we first started going out together, 'Some day you'll outgrow me.' I was adamant that would never happen, of course, because I loved him, or at least I thought I did. He broke up with me a few times after we starting going out together, saying I was too young for him. I said to him once, 'You're only breaking up with me because you can't have sex,' and he replied, 'Well, I am a man.' I don't know why he stuck with me. At the time I was living in Tallaght, sharing a house with a group of nurses, while Brian was still living at home with his mother. He used to come and stay over at my place, but nothing ever happened. He was the perfect gentleman.

One night, after we'd been out drinking at the Dragon Inn in Tallaght village, I suddenly gave Brian the green light for sex. I must have just decided impulsively, Right, come on then, let's get it over with! It was wintertime and it was cold and frosty and there was a full moon. Maybe it was the full moon that got me going! We didn't even wait to get back to the house, just slipped into the first place that afforded some privacy. And that's where I had sex for the first time, in the freezing cold, lying on his coat under a huge leafless tree, with the headstones poking through the ground all around us. Now, this is no reflection on Brian, but when it was over I remember thinking, 'Oh my God, is that it!' I think that's a very standard reaction for most women after their first time. It's just different for women, we have to work harder at it to get to those soaring heights we're promised. I do remember thinking how beautiful it was in the graveyard. I really loved that graveyard and whenever I was walking by, which was often, I couldn't help wandering in for a look around. The graves there were very old. My mother, God rest her, would have killed me if she'd ever found out that I'd had sex there – I'm sure it's forbidden in some part of the Bible!

Brian was a lovely guy and we were good together for a long time. He treated me very well and we were a good match, despite the seven-year age gap. We even had a stroke of good fortune when we were at a festival in Tallaght one night. Brian bought me a raffle ticket for twenty pence and to our shock and amazement we won first prize … a brand new Datsun 120, four-door car! It was an incredible win, but when the car was delivered, we realised that we couldn't afford the insurance, so we were left with no option but to sell it. We were sad to see it go because we had both fallen in love with the fabulous motor. However, with the £6,000 cash from the sale of the Datsun, Brian splashed out on an engagement ring for me, and we used the remainder of the money to put a deposit on a house in Springfield, Tallaght.

I remember the evening Brian sprung the surprise proposal on me. We were watching television in the house I was then sharing with a couple of other girls. That evening it was just Brian and myself plonked in front of the TV. I was totally engrossed in 'M★A★S★H', which was one of my favourite TV shows at the time. Brian was lying back in an armchair and I was sitting on the floor. He tapped me on the shoulder. I kind of shrugged him off because he was disturbing me from my programme and there were some dramatic scenes going on at that moment. Brian interrupted me again, and now I was getting annoyed. Feck off and let me watch me programme, I thought. I turned and looked at him and then he said straightaway, 'Do you fancy getting married?' I bolted upright. 'Yeah, why not!' I blurted out, delighted, as I believed we were heading in that direction anyway. Next he produced a little box and when I opened it, my gaze fell on a beautiful engagement ring he had bought. It was a brave thing for a man to do, as women like to choose their own ring, but he was on safe ground because I had already admired that ring in a shop one day, when I was out around the city window-shopping with him, as young couples do. It was a gorgeous sapphire ring in the shape of a star with tiny diamonds around it. As I gazed at it, I suddenly became very emotional and I did cry a little, as I always do. I'm an awful whinge-bag!

I was immediately caught up in the whole fairytale of the wedding and I couldn't wait to break the news to my family. It was mid-week, so I decided to hang on until the weekend when everybody was together. On the Friday night, I met Tomo and Geraldine and told them at a pub in James's Street. They were both delighted. We then arranged for all the family to meet up in the County Bar in Ballyfermot on the Sunday. Other than Tomo and Geraldine, everyone else thought it was just a family get-together for no particular reason. When we walked in the door of the pub and I flashed the ring, Mammy got all excited, gave me a big hug and congratulated me. The demon Aunt Mary was there, too, and she made her presence felt in her own inimitable way. 'So is there a bun in the oven?' she called out loudly, so that everyone heard her clearly. Well, do you know what? I had never seen my mother so proud or so thrilled in all her life as when I replied firmly, 'No!' From that moment on, Mam had Brian on a pedestal. He became part of our family, stayed over at the weekends and went drinking with my brothers. Mam would make him his breakfast the morning after the night before, and the two of them would sit at the table chatting together. He absolutely loved my mother, and she loved him.

From the outside, it looked like I was all set for life as a newly married housewife, with children to follow in short order – the norm, in other words. But it didn't work out like that. We had another two wonderful years, but then I started to feel unhappy in the relationship. He had told me that I'd outgrow him, and he was right. On my nineteenth birthday, Brian threw me a big party in our house and I got really drunk. A friend of his had brought her brother with her, who was the same age as me, and I ended up kissing the face off him on the stairs. Brian came out, saw us and hissed, 'Oh for God's sake!' He walked away; he knew I was drunk. It had been a long day of drinking, with dozens of people in the house, a really great day. When I woke up the next morning, the young fella I'd been snogging on the stairs was sitting on a chair in front of me, and he blurted out, 'I love you!' *Arrrghh!* I roared inside my head, then told Brian to get rid of him out of the house.

Incredibly, Brian didn't dump me for that, just put it behind him and looked ahead, to our wedding. I still had the fairytale racing around in my mind as I set about making plans. I wanted a wedding close to Christmas and I was going to have a beautiful white dress and a hood with fur around it, instead of a veil. The bridesmaids were going to be in red dresses with red hoods framed by red fur. It was going to look like *White Christmas*, even if the snow didn't arrive to complete my perfect picture. I planned everything with excitement, with Brian and myself booking Wynn's

Hotel in Dublin city centre's Lower Abbey Street for the celebrations. Everyone got measured for the dresses and Brian organised the suits for himself and his best man and groomsmen; we paid all the deposits. Of course, most importantly, we booked my local church in Ballyfermot for the big ceremony. With all the fuss involved making the various arrangements, I didn't give much thought to the relationship I was signing up to for life. It was Brian who jolted me out of the fairytale and made me really think about what we were doing.

One night, about a month before the wedding, we were relaxing in our sitting room and he turned to me and asked, 'Do you think we're doing the right thing, about this wedding?' I reassured him that we were because I wanted my wedding day, but deep down I knew he was getting at the truth. At that stage, we weren't even having regular sex anymore because it just didn't feel right. It did to him, I think, but not to me. After he asked that question, I began to think he was right about the doubts he had. Now that there was a wedding date set in stone, I started to give it some serious thought. 'Is this the life I want?' I asked myself over and over before deciding … it wasn't! Slowly I realised, and admitted to myself, that I didn't belong with him. I realised that I wanted to get up and go and leave this whole situation.

I broke up with Brian just before I turned twenty in 1979, and just three weeks before our wedding day. When I told him I wanted to leave him, it was obviously a big blow, especially with a wedding set to go ahead shortly, but as ever, he was a gentleman about it. He accepted my choice and got on with it. It wasn't a bitter parting, he never tried to make me feel bad or guilty about it – he just put his own feelings aside and supported my decision. That's the kind of man he was.

Of course, then I was faced with the job of undoing all the wedding arrangements, forfeiting all the deposits we had paid, and letting all the guests know there wasn't going to be a big event after all. It was all very stressful and embarrassing, but at the same time I was hugely relieved to have taken the decision not to go ahead with the marriage. By now I felt 100% sure the decision was right and that if I hadn't had the guts to stop it then, it would all have ended in tears somewhere down the line.

I was so caught up in all the madness surrounding the separation and the undoing of all the arrangements that I didn't have a moment for the emotional impact to hit me. I tried to put off thinking about it even longer by impulsively booking a holiday with some girlfriends – I was flying out that night. I couldn't escape my own head and heart forever, though. On the morning of the wedding day I was lying in bed at my family home in Ballyfermot, trying to keep my thoughts on the holiday in Spain, but unable to keep out all the other thoughts about Brian and the future we weren't having together. I was lost in my emotions, feeling everything all at once, when suddenly there was a knock on the front door. I heard my mother going down the hall, then pulling open the door. The sound of the male voice that drifted to my room was that of the local priest. I shot up in bed with the shock. Oh dear God!

I heard him say cheerfully, 'Good morning, Mrs Byrne, have you got a wedding here?' I swear I could feel my blood turn cold in my veins. There was an awful silence before my mother stammered an answer and explained what had happened. I sat there, unable to move a muscle, shocked rigid. Their voices murmured on, until eventually I heard the front door closing. Then I listened as Mam's footsteps came down the hall, up the stairs and to the door of my room. 'You bitch!' she cried as she flung open the door. 'Oh, Ma,' I wailed, 'I forgot about the church!' She was mortified and gave out yards to me. Thinking about it later, I couldn't understand why he hadn't realised there was a problem when I hadn't been down there for the past three weeks and hadn't paid any money or decorated the church or anything. Just as well I'm going to Spain tonight, I thought to myself as Mam ranted at me for being selfish, 'otherwise she'd probably kill me.'

I flew out to Majorca with my friends that night and felt a weight lift off my shoulders as the plane rose into the sky and I left Mam, Brian and Ireland behind. My four girlfriends and I were headed for Santa Ponça, on the south-west coast of Majorca. It should have been my honeymoon I was going on that night, but instead it was a girly holiday to help me get over all the whole sorry saga. It was exactly what I needed – non-stop laughs and fun, with no pressure to do anything other than laze about, suntan and eat and drink. I had two great weeks there and I loved it. We met twelve Irish guys who were on a lads trip together and we christened them 'The Apostles'. We used to have great craic with them. You'd be lying face-down sunbathing, with your top unclipped, and the next thing you knew you'd be picked up and flung into the pool, topless. Of course, you'd end up getting off with one or two of them, or maybe three or four of them, as the week went on, but it was all very innocent – no sex, just kissing. I certainly had no interest in getting involved with anyone. I felt it would be a long, long time before I'd want to try another relationship, so I couldn't in a million years have imagined what was going to happen next.

6. The Love of A Good Woman

After the holiday and the drama of the break-up, I was back in Dublin and it was a huge anti-climax. I was in a state of confusion about what I was doing and where I was going in my life. I suppose I turned in on myself a bit at the time, not wanting to attract attention from anyone because I needed to just be on my own for a while. While it had been my choice to leave Brian because I knew, deep down, that he wasn't the right man for me, I still felt very upset and traumatized by the ending of our five-year relationship. It's a hard situation to be in – because you're the one who left, everyone thinks you're doing just grand, but the truth is you're hurting just as much inside as the other person, but you're not really allowed to show it or expect sympathy for it. So I was kind of floating along in a daze, unsure what to do or think or feel. I certainly wasn't looking for a relationship, and I most definitely wasn't looking to have a lesbian relationship. But that's what happened.

After the break-up I left the house in Tallaght I'd shared with Brian and started sharing a rented flat in Inchicore with a girl who worked in CB Packaging. When I moved in with her, I had no inkling that Lorna (not her real name) was gay. She was just my friend and we got on brilliantly. I only found out about her sexuality when she confided in another girl in work. That girl, whose first name, comically enough, given the situation, was Gay, came to me and told me that Lorna was gay. 'You're joking me!' I said in disbelief – lesbians weren't exactly ten a penny in 1970s Dublin. I genuinely had no idea Lorna might fancy girls, it had never even occurred to me. 'No, I'm not joking,' Gay said, 'and she's in the toilet right now, very upset.' Gay then looked at me for a moment before adding that Lorna had said she fancied me. I went off to the toilet, to try to comfort her. I remember I said, 'So what if you're gay? You're still my mate.' Then I said to her, 'You don't fancy me, do you?' 'No,' she sobbed, 'I fancy bloody Gay.' I went back out to Gay and said, 'It's not me she fancies – it's you!' Gay, who wore trousers all the time but was very feminine, started shouting, 'I'm not gay! I'm not gay!' It was like a comedy of errors. Later on, after we became involved in a relationship, Lorna admitted that it was me, not Gay, she was besotted with, but when I asked her straight out that day, she was afraid she'd lose my friendship if she confessed how she felt about me, so she pretended Gay was the one she wanted. You couldn't make it up!

We continued to share a flat and be great friends, but that was all. Lorna did like me, though, so it was only a matter of time before something would happen. The very first incident between us happened when we went away on a holiday in the summer of 1981, backpacking across America for six weeks. We saved for it and went without holidays for a whole year so we could take all our holiday leave in one go. We flew into John F. Kennedy International Airport in New York, then we hopped on a greyhound bus that would take us across the States as we headed for the bright lights of Las Vegas. I remember the excitement of stopping off in places like Amarillo and Cheyenne, which until then I had only known from the movies and TV. I have a vivid memory of driving through Kansas and the driver announcing, 'If you look to the left, folks, you'll see a tornado!' Even though it was only a small tornado in the middle of a massive field, Lorna and myself were all excited and had our faces pressed against the window of the bus as we followed its path. 'That's Kansas for you, girls!' the driver added.

When we got to Las Vegas after our four-day bus journey, we immediately looked around for a place to eat and found The Plaza Hotel at the top of The Strip. When we looked at the menu, we realised we couldn't have picked a more expensive place to eat. Then, we got chatting to a big Irish-American guy who was working in the hotel. 'You two are travelling around America by yourselves?!' he exclaimed, when we told him about our grand adventure. We didn't think we were doing anything special, but two young Irish women travelling alone across the US was a big deal. We shared a drink with the guy and the two of us got quite drunk. It was still early in the day at this stage and we hadn't booked any accommodation for the night. The guy we'd been chatting with suggested the Orbit Motel, off The Strip, so we set off, giggling and laughing, full of the joys of alcohol.

The Orbit had vacancies and we booked a double room. Our plan was to dump our bags, freshen up and change and head back out on the town. I took a quick shower and as I was coming out of the bathroom with a towel wrapped around me, Lorna passed me on the way in to have her shower. We brushed up against each other and without any warning, she kissed me on the lips. Nothing was said between us and she continued on into the bathroom to take her shower. I was left standing there in shock and embarrassment, thinking, Shit! What am I going to do? When Lorna emerged from the bathroom, nothing was mentioned by either of us. Although that kiss on the lips frightened me, when we returned to the room that night, very drunk after painting Vegas red, we had a really passionate kiss. What happened then was all a bit of a blur afterwards, but I think we were just trying it out, experimenting to see what it was like. Nothing else happened between us on that holiday. We mentioned the kiss briefly at the end, before returning home, but we never spoke about it again for a long time after that.

At that time, Brian was still in contact with me because he wanted to stay friends, but it made things confusing and unsettling and I used to get very upset after talking to him. Through it all, Lorna was there for me, being a good friend and a shoulder to cry on. The November after we'd spent the summer in America, I celebrated my twenty-first birthday with a big bash in our flat. I invited Brian to come along because he was still a family friend, still going for drinks regularly with my brothers. Lorna and I weren't in a relationship at that point, we were still just sharing a flat, so it didn't feel odd to invite Brian to be there. It was a huge party and a big gang of people stayed over with us that night. All the beds were full and there were bodies crashed out all over the place. When I tried to crash out myself, I discovered my own bed was full, so I headed off to Lorna's room. She was there, with only one other person taking up space – a fella who was in a deep, alcoholic slumber at the foot of the bed. I squeezed in beside her, and just then Brian wandered into the room. When he saw us in the bed, a look of disgust crossed his face. He didn't see the guy passed out on the bed – just me and Lorna cuddled up side by side. Brian knew that she was gay because it was now public knowledge, and he jumped to the conclusion that we were being intimate. He left immediately and I'm sad to say that we didn't talk for years after that.

One night, about a month later, Lorna and I went to a hen party in Ballyfermot and stumbled back to the flat in the early hours, both of us very drunk. She kissed me … and it didn't feel bad. So, that was the start of it. I suppose it was inevitable, after sharing the intimate kiss and the emotional support she gave me in the aftermath of the split with Brian, that we would grow close. I just hadn't banked on it being that close! We became very comfortable with one another, though we both knew I wasn't gay and I didn't know why I was doing it. I suppose she had helped me through a bad patch in my personal life, and I didn't want to move out of that comfort zone in case I got hurt again. She was my comfort blanket.

Lorna wasn't a classic beauty, but there was something about her that stood out and was really attractive. I would describe her appearance as funny prettiness. She was nice-looking, with a smiley face framed by sandy-coloured, curly hair, and she was quite tall. She was a really nice person with a big, warm heart. She was gentle and more understanding than a man would be. I enjoyed all of that while we were together, even though I didn't have the feelings for her that she had for me. I needed her at the time, but I wasn't gay or bi-sexual. She would even say to me from time to time, 'You're not gay.' I would reply, 'I know!' Then she'd ask, 'Well then, what are you doing with me?' I would shake my head and smile, 'I don't know, you started it!' We used to laugh about it. That said, it was also a full-blown relationship that lasted for two years. In terms of the intimate side of it, to be honest, I don't even know if we did it right. For me, it was more about the hugging and kissing and just lying there together and being held. I don't think I fulfilled her sexually because I didn't know what to do, and she didn't know what to do either because I was her first. So while we were intimate and close and comfortable, it wasn't red hot sizzling lesbian sex – I didn't mind that, but I'm sure Lorna must have.

My family had their suspicions about us for a long time before they actually knew for definite that I was in a relationship with Lorna. Mam and Dad never admitted to me that they were aware of it, but Betty and my brothers did. Their reaction was typically laidback and generous: 'You're my sister and I love you and if you're happy, that's grand.' Towards the end of the second year, our relationship began to fizzle out. We both knew it was inevitable, given that I wasn't homosexual. Our 'final fling' together was a trip to the Canary Islands that Christmas. We flew out the week before Christmas and stayed right over the festive period, coming home the day after New Year's. We had become so used to travelling abroad together that it was a natural thing for us to do, even though we weren't getting on the same way anymore and even though her sister and brother came along, too. During that holiday I started having weird dreams and sensations – it was horrible. I couldn't sleep and if I drank alcohol to help me sleep, I had nightmares. On Christmas night I rang Betty at her home in Tallaght, as I had arranged to do before leaving on the holiday. She was the only one in the family with a phone at the time and Mam and Uncle Willie were there with her. Willie got on the phone to me and said, 'I can't believe I'm talking to you all the way over there in the Canaries. I think you're messing with me and you're only down the road!' We laughed, and at the end of the conversation I told him that I loved him. That night the horrendous nightmares came back. Apparently, I was screaming in my sleep and Lorna and her sister were trying to wake me. I woke up crying inconsolably, with no idea why. Later I would learn that Uncle Willie died suddenly the following day, from a massive heart attack.

I worshipped my Uncle Willie. He was Mam's brother and growing up, I didn't know a time in our house that he wasn't living with us. He had also lived with us in Manchester, where he was the one who had saved me from being flattened by the marble fireplace. He was like another parent to me, who had been there all my life. Mam and Willie were extremely close, too. Poor Willie had been through the mill in his personal life as a young man, and it was his sister he turned to for help and support. He had married an Irish girl and was head over heels in love, but his whole world collapsed when she left him. She did a bunk on him to England with another fella and later sent him divorce papers, but he refused to sign them. Willie never became involved with another woman after that – she had been the love of his life and he just shut down after she left him. He was a lonely man, but he loved being part of our family. He had lived with Aunt Mary for a time and then in a flat on his own. Living alone ended after he nearly burned down the flat one evening. He had been in the pub and when he arrived home, he put a pot of traditional

Dublin coddle, made for him by my Mam, on the stove to heat up. Then he fell asleep. Luckily, my brother, Jimmy, happened to call in and he rescued Willie before there was a tragedy; the only damage suffered was a hole in the bottom of the pot. Jimmy packed Uncle Willie's bags and brought him straight home to Mam, and that's where he stayed.

Sometimes there would be arguments between my father and Willie because, obviously, the husband and the brother-in-law living together could lead to tensions. Dad was very aware that Mam cared about Willie as much as she did about him, and that made him jealous. There was even the odd punch thrown here and there in their younger days, when someone would get drunk and say something they shouldn't, but those incidents were few and far between.

Willie adored his grand-nieces and nephews and looked forward to them visiting the house – Betty's children, Diana and Brenda, and Tomo's son, Gordon. Willie loved playing with them and he'd have them mesmerised by the stories he'd make up for them. We had a big, old television with a door covering the screen and he used to tell Gordon that there was a man living in it and that he'd come out the door after him if he went near it. Gordon didn't mess with the telly after that! Willie was always very good to my mother. Whenever he won money in the bookies or got extra in his wages, he'd always throw her a few pounds. There was a great mutual love there.

I celebrated the New Year in the Canaries and flew back home to Dublin, blissfully unaware that my Uncle Willie was dead. The family had decided not to spoil my holiday by telling me the bad news because they knew that I would be devastated. I arrived back at my family home around ten o'clock at night, to find all the clan there having a party. I remember thinking how it was unusual for everyone to gather like that to welcome me home. They were all drinking and I had brought home bottles of duty-free Blue Label vodka, so I opened one and joined them.

With so many people in the house, it was the best part of an hour before I noticed that Willie was missing. I suddenly said, 'Where's me Uncle Willie?' The hum in the room fell silent and Mam said, 'Oh, he's up in Aunt Ellen's.' I asked why, saying to my dad, 'Did you have a fight with him?' Dad said, 'No, I'm not fighting with Willie.' So, it was around 3.00am and we were having a sing-song, when suddenly my eldest brother, Jimmy, said, 'This is ridiculous, you have to be told.' Jimmy broke the news to me that Willie was dead and buried, and I fell to pieces.

Willie's passing was the first close death that I had experienced. I remember my Uncle Tom, Willie and Mam's brother, dying when I was younger, but although he lived around the corner from us, I wasn't close to him. I was away on the Oakwood farm in County Wicklow when he died and, just like with Willie, I was only told when I arrived home, which was a few days after his funeral. Mam told me and I ran upstairs and cried, but the tears weren't for Tom; I wanted to be back in Oakwood. This time, I had lost someone to whom I was very close and loved very much. It was like the moon not rising, to have Willie not there with us. I couldn't cope with the grief and his loss completely unsettled me. Two weeks later, I left Ireland, with Lorna, and went to a kibbutz in Israel.

7. The Commune and the Calling

**W**hen I decided, pretty much on a whim, to leave Ireland for Israel, I hadn't a clue what a kibbutz even was. It was a blind adventure into the unknown, but it would turn out to be one of the great experiences of my life. Over the next year I would lose a woman, but gain a man and some great friends and a wealth of fantastic memories. But as I went through the motions of packing and saying goodbye to everyone, I had no idea what I was doing. After the shock of Uncle Willie's death, I just wanted to run away from my life. I was depressed and in mourning, and I hated seeing my mother so sad. So I ran away, as people do. It was Lorna who had done all the research about the kibbutz, and when she read out the basics to me I immediately said, 'Let's do it. I want to get out of here.'

I left Ireland in the second week of January, with my mind in a whirl. As we flew out of Dublin Airport on a frosty morning, even my relationship with Lorna was drifting away, if not already over. I couldn't think about that, though, or I'd lose my mind altogether, so I just focused on the flights and the connections and the travel plans. We flew to Luton and on to Tel Aviv, in Israel. Once there, we were greeted by a smiling Lustique, the big Israeli guy who ran Kibbutz Geva in the Jezreel Valley, near the city of Afula. Lustique threw our bags into the back of a big, old American bus and drove us the two hours to the kibbutz, talking nineteen to the dozen about how great it was going to be and all we'd see and do.

When we got to Geva, the first thing I noticed was the amazing countryside, the fabulous views and the beautiful backdrop of Mount Gilboa. My dark mood lifted and I had a feeling that life was about to get a lot better. During my time there, I would have my breath taken away as I witnessed the sun rise from Gilboa; it's an unforgettable image, a memory that has stuck with me from my stay in the valley. But it was the community spirit in Geva that made the biggest impression on me. There were Germans, French, Swedish, Australians, South Africans, English and us two Irish women, all living together in the one community and all getting on brilliantly. It proved that there doesn't have to be violence in the world over religion, and that all human beings have the same basic needs, irrespective of race, colour or what god they worship. As far as everyone there was concerned, we all believed in the one God. If religion did come up in conversation, it was a case of, 'What do you believe in?' 'I believe in a Master of the Universe.' Everyone would nod and say, 'Yes, same here', 'Same here', 'Same here'. There was never a debate about it.

So, I finally got to find out what a kibbutz actually was. It's basically a self-sufficient group of people, where everybody is treated as an equal and all the income goes into a common fund. One of the jobs I had in Kibbutz Geva was out in the fields, collecting grapefruits, and I also worked in their factory, making nuts and bolts. When we arrived, we were given old army outfits to wear, which were our working clothes. We were given the equivalent of £3 and three packets of cigarettes a week, but we didn't need much money because everything was provided free for us, including our food three times a day. I was brought to the kitchens at five in the evening, twice a week, to help get the meals ready, but I didn't mind that because they were air-conditioned and you could snack on pieces of chicken here and there as you prepared the food. We lived in huts, two or three to a room. We worked from six in the morning till twelve noon, when it would become too hot to carry on doing outdoor labour. Then you had the rest of the day free to do what you liked, including sunbathing and cooling off in the big swimming pool. Some evenings we'd drink Dutch beer, which cost tuppence a bottle and was like rocket fuel. You couldn't drink every night, though, because you had to be up at six in the morning. Saturday was the Jewish Sabbath, which was celebrated with festive meals, so Saturday night was our big night to have a drink. Even though I couldn't speak a word of Hebrew, I got on well with the Israelis and I was quite proud of the relationship I built up with them. They liked me and that was a good personal lift at a time when I really needed one.

Another boost to my ego came in the form of a gorgeous big English bloke called Dave. He was tall, had a beard – I always went for guys with beards when I was younger – black hair and big brown eyes. He was built like a house, with not an ounce of flab on him. Oh, he was a fine thing! By this stage, we had been three months in Kibbutz Geva and Lorna and myself had more or less accepted that we were no longer together as a couple, although she hadn't fully come to terms with this. I was her first big relationship, so it was harder for her to deal with the split. As we both knew, I wasn't gay, so that also made it easier for me to accept that our relationship was at an end. It was obviously difficult for Lorna, watching me getting close to the gorgeous Dave.

It wasn't all plain sailing with Dave either, though. One of the first things he said to me was that he didn't like Irish people. It turned out he had been a soldier in the British Army and had served in Belfast while the Troubles were raging in the 1970s. Long before we got together, Dave and I would have big arguments about this, with me telling him that he shouldn't judge books by their covers and tarnish all Irish people with the same brush. I also argued that his views went against the spirit of the kibbutz. Dave could be quite big-headed, but I soon knocked that out of him. Later, he told me that my constant arguing with him was what attracted him to me. Apparently, I was the first woman who had ever stood up to him and said, 'F*** you!' He used to say, 'If there's any Irish I like, there's only one, and that's you.' Back home in England, Dave had been going out with an Israeli woman, but they had broken up before he arrived in the kibbutz. He was nursing a broken heart when I came along, so I suppose I filled that gap for him.

When we finally got together, it wasn't easy for Lorna, who was still with me on the kibbutz. Our relationship was over, but she found it difficult to let go and it was hurting her terribly to see me with somebody else, even though it was a man and not another woman. One night, as I was sleeping next to Dave, she burst in on us. She was a bit drunk and in a rage, ranting and raving at us. The following day she was embarrassed and apologised for creating such a big scene, but we both understood where she was coming from. It was just normal jealousy and hurt that she was trying to deal with at the time. Lorna wasn't one to hold a grudge, so as time went on, she became more comfortable around Dave and myself, particularly when we started to travel around and she began to meet other people. It was then that everything settled into place.

Travelling was part of the experience of living on the kibbutz. When you had worked for three months, you were entitled to a week off. The Israelis used to pack us into their big buses and take us off to show us their Israel. It was a great way to experience the country and we were treated like kings and queens; they were lovely people. I remember when we visited Jerusalem and Bethlehem, and I couldn't believe I was actually at the place where Jesus Christ was born. That was a huge thrill for me. A crowd of people were singing 'Silent Night' in different languages and I cried the whole way through because it was so emotional and so touching. We also took a trip into Egypt, where we went sight-seeing around Cairo. You could travel for little or nothing money-wise, so it was a great opportunity to see the different countries and cultures.

When our time was up on the kibbutz, after nearly a year, Lorna travelled around Europe with Dave and me, visiting Greece, Turkey, Italy, Germany and Norway, before I returned to Ireland. Dave and I parted on good terms. There were lots of promises made, of course. I was supposed to go to England and we'd get engaged, all that kind of thing. I never did. Once we went our separate ways, I realised it was just a holiday romance. It was obviously the same for him, too, because he never came looking for me in Dublin. Eventually, I lost contact with Dave and I have no idea where he is now, or how his life turned out. I'm sure there were times when he must have wondered, 'Whatever happened to that mad Irishwoman?' I'd like to think that he watched me on 'The X Factor'. I hope he was looking in, and that he remembered the good times we had together. I remember him putting his hand on my head when I was going home and telling me, 'No matter what happens in life, Mary, I'll always have a great memory of you. You're a great woman.'

It's only now, as I reflect on my life and recall those memories, that I realise I had so many positive things going on way back then. Now I see all the good things that were given to me – like that massive compliment from Dave. It was fabulous, but it didn't register with me at the time. Back then, I was a sponge that only soaked up the bad stuff. The negative side got me nowhere, except deeper and deeper into a person I shouldn't have been. I should have held on to the positives, like I do now. But when you're young, it's easier to take things for granted and ignore life's little gifts and adventures. I wish it had been different, but that's just the way I was.

I got back to Dublin in 1982 and the sameness of everything immediately got me down. Lorna and I had gone our separate ways as partners, but we remained friends and were now working in a factory in Tallaght, I-Tech, which made security alarms. Not long after I got home, I went to Ballyfermot church to pray. I knew I was at a crossroads in my life, even though I was just twenty-three. After having romantic entanglements with both male and female partners, there was a lot of confusion in my head to sort out. Strange as it might sound, I was drawn back to the Church because I still hadn't given up on my childhood ambition of becoming a nun.

This idea had started way back, in primary school. I always thought the nuns in school looked special, but there was one in particular who made a big impression on me when I was very young. She was a novice, and sometimes when our teacher was out, this young nun would fill in for her. I remember she was very pretty, small in stature and she looked really elegant in her black habit. I think that as she was the first person to make such an impression on me, I wanted to be just like her, which meant being a nun. She looked like a happy bride, not that I knew what a bride was then, but when I think back now, that's what she looked like to me, this pretty little thing who had given up her possible life of sex and children (I didn't know all that then, either), all the normal things that women do. To me, she looked so joyous and contented, and I wanted to feel like that. When she read a story to us, her soft voice enchanted me. The book she read to us each day was *Heidi*, and I still love that book and the movie that followed. Every single day she was with us, she would make time to read to us for an hour, and I would be transported into the imaginary world of *Heidi* as the story unfolded. I couldn't wait for the next day to come so I could hear the next chapter. The story captivated me because of the way she read it, and as I listened, I felt a pull towards this woman and her chosen vocation.

It had gone further than that, too. When I was fourteen, I decided it was time to do something about becoming a nun. I had my heart set on it.

When I told my mother, she had mixed feelings about it. On the one hand, Mam seemed quite proud of the fact that I had a religious calling, but I could see that she was also upset at the thought of me leaving home. 'Are you actually going to do this?' she kept asking. 'Are you going to leave me?' I nodded. My mind was made up. I had always loved my Catechism, I believed in Jesus, I believed that this man was going to help me through my life, and I still do.

Mam arranged for me to go up and see our then local priest, Father Wall, who was a lovely, gentle person, very kind and everyone's favourite. As I fidgeted with my cardigan, I remember him explaining to me the difficulties of being a nun. He pointed out the downsides, to try to make me understand the reality of what I was choosing, in case I had some kind of romantic notion about the life I wanted to take on. In hindsight, it was a romantic notion. But at the time I was having none of it, insisting to Father Wall that I definitely wanted to be a nun. He just smiled, then said he would arrange for me to meet with the local order and they would take it further.

Father Wall got back in contact shortly afterwards and sent me for a meeting with some nuns at a convent in Seven Oaks, in Ballyfermot. My sister-in-law, Geraldine, came with me and I was all excited. The nuns invited us in and gave us tea and buns, and the more I watched them potter around, the more I wanted to be a nun. In fairness, they took a very practical approach to my interest in joining the sisterhood. 'You're very young,' a quiet-spoken nun said to me at the end of tea and after a lot of chit-chat. Then she offered me some sound advice: 'What we'd like to see you do is go out in the world and live your life. And if, by the time you're 18, 20 or even 30, you'd still like to be a nun, come back to us.' I don't know how planned it was, but I had definitely taken that advice.

Now here I was, in Ballyfermot church at the age of twenty-three, with plenty of life experience under my ... well, the chastity belt was long gone

… and still wondering if God wanted me to be a nun. I remember feeling a strange sensation as I sat there talking to Him. 'I don't know what to do with my life,' I told Him. 'I'm sorry for the sins I've done. Please show me the way. Even if it takes a long time, guide me to the right path …' As I spoke, I got this feeling that there was someone standing beside me. I can't describe it, but I felt as if, in my eyes, it was God, it was Jesus. A beautiful, warm glow came over me and I felt very close to Him. I looked up at the crucifix in the church and I said, 'Do you want me to be a nun? Is that what you're calling me for?'

I honestly believed that I had something to give as a nun, be it the gift of the gab or a bit of love and caring and compassion. On the other hand, maybe I was searching for love and I saw it in Christ? He couldn't put his arms around me physically, like I wanted someone to put their arms around me and look after me, but His was a love I could accept. Sitting in the church that day, with the candles flickering and the incense hanging heavy in the air, I made the decision to go and find out if this was what was being laid out for me in life by God. I contacted a convent in Clondalkin and the head nun there, Sister Nuala, arranged for me to come and see her. I went up on a Sunday morning after Mass and Sister Nuala answered the door. She was a very jolly person.

'Follow me into the kitchen, Mary,' she called cheerfully and I trailed in after her. The kitchen was a hive of activity, with several nuns busy cooking the dinner, or lunch as we call it these days. If I'd any doubts about what I was doing, they disappeared in that moment. There was a lovely 'family' feeling and a warm, happy atmosphere as the nuns worked, chatted and laughed side by side. I would have joined up that very second if Sister Nuala had given me the invitation. I felt really safe and secure among those chirpy nuns in that lovely kitchen, which was filled with the mouthwatering aroma of a delicious Sunday roast that was cooking gently in the huge Aga.

As the other nuns flitted around us in a very industrious fashion, Sister Nuala sat with me and we had a long, deep conversation. She asked me all about my background and what I had been doing in life up to that point. I told her about my experiences, although I felt there were some things she didn't need to know, at least not at that moment. I didn't tell her any lies, but I didn't tell her everything at the same time. There are some things a nun shouldn't hear before she has her dinner! Sister Nuala was, I felt, taking a very serious approach to my vocation. She discussed my education and I told her about my problem with spelling. I was delighted to hear that more education could be arranged for me, so that wouldn't be a problem. It was all sounding very good and I left the convent that day feeling great. It looked like my life was going to take a turn for the better and that, after all these years of dreaming about it, I was finally going to answer my calling and become a nun. I felt happy and more hopeful than I had in a long time.

Before I left the convent that morning – they didn't ask me to stay for dinner! – Sister Nuala suggested that I should take six months to think things through. After that, I was to return to her with my final decision. I was happy to take this course, even though I had my mind made up at that moment and was certain that I wanted to be part of convent life. Six months won't make any difference, I thought confidently as I made my way home. I couldn't have been more wrong.

8. Mr Irresistible

As I slipped through the door of our neighbourhood pub for a mid-week drink with my friends, a stranger at the bar was about to change the course of my life. I had settled back into a routine in Dublin, working in Tallaght, living and socialising in Ballyfermot. Mam and Dad were thrilled to have me back in the house, and I didn't mind it as much as I thought I would. I was floating along nicely, still seriously thinking about the nunhood since my talk with Sister Nuala three months earlier. Right at that moment, though, I was looking forward to having a few drinks, a laugh and a good gossip with two of my friends, Maggie and Julie, down at our local, The Lawns, in Ballyfermot.

I walked into the bar and instantly spotted the finest-looking backside I'd ever seen in my life. The fella it belonged to was standing at the counter with two other guys. He was 6ft tall with long, dark hair. I generally wasn't into men with long hair, but this guy was something else. When he glanced around, I could see that he was very good looking, with chiselled features – a real matinee idol. It was like he had just walked out of a Hollywood movie and into our grey world. With his height, strong build, handsome features and warm look, he reminded me of my father to a certain extent. All I could think was, 'Oh God, I want him!' Talk about being hooked – he had me before he even said a word!

I was in a fluster and nudged the girls, muttering, 'Ooh, look at him. Fine bit of stuff!' Suddenly, he turned around fully and looked straight at me. Well, he might have been looking at the other girls as well, but as far as I was concerned his eyes were on me – and I had one of those movie moments, you know, when a couple spot each other across a crowded room and romantic music starts playing? Well, that was my moment – without the music, obviously. I was incredibly attracted to him and couldn't stop staring over at him. 'He's the one I'm going to marry,' I told the girls, as they split their sides laughing at me

It turned out that Julie actually knew this beautiful man, and she told me his name was Robbie. Julie eventually went up to the bar and chatted with him and his two friends for a short time, before inviting them to come over and join us at our table. They did, and soon we were all yapping together. I was still almost spaced out with desire – words were coming out of my mouth, but I had no idea what I was saying. I was in awe of the guy; he made me feel like a love-sick teenager all over again. I remember how I was thinking stuff like, 'Oh my God! He is a god!' Julie had told me that Robbie wasn't married or even in a relationship, which was music to my ears. Before our time was up in the pub I turned to him and said, 'You're walking me home tonight.' Then I thought, 'Did I just say that? Out loud?' The words had just spilled out of my mouth. I don't ever recall being so cheeky with a fella I'd just met, but I wanted this guy and I wasn't going to let him get away. His answer seemed to take an eternity, but when he did reply it warmed my heart. 'Yeah, okay,' he said simply, but those words sent my pulse racing.

Our conversation on the walk home is a blur to me, but when we reached my house and said goodnight, we kissed. To me, he was the best kisser I'd ever experienced. I was now beyond rescuing from this man. As we parted outside my home that night, I was a bit disappointed that Robbie didn't ask me out on an official date. Instead, there was a very loose arrangement – he just said he'd be in The Lawns the following Saturday night. Not to be put off, I took that as an offer to come meet him there. Over the next couple of days, in the countdown to Saturday night, I couldn't stop thinking about him. I could barely concentrate on my work in the factory. I kept thinking, 'What if he's not there? What if I never see him again?' I was consumed by thoughts of him in the foolish way people are during the first throes of passion, love and, the most deadly of all … lust.

I was on tenterhooks as I made my way up to The Lawns that Saturday night, all dolled up, wearing an outfit that included a short skirt and high heels. My heart was thumping against my ample chest and I was on fire as I went through the door. Robbie was standing by the bar, with a smile on his face. I nearly let out a yelp, I was so relieved to see that he'd turned up to meet me. Even though I knew nothing about him or his personal life, I was now certain of one thing: this was the man I was going to marry. I also knew that I wasn't destined to be a nun. I'm not sure whether it was God or lust that had decided that for me – probably the latter.

We hit it off together and after that Saturday night, we continued to meet up for drinks at The Lawns with our friends. We didn't leap into bed straight away or anything like that. The relationship developed casually and slowly over a few weeks. There were social drinks with our mutual pals, but nothing much else was happening. Actually, I still wasn't a hundred per cent sure that I had landed him at that stage. Then out of the blue, he finally asked me to meet him for a drink, just the two of us, and we got on brilliantly. He left me home, there was some kissing and cuddling, and I was even more sure that this was the man for me. After that, we started going out on regular dates and it was the happiest time in my life. I was floating around on a cloud.

A few weeks later, I brought Robbie home to meet Mam and Dad. Mam liked him immediately. Dad just said, 'How'ya!' I don't know if they saw how gone I was on him, and how it could all end in disaster as a result, but if they did, they kept it to themselves and let me have my wild romance – at least for a while.

Even in those early days, the relationship didn't run smoothly. I was left confused and hurt when he stood me up on a couple of dates after only a few weeks. I obviously didn't do a very good job hiding the pain from my parents. 'That fella is going to break your heart, he's going to tear you apart,' Mam told me after another letdown. 'Oh yeah, you think you know everything,' I said angrily, annoyed at her for saying such a thing. Even though he was messing me around, I didn't want to hear a bad word said about Robbie. So I was relieved and felt vindicated when Robbie started to become more reliable, stopped missing dates and we started to grow closer and closer. After those early hiccups, we had a great year together, and for the first time in my life I felt really blessed and content in my world.

Then came the bombshell to wreck it all. I was completely floored when Robbie confessed to me one night, out of the blue, that he had been seeing another woman and that he was torn between the two of us. He wanted her, but he also wanted me. Words can't express the pain and devastation that ripped through me at that moment. It felt like someone close to me had just died, like a death in the family, and I went into convulsions, crying my eyes out. I could not believe it. It wasn't just sex or a one-night stand with another woman, he was emotionally involved with her. Apparently, he had been seeing this woman on and off before he met me, but this was the first I'd heard of it. The worst thing was, I had never suspected for a moment that he might be seeing someone else when he was with me. I couldn't take in what I was hearing. Why did he want to be with her now, when he had me? For the first time in my life, I had met someone who I really, really wanted to be with … and he had someone else on his mind. That night, I came home from the pub, went to bed and cried myself to sleep.

I decided I couldn't have anything to do with him then and we split up, which was a big blow after a happy year together, at least for me. I drifted around aimlessly for a while after that, with a big, black cloud hanging over me as I struggled to pick up the pieces and live without him. When you're used to a way of life, including another person in the decisions you take week in and week out and investing all your emotions in that person, it leaves a huge, gaping hole when they're gone. Mam and Dad were great, though. They just quietly supported me and gave me the space to sort myself out.

Two months later, and I was still miserable. The green-eyed monster had come out and I was very jealous that some other woman had taken this beautiful man from me. Even so, I still couldn't bring myself to hate Robbie. One day, he rang me, completely unexpected, to tell me he had finished with the other woman. He said it had been a complex relationship and he never knew where he stood with her, so he had decided to end it. He was calling to tell me this because he wanted us to pick up where we had left off. Well, there's no fool like a besotted fool, is there? I took Robbie back. The way I saw it, with my twenty-six years of experience of the world, there was no such thing as a perfect life and nothing was black and white. I accepted that people could lose control and get caught up in all kinds of relationships as I thought about my own past with Lorna and Dave. So I decided to forgive Robbie. I couldn't really do anything else – I was still mad about the man.

After the break-up and make-up, I felt more secure with Robbie because he seemed very happy when we were together. One weekend, I went off camping to Killarney, County Kerry, with some of my friends, and when I arrived back I met up with Robbie and we ended up having sex at my house, after which he went off home. For some strange reason, I remember thinking to myself straight away, 'I'm pregnant'. I don't know why I thought that, but I did. There was no conflict in me about this. I wanted the baby from that very first thought. I'm sure some would argue that I wanted his baby in order to have a hold on him, others might say I was the right age to settle down and start a family – I don't know the full truth of it myself, but I was happy to have a baby and as far as I was concerned, it wasn't going to be long before I became a mother.

Even though my instinct kept on telling me that I was pregnant, there was no way I was going to mention it to Robbie until I was absolutely sure that there was, to quote Aunt Mary, 'a bun in the oven'. There was only one way to find out, so I went to the doctor and had a test done. I was told that it would be a week before the results came back. *A week!* I was never going to be able to live through an entire week to find out whether or not I was expecting a baby. I was right – I lasted three days and then I cajoled and persuaded Tomo's wife, Geraldine, to ring the Coombe Maternity Hospital on my behalf and plead my case with them. Geraldine lied to the person on the other end of the phone and said that I needed to know the result as soon as possible because I was on my own and was in a terrible state. Geraldine was obviously convincing, because they went off, got my file and gave her the news … the result was positive. My sister-in-law went white in the face and put down the phone. I instantly felt a crazy rush of emotions and was a bit overcome. I didn't know how I felt. I wanted to hear the test was positive, but I wasn't prepared for the reality of it when Geraldine actually said the words. My first reaction was, 'We have to go home and tell Mam.'

My head was spinning as I made my way to Ballyfermot. I was smiling one minute, then filled with fear the next. I wasn't sure how Mam was going to take it. When I arrived, she was relaxing on the sofa and I think she could tell from the look on my face that something was up. 'Mam, I have some news,' I said. When I finally managed to get the words out, her reaction couldn't have been better. She got up, put her arm around my waist and said, 'Ah, don't worry about it, Mary, we're here for you. You know you'll always have us.' Then I told my brother, Willie, and he just said, 'So!' I had sort of already said to my Dad, a few days earlier, that I thought I might be pregnant, so he wasn't shocked either. I was always very open with my parents, but when Mam heard that Dad knew before her, she was livid. 'Why didn't you tell me?' she demanded in a rage – he probably got what she wanted to give me.

The next person I had to tell was the father himself. I rang Robbie at work and asked if he would meet me that evening. I was terrified about telling him, not knowing how he was going to take it. To add to my discomfort, it was an absolute scorcher of an evening as I walked to St Matthew's Church, to meet him off the No. 78 bus from his home in nearby Blackditch. As I neared the church, I got more nervous by the second. My heart was in my mouth when the bus arrived and I saw Robbie getting off. 'How'ya, how's it going?' he said, which was his usual greeting. Before he said another word, I just blurted it out there and then on the street. 'Look, I'm pregnant,' I said quickly, and I'm sure I was ashen-faced by this stage.

Robbie didn't react immediately. He said nothing for a few minutes. I was sweating. Oh God, please say something, my head was screaming When he eventually did, the words that came out of his mouth weren't what I wanted to hear. I don't know what I had expected from Robbie, but I hadn't been prepared for his negative reaction. Even though I would have loved it, I never expected him to fall into my arms and tell me our world was about to get a lot better. I wouldn't have been surprised if he'd said he was shocked and needed a bit of time to get used to the idea that he was about to become a father. That wouldn't have been an unnatural reaction in the circumstances. But even though he had helped to make this baby inside me, Robbie simply wasn't able to accept the reality of what he was hearing. I think anger welled up in me then and I snapped at him, 'It's alright, just forget about it' and walked away. When I looked back, he was still standing there, in shock. For a brief moment I thought,

'Maybe he'll have a change of heart and come after me', but he didn't. I held in my emotions until I got home, but once I was in the safety of my own bedroom, the dam burst and I cried my heart out. Even though my family were in the house, I had never felt so alone in all my life.

As soon I discovered that I was pregnant, I changed my lifestyle to make sure that I'd have a healthy baby, although Mother Nature had a part to play in that, too, because I was very sick for the first three months and couldn't look at a drop of alcohol or at any sugary, fatty foods. I didn't socialise for about the first six months of the pregnancy, but then one evening I decided to put on my best maternity dress and go down to The Lawns for a night out with my sister-in-law, Geraldine. I thought I looked great that evening, in my dress and with my now very obvious bump. When I walked into the bar I got a lovely, warm reception from the staff and customers. They all knew me well, especially because I'd sing the odd song for them, so they were fond of me as a regular. I was saying hello to people, smiling at them all, delighted to be out again, when suddenly, I noticed Robbie standing at the bar. My legs went to jelly, but I stayed calm and just ignored him. Even though I was now going through a terrible time, worrying about my future on my own with a child, I hadn't a single regret about our baby. I was proud of my decision to be this baby's mother, even if I had to do it all on my own. The child in my womb had been conceived out of love. I loved Robbie, and the baby we had made would be born out of the love that I had for him in my heart. I was crazy about him, no matter what.

My beautiful little baby daughter, Deborah, arrived into the world on 2 January 1987, weighing 7 pounds. All through the pregnancy I thought I was having a boy, but when the nurse asked what did I think I'd had, I said without hesitation, 'A girl!' She held my baby up to me and I thought she looked perfect, from the gorgeous hair on her head to her little tiny toes. Every mother thinks her baby is beautiful, but Deborah really was a

Above: My handsome
dad, Thomas Byrne, and
beautiful mother, Lily
White, pictured in their
young days at the
opening of The County
Bar in Ballyfermot.

Right: Mam, aged 16,
with my Granny White,
her own mother.

Left: A cherished memory –
Dad on our holiday together in
Orlando, Florida.

Below: Proud grandmother –
my Mam with my niece,
Diana. All the grandchildren
adored their Nanny.

Right: A family get-together –
my brother Jimmy and my
Uncle Jim from Manchester.

Below: A pair of Jokers!
Tomo, my brother, having a
laugh with our niece, Diana.

Left: I'm trying my best to look like a little angel on the day of my First Holy Communion.

Right: Oh God! I look like I have the worries of the world on my young shoulders.

Right: I was a busty teenager, which made me popular with the boys.

Below: Enjoying a night out with my gorgeous brother-in-law, Liam, my sister, Betty, and Dad.

Left: My beautiful baby daughter, Deborah, on her 1st birthday.

Below: Deborah's First Holy Communion, with Dad and myself. Our smiles hide our heartaches over Mam's recent passing.

Right: Two peas in a pod ...
I love the relationship I have with Deborah.

Below: Sisterly love ...
I've always looked up to my big sister, Betty.

Karaoke Queen: Singing in a pub on holiday, before 'The X Factor'.

beauty. I fell head over heels in love with her at first sight. This was the child I had talked to for nine months, telling her all about the family she was going to join very soon. I kept promising 'the bump' that I would do my best, and that I was so sorry there was no Daddy around.

At first, I was euphoric, on a complete high to have met my daughter at last, so happy that she was healthy and I was well. After that initial high, there came a low and I got the baby blues. It was like it suddenly hit me that I was going back out into the world to rear a child, on my own. I felt so scared. I was gripped by a terrible depression and started to scream and scream as I sat there in the bed, paralysed by fear. The nurse came running into me, pulled the curtains around my bed and listened as I spilled out my guts to her about my fears and anxieties. I got it all out of my system, and eventually calmed down.

When the time came to leave the hospital, I thought I wasn't going to be able to take Deborah home with me because she kept vomiting up her bottles. I remember sitting up in bed, with her in my arms, and I was whispering in her ear, 'Come on, baby, just take this bottle. It's only a few ounces and then I can take you home.' I was really worried about her, but then she suddenly perked up and was fine. I'm sorry now that I didn't breastfeed, but it wasn't really the done thing back then. Nonetheless, Deborah was a very healthy baby, which surprised me because I thought with me being so sick for the first three months, it might have affected her. I was very green about all that kind of thing at the time. I was about 11½ stone when I got pregnant, but as I couldn't keep down food, the weight dropped off me. Once all that sickness passed, though, I looked better and felt healthier than I ever did in my life. When I went into the Coombe to have my baby, I weighed just 9½ stone. There's a photograph of me at the I-Tech Christmas party in my maternity dress, with my hair cut very short, and even if I say so myself, I think I look really well in it. So being pregnant had suited me.

It was snowing the evening I left the hospital with Deborah. Liam and Betty came to bring us home to Ballyfermot. Deborah was wrapped in a huge pile of blankets and I was determined to carry her in my arms from the car to the house, ignoring Betty, who kept offering, 'I'll carry her.' One of the neighbours distracted me as she rushed out to have a look at the child and I slipped in the snow. I saved Deborah from harm, but I cut the feckin' knees off myself. We got into the house and it was stifling hot. There was no central heating, but Mam and Dad had a blazing fire in the grate, as well as a gas heater blasting away like a furnace. All the floors had been scrubbed, everything was spotless, and the family had gathered in excitement to see Deborah. I had only expected Mam and Dad to be there, but Jimmy and Kathleen were waiting for us, too, as were Tomo and Geraldine, and Willie, of course. It was like a family reunion to welcome Deborah into the house and into the clan. I forgot about all my cares that night as Deborah and myself were smothered with love. It was lovely and I really enjoyed those first few days.

Deborah was christened on 23 January, three weeks after she was born. I still hadn't heard or seen anything of Robbie. But about a week after the christening, I went up to The Lawns with all my friends, and there he was, standing at the bar, large as life and still as handsome. Hard as this is to believe, all my old feelings for him came flooding back the moment I laid eyes on him. Robbie nodded to me across the room, and I found myself smiling back at him. My friends were appalled, 'Oh, Mary, will you ever cop on?' But there was no talking to me. I was a fool in love all over again. Before the night was out, Robbie had made his way over to me and I had agreed to let him walk me home. It was as much my own fault as Robbie's that I continued to see him, on and off, for the next year, even though he wasn't part of Deborah's life. Thanks to my stupidity, I denied myself the chance of developing other, more serious relationships. In the course of that year two really good men came into my life, one after the other, and both wanted to take care of me and my child, but I fobbed them off because of Robbie, and the empty dream I clung to that eventually, we would be together as a family.

That dream kept me going for a year, but one day I woke up and came to my senses. I finally accepted that I was wasting my time and that there was never going to be a happy ending with Robbie. He wasn't a bad guy, but I knew that he was never going to commit to me and our child. So I ended the relationship, such as it was. I still loved the man, but he didn't feel the same way about me. We couldn't keep going like that.

Several years later I was at home alone with Deborah in a house the Corporation had provided for us in Cherry Orchard. The phone rang, and it was my friend, Monica, calling from The Lawns. She said she was going to drop up to see us; I was delighted to have the company. When the doorbell rang, I went out to find Monica on the step … with Robbie, and a male friend of his whom I didn't know. I couldn't believe it. Poor Monica thought she was doing a good deed, but I was rocked back on my heels by the sight of him, thinking, 'What the f*** is going on here!' Deborah, who was about six years old, was sitting on the couch in her nightdress. I said to her, 'This is Robbie.' She knew who he was because I had spoken so much about him. She kept looking from me to him and back again. I think he spoke to Deborah for about ten minutes then, and she asked him to write something to her in her notebook. When he left, I looked at what he had scribbled: 'Robbie was here.' Deborah has never forgotten that night.

I often asked God why he let me meet Robbie, if he wasn't meant for me. That relationship has affected me more than any other – it gave me the one person in the world I adore above all others, Deborah, but it also gave me years of heartache and uncertainty. Whatever the reason, it's all behind me now. If I passed Robbie on the street today, it wouldn't bother me because, thank God, I'm finally free of any feelings for him.

9. Single Mum Blues

Being a mother wasn't the fairytale I had imagined in my mind. After our lovely homecoming that first night, the harsh reality of life as a single mum soon set in. As much as I adored my gorgeous little Deborah, I felt trapped in the house and I resented that so much. I was twenty-seven years old and used to being my own person, so I wanted to go out with my friends and do the things I had always enjoyed. I started to miss my freedom. For nine months I hadn't been able to do anything much at all, and now I was dying to get back out into the world and have some fun. Naturally enough, this led to friction between me and my mother. We were all living together under one roof, and the doting grandmother couldn't accept that the mother might want time out to herself.

The week after I brought Deborah home, I asked my mother if I could go have a few drinks with Geraldine and Tomo. She agreed on the condition that I came home early. Going out the door, those words were ringing in my ears. I felt like I was a child again, being told what to do by my mother and having to obey her. Little by little, I started to feel like a prisoner. Most mothers who are married young and start families young have their husbands or partners around them, so they can settle into that way of life. But as I was a bit of a wanderer, liked my freedom and had no man, it was a shock that I had to stay put and look after this baby. It was particularly hard in the beginning because I still wanted Deborah's daddy. That was probably the biggest reason behind my desire to go out so much.

The reality was that I wanted Robbie to see me looking slim and radiant after giving birth to our daughter. I still kept hoping against hope that he would change his mind and come back to us.

The other thing that got to me was my love for my baby. Over those initial weeks and months, a firm bond was growing between Deborah and me. The love I felt for her almost frightened me. I think it's a very special kind of love, one that only mothers and fathers experience. This was the very first time in my life that I felt real, burning love for someone. I was constantly in terror of something bad happening to her, that she would get hurt in some way. The problem was that I didn't know how to embrace this incredible emotion. I knew this little bundle was mine, but what I felt was so overwhelming, it made me want to escape from it. There were moments I believed that I wasn't worthy of my child, that I wasn't able to look after her properly and give her everything that she needed. Mentally and emotionally I felt very alone because at the end of the day, this child was my responsibility, no one else's. It was terrifying. Up until then I had only ever had myself to look after, so this was a big shock to the system.

I think young girls can have very romantic ideas about what it's like to have a baby. I know I did. I dreamt of changing simple nappies and dressing her up in pretty dresses, but it was nothing like that at all. For one thing, she developed colic after I went back to work. My poor mother used to come into the bedroom, in her nightdress, in the middle of the night, and walk a screaming Deborah up and down for hours, trying to soothe her. I was almost comatose because I had to get up at seven to go to work. During the day, when I was at work, my friend would have to nudge me hard to wake me up when I dozed off as I sat over my machine. That happened a lot because I was so tired all the time.

When I was pregnant with Deborah, I used to relax in my room by listening to music on an old-fashioned record-player. I'd play all the records of my favourite singers, like Tom Jones, Elvis Presley, Shirley Bassey, Neil Diamond, Elaine Paige and Frank Sinatra. I'd listen to some 1970s and 1980s artists as well, but not as much as to the great singers. After Deborah was born and came home, I discovered that whenever I'd put on Tom Jones or any of the other singers, she'd settle down and fall asleep. She obviously recognised that music from the nine months of me playing it for myself. I have no doubt that babies can hear things when they're in the womb and that Deborah found those singers' voices soothing and familiar. Today she's a big Tom Jones fan, a big Elvis fan and she loves Neil Diamond and Shirley Bassey. She loves her pop music, too, but she always goes back to all the old stuff that I reared her on. I remember one incident shortly after we got out of the hospital, and she was lying in my bed, screaming her little lungs out. I put on Tom Jones, singing 'It's Not Unusual', and within seconds she fell quiet and was content, almost as if she was thinking, 'Oh, I know this. I love this!' People say that it's the mother's heartbeat that relaxes the newborn, but in Deborah's case, it was Tom Jones.

The great singers couldn't save us from colic, though. It was a really difficult time for the whole household, and added to the weary conflict between my mother and myself. I insisted on carrying on a social life and she insisted that I was wrong. It's only now that I can understand what she was doing, or trying to do, but at the time I was hugely frustrated with her. She wouldn't let me go outside the door after a certain time of night. There was murder if I came home after her curfew. It was like I was a teenager again … and a bloody rebellious one at that! If she said to me, 'You better be back here by one!', I would get my niece to look after Deborah, in Mammy's house, and she would stay in my room while I might go to my sister-in-law's and stay there *all* night. I knew what I was doing was wrong, but I was rebelling against my mother telling me what to do. That probably went on for the whole first year of Deborah's life.

The rows got worse and worse and I'd end up in my bedroom, screaming and crying, while Mam was downstairs, shouting, 'It's not my child!' Sometimes I'd try a different line for getting out of the house: 'If I was a married woman, I'd be able to go out with my husband!' Of course, Mam would roar back at me, 'But you're *not* a married woman! You're a single woman and you have a child.'

It was only many years later that Mam confessed that during that time, her biggest fear was that I'd go out and get pregnant again. This was something she had seen my Aunt Mary do in her youth. Before she married my Uncle Phil, Mary had had four children with different guys, as I mentioned. Her father was very strict and it was her way of rebelling against him. Mam had watched all this and so when I was acting up she was thinking, 'I'm not having Mary go down the same road as my sister.' In order to 'save' me, she threw everything she could at me, to try and control me. She was also worried that I would miss out on every little change in Deborah's life because I was focusing so much on wanting to be out with my friends. I hadn't realised how much I wanted a child until I conceived one, but now that she was here, suddenly I wanted to run out the door and enjoy myself. I've often wondered would I have been more content to stay at home if Robbie and I had been together, and I'm inclined to believe that I would have. It wasn't Deborah who made me feel trapped, it wasn't even my mother, it was me. I wanted to have my baby and still be free to do what I had always done, as a young, free and single girl.

Although she tried hard to keep me in line, Mam did understand where I was coming from. She told me that after the twins, Jimmy and Betty, were born, she felt her life was no longer hers, that it was changed completely, forever, and that she would never enjoy herself again because she had to look after these bundles. She tried to reassure me by telling me that things did get better for her and would get better for me, if I just gave it time. Meanwhile, my poor Dad was caught up in the middle of all this strife. Mam complained to him endlessly about me, but Dad understood the two sides of the story. He loved the both of us and just wanted us to get on, because he wanted a peaceful life. I don't know how the poor man coped, stuck between two very stubborn women.

My brother, Willie, did his best to ignore the trouble with the help of alcohol, but if he was plain sober he used to pick on me, too. I assumed he was just taking my mother's side against me, but years later he told me that he had been envious of me. He envied the fact that I had travelled and seen a bit of the world and now I had this beautiful little package, Deborah. He was a bit lost around that time and the alcohol wasn't helping at all. Then he transformed himself and I think that was down to his love for Deborah. When I brought her home, that first night, he couldn't take his eyes off her. 'My God, isn't she tiny!' he whispered when he saw her. Minutes later she was in his arms and he was gazing at her, oblivious to the rest of us sweltering in the heat of the house. Within eighteen months of Deborah's birth, Willie had gone back to Alcoholics Anonymous and had turned his life around as a recovering alcoholic. He was just mad about her from the first moment he looked at her. I remember, on Deborah's first day of school, that he handed me £20 for her books, when he hadn't a penny for himself. He would have given Deborah his life, if she'd needed it.

Willie and myself had fought and argued all the time as kids. When I was six, he used to lock me in the coal shed until Mam came home, but in spite of everything, I think we were a lot closer than either of us realised. I remember when I got the measles and he said, 'I suppose I'd better look after you, since you're sick.' I think that was his way of showing that he cared about me. Willie admitted to me once that he was jealous when Mam arrived home with me, his new baby sister. He had been the baby for six long years, but then I arrived and spoilt his fun. But I loved the way he took to Deborah – they got on great and still do, to this day. Willie later went on to have a child of his own, his son, Mark, and when things didn't work out with the child's mother, he didn't turn his back on them. He made sure he was always there for Mark, and that his son came and stayed with him. He still has a great relationship with Mark and I think that's a tribute to the way we were brought up, that we take our responsibilities as parents very seriously.

So, Mam, Dad and Willie had adapted to our new life with Deborah, but I took a bit longer to get my head around it. When I think now of how sorry I used to feel for myself back then, it was ridiculous! I had this beautiful, healthy baby and all I could do was cry about my friends going out and having a great time without me. As Willie pointed out often, I had lived a great life, had been to America, France, Germany, Turkey, all over Spain and I had lived on a kibbutz in Israel for a whole year. What had I got to cry about?

Maybe two years passed before I began to cop on to the fact that Deborah was the best thing that had ever happened to me, but I can't romanticise the experience because it was hard work. I worked all day, five days a week, while my mother minded Deborah, and then as soon as I got home, tired from a full day's work, I had to look after a baby that was handed to me the moment I came through the front door. I don't think I fully came to terms with the responsibility of being a single parent until the Corporation gave me my own house in Cherry Orchard, which I got in 1992, when Deborah was five years old.

By then, Mam was hitting sixty and her health wasn't great. She smoked an awful lot and though she wasn't actually sick, she wasn't in great condition. She did her best by me and Deborah, but I soon recognised that she wasn't really able to mind a baby all day. I had to make some changes. I gave up my full-time job and took a part-time job as a cleaner in The Lawns pub. The amazing thing about Mam was that she never complained once about having to look after Deborah. She only complained about me wanting to go out at the weekends, when she felt I should be happy to stay home and spend time with my daughter. I'd whinge at her, 'But I've been working all week. I came home every evening on the dot of 5pm, and then I minded her every night.' Mam would shout, 'But she's *yours!*' She was right, of course, but I wouldn't have said that back then. Now, I regret my behaviour at that time, but I can't turn back the clock and change things. We all make mistakes, but thank God for the family I had around me. I would never have been able to cope without their support.

It wasn't all bad, of course, during those early years in the family home with my baby. I have great memories of that time, too. I especially recall the Christmas when Deborah was two, almost three. There was a children's programme on television called 'Teenage Mutant Ninja Turtles' and she watched it every day with Willie. They both loved it, though I think he was a bigger fan than she was. This particular Christmas, it was seven o'clock in the morning and I was up and getting the preparations underway for the dinner. The television was on because I was recording *White Christmas* for Mam. Willie was on the couch, watching the film, and Deborah was under the tree, poking at her presents. My mother had bought her a beautiful, golden-haired doll that could walk if you held it upright. The doll came in a huge box and Deborah was dying to unwrap the big present. When she finally ripped off the wrapping paper, she *Ooohed* briefly, then took the doll out of the box, dumped her on the floor and climbed into the box herself and began to roll around. 'Where are you going?' I asked her. 'I'm Leonardo [one of the turtles]! I'm going to the sewers!' The poor doll was neglected for the rest of the day. Mam came down and asked, 'Does she not like her doll?' 'Oh, she loves it,' I said quickly. 'It's just that she loves the box, too!'

One of Deborah's favourite things to do was to get into my Dad's big boots, put his cap on her head and his scarf around her neck and then march around the room. We have lots of photographs of her dressed like that. Her face is dirty in one of them and it looks like she's wearing a moustache, and with that and the clothes, you'd swear she was Charlie Chaplin. She started to sing before she could walk, singing the songs from ads on the television, loving the claps and praise she would get.

Deborah was a brilliant addition to our house in Ballyfermot and to the whole family. She was great company for my mother, who had by then stopped going out to the pub. She spent hours teaching Deborah how to colour in pictures and play cards. This is what she did with all her grandchildren. She used to say that Deborah was the double of me, in terms of how I used to go on. Daddy idolised her, too. He would sing to her and she'd fall fast asleep in his lap. Willie would watch TV with her and keep her occupied while I was cleaning and Mam was making the dinner. Deborah became a very important part of our family, in that she gave each of us something. You got up in the morning and her smiling face would set you up for the day.

Deborah's day would start with her running straight to my mother: 'Nanny! Nanny! I want me brekkie.' It wouldn't matter if I was downstairs in the kitchen already – she had to see her Nanny first thing. Once they'd got a look at each other, Nanny would send her down to me. Dad would be with me in the kitchen, making a cup of tea for Mam, and Deborah would race in. 'Granda! I want me brekkie!' He'd get her breakfast and she'd eat it in front of the TV. I could see their delight in her, in their faces. She brought a warmth back into the house that hadn't been there since Betty, Jimmy and Tomo had left to get married.

I put her into the playschool just across the road from our house. There wasn't a bother on her for the first two months, but then she got bored and didn't want to go anymore, so I let her stay home. One morning the girl from the school knocked at the door to ask if I couldn't afford to send

Deborah anymore. I explained that it was more that Deborah didn't always want to go across. The girl just said for her to come over anytime she felt like it. So in the morning I'd ask her, 'Do you want to go to playschool today?' Some days she did and some days she didn't, but I didn't push her either way.

When she went to 'big school', the local primary, she already knew some of the children in her class from the playschool. A couple of the little boys lived on my mother's road and it was those she played with, which helped keep her happy. I hadn't got much money when she started school because I was only working part-time, but as usual my family helped me out. As I mentioned, Willie, who had nothing, gave me £20, and Mam bought Deborah her first schoolbag and other bits and pieces. When she stood in front of me and Mam, in her school uniform, for that very first time, I burst into tears and my mother wasn't any better on the other side of her. Willie had to turn away so we wouldn't see that he was crying, too.

Most of the time, I enjoyed living at home with Deborah and my family, but I knew in my heart that it couldn't continue. I had had my name on the housing list for quite a while, and when Deborah had just turned five, the offer came through for a Corporation house in Cherry Orchard, and I accepted it. I don't know why I accepted it, and it's something that I still regret. When I think back, it was probably because I wanted to be able to bring Deborah up my own way. I used to have battles with both Mam and Dad when I'd say something to Deborah and they'd say something different, contradicting me. It wasn't very serious, but new mothers can be a bit territorial, and I think I just got it into my head that I had to bring up my own child myself, without 'interference'. But I know it went very hard on them to see us leave. The day we were moving out, Mam said, 'I don't want you to go. I don't want you to take that baby out of the house.' I say I regret it now, and I do, but I'm still glad

I did it. I had to do it. I had to learn how to take care of Deborah and me by myself. Moving out was the biggest decision of my life, but I knew I had to stand on my own two feet. Mam and Dad weren't going to be around forever; I'd have to get onto the high wire without the safety net at some point.

10. On my own

My new house in Cherry Orchard was only a half-an-hour away, but it felt like a different world from Ballyfermot. Living alone with Deborah was a huge leap for me, and for the first time in my life I was surrounded by people I didn't know. I could see that Deborah wasn't happy in Cherry Orchard, but she never said anything to me. She loved visiting Nanny's house and going out to play with her friends on the road there. We spent a lot of time in my mother's, just so she could see her pals.

Over the next year, I began to notice that Mammy wasn't herself. She wasn't well and for a long time we couldn't figure out exactly what was wrong, but eventually it was discovered that she had Alzheimer's. She went downhill rapidly after that. It was Dad and Willie who really took care of her then. I was finding it difficult to settle in Cherry Orchard, even though I had some great neighbours there. I wanted to move back home, to Ballyfermot, but I reckoned that it wouldn't be fair on Mam as she didn't need a child running about the house at this stage. Deborah missed her Nanny terribly, but it quickly got to the stage where my mother couldn't relate to her grand-daughter when we visited the house. Alzheimer's had taken hold of her and was slowly taking her from us. There were times when I would be washing her and she'd think I was her sister, Mary. It was very sad, but I have to say there were funny times with it, too. She'd think that Deborah was her niece and as for Daddy, she'd be saying to us, 'That fella fancies me and keeps pestering me to go to the pictures with him.' We'd have a right laugh about that. She'd actually see Dad as a young man and would say to us, 'See that good-looking fella there, he fancies me!'

Of course, in her head she was also young, so she was actually quite happy in herself at that stage. In the beginning, before it really took hold of her, she knew something was wrong but didn't know what. Then, I suppose, she went into her own world, where she and Dad were young again. That's why it was sad, but we also had a good laugh in the early days about the stuff she'd come out with. I mean, you had to laugh when you could, otherwise you'd just roll up in a ball and cry. In the beginning we'd argue with her and say, 'No, Mam, that's wrong', but over time we realised that she didn't really know what she was saying, so we might as well agree with her. The good thing about laughing over some of the odd things she'd come out with was that she'd laugh along with us, and that, we felt, could only be a good thing. She wasn't hurting like we were. We were losing the person in front of us, but she went happily about her day, thinking that all was fine with her world.

One night, Mam said she wanted fish and chips. If my mother had said she wanted the moon, Dad would have found a way of getting it for her, that had always been the way, so he got up on his bicycle and went up to the local chipper. Whenever he went to the chip shop he always left the bike in his friend's garden, on Ballyfermot Road. He got the fish supper and came out, picked up his bike and got back up on it. There were two cars parked on the side of the street and as he pulled out between them, a stolen car came out of nowhere, knocked him off the bike and shot off, leaving him there to die on the road. Later, Dad would tell me how he remembered lying on the cold, hard ground and seeing himself float above his body, and thinking that he had to go back because there was no way he was leaving just yet. The next thing he remembered was waking up at home. His friend had come out, found him unconscious and brought him home to Willie and Mam. Willie wasn't able to take him to the hospital that night because he couldn't leave my mother, so they put him in his bed. Dad was all bruised, in a lot of pain and looked terrible, so the next morning Willie rang us all and when we arrived to take care of Mam, he took him to the hospital.

When the doctor saw the state of Dad, he gave poor Willie a roasting for not bringing him to the hospital immediately after the accident, adding that had Dad not been found by his friend, he would have surely died. Willie did his best to explain that he couldn't leave my mother, who had Alzheimer's. Dad needed work done to his hips and his knees and eventually came out of the hospital on a Zimmer frame. But he was hell-bent on getting back to his normal self as soon as possible, and he did, too, within a couple of months. He wasn't one of these people who sat around; he was used to being active and cycling everywhere. His recovery period was a very stressful time for everyone, all the same. Willie was now trying to be nurse to Mam and Dad, while I was juggling being Mam and Dad to Deborah and helping Willie out as much as I could.

Mam wandered off a lot and we had all our neighbours, on the Avenue, the Crescent and the Parade, on high alert. There were many times when someone in the neighbourhood would find her rambling around and bring her home, God love her and them. They all knew her, and even before we told them about her condition they were aware that something was wrong because sometimes she'd go out walking wearing just her slip and coat. When we asked her where she was going, she'd tell us, 'I was going home to my mammy.' She'd be out looking for the house she grew up in. After a while, we took to hiding the door key from her, which drove her mad. She'd tear the place apart. 'Where's the bloody key? Yous are always trying to lock me in.' Whoever was free would take her out on a walk, saying, 'Just give me a minute, Mam, and I'll go out with you.' If you met someone and stopped for a chat, you'd have to keep a close eye on Mam because she was liable to disappear in a flash when you were distracted. More often than not, I'd have to cut a conversation short and go running after her. It was like looking after a little child.

In the end, Mam's physical health broke down. She picked up a cold and just couldn't shake it off. We got the doctor out and he told us that there was a slight touch of pneumonia to the lungs, and that we just had to keep her warm with lots of fluids. He wanted to put her into hospital, but Mam had said to us, 'Don't let me die in hospital', so we were determined to put it off as long as possible.

The night before Mam passed away, I went down to help Willie give her dinner. At this stage, she and Dad were sleeping downstairs, in the sitting room. They'd also recently had a bathroom built downstairs. She was just lying there, unable to eat. When I was leaving I said, 'I'm off home now, Ma, I love you.' Up to that point she hadn't recognised me for some time, but she immediately replied, 'I love you too, Mary, look after yourself.' In that moment, she knew who I was. After I left, Willie washed her, because she was going into hospital the next day. I said a prayer to God that night: 'Please God, if you can't heal her, then just take her away because that's not my Mammy lying there anymore. She doesn't need to suffer like this.'

During that night, Dad got up, at about two o'clock, to use the bathroom and she called out to him, using her usual name for him for the first time in ages, 'Daddy'. At this stage she had forgotten his name and almost everything else about him. He was passing by her and she said, 'Daddy, come in beside me. It's cold.' He said, 'I can't get in there, Ma, the bed is far too small.' He sat down beside her for a few minutes, gave her a kiss and went back to his own bed.

By the time he woke up the following morning, she was gone. Willie had gotten up early, put on the kettle and looked in on her. At first he thought she was sound asleep, but then he felt there was something wrong and called her name. There was no response. He went over to the bed and touched her; she was cold. The doctor reckoned she had died sometime between two and four o'clock in the morning. She was sixty-nine years of age.

Willie rang everyone in the family, except me. Betty, Jimmy and the others arrived at the house and told him to ring me, but he didn't want to tell me over the phone. He went out and got Dad's push-bike and cycled up to Cherry Orchard, where I was busy getting Deborah ready for school. I remember it was a gorgeous morning, by far the best day we had seen in a long time. James, my young nephew, was staying with me and I heard him say, 'Here's Willie on the bike'. It never occurred to me why Willie was there at that hour of the morning. I opened the door and he came into the hall. He kept staring at me and I asked him what was wrong. Eventually he just said, 'Mammy is dead.'

I didn't cry. I just stood and said, 'Well, I know what she wants because she told me.' He nodded. After asking James to lock up the house and mind the four dogs I owned, I grabbed Deborah and as the three of us started walking, I kept talking at a fast pace. 'Now, she wants a wake, and she doesn't want to be put in Massey's funeral home. [She had always said she didn't want anyone from the County Bar gawking at her in the coffin!] She wants us to have a load of drinks, sing all her favourite songs and have a good a laugh, a good joke, as well as a good cry over her.' Willie just kept nodding and walking.

When we got to the house, the family was outside in the garden. Brenda, Elaine and Diana, my nieces, were crying bitterly. I went inside and Mam was there, lying in the bed. She did look as if she was asleep, with her mouth slightly open. We think she must have got a pain because one of her hands was gripped at her nightdress. I bent down, kissed her and said a few words, but I still didn't cry. I don't understand that.

Deborah followed me into the room but ran out again; she couldn't deal with it at all.

Dad was sitting beside her, staring into space. He didn't know what to do or what to say. The priest, a lovely little man, arrived to give her the Last Rites, and that's when I broke down. I had a medal of Our Lady around my neck and I prayed to Our Lady to be with Mam, and not to leave her in the dark by herself. She hated the dark; she always had to have a light on at nighttime. When, years earlier, Dad had hung a picture of the Sacred Heart over their bed, with the little red bulb in front of it, that bulb had to be lit every night for her or she wouldn't sleep.

Mam died on 2 May 1995, just one week before Deborah made her First Holy Communion. That was awful. As I was going through the city with Carol, a friend of mine, looking to get myself a jacket for the Communion, we ended up in the old markets in Queen Street. I was suddenly filled with memories of walking through this area of town with my mother. Everything came back to me – the visits to the pawn shop, the red lemonade in the pub on the corner and buying fresh fish in the market for Daddy's dinner. Poor Carol was left standing there, not knowing what to do or say, as I broke down in floods of tears.

On the morning of the Communion, I was doing Deborah's hair and trying to be happy about her big day, but I kept having to escape into the kitchen for a cry. I brought Deborah down to the church and then, after the ceremony, back to my Dad's house, where she was having her photograph taken with him. I stood in behind them and managed to smile for the camera, but then I couldn't stop looking at the empty chair that Mam used to sit on. It was heartbreaking. On the one hand, I was so happy for Deborah and so proud of her, but the tears for Mam were never far away and I had to keep forcing them back. I couldn't let them out because I didn't want to spoil Deborah's special day. I couldn't help thinking, 'If only my mother had held on for another week.' But Mam had been suffering, and I consoled myself with the knowledge that now she had no more pain.

The first few months after my mother's death were horrible, there's no other word for it. I missed her terribly and I struggled to keep my head together. It was worse for poor Daddy. He kept saying, 'I miss Mammy', a phrase he would repeat for years afterwards. Shortly after we lost Mam, Dad started to cling on to me. I could see that his heart was broken and that he was unbearably lonely without her. Like every couple, they'd had their ups and downs in life, but they had been great together and really united as a husband and wife. It was the end of life as Dad had known it throughout all his adult years, and you could see the sadness taking its grip on him. At least he had the company of Willie in the house, and my brother was so good to Dad, taking on the huge responsibility of looking after him.

I went down to the house every day, to give Willie a break, or else Dad would come up to my house in Cherry Orchard and we'd watch old films together. He'd drink the few bottles of stout that I bought him, and then Willie would send a taxi down for him. I was now working in Centra, which used to be a shop called Sesame Street, in Ballyfermot, and Daddy would meet me there on a Friday when I finished work and I'd take him out for a few drinks and a good old sing-song. Those evenings lifted his spirits, at least while they lasted. But it got to the point that he wanted me to be around all the time. There were times when he'd beg me to come home and live in the house again, but I couldn't. Willie was now running it and it wouldn't have worked. As much as we loved each other, if we were living together, Willie and myself would have killed one another.

In truth, I wasn't coping very well myself with all the trauma. It felt like a load of tragedies had happened at once. I was still upset about Dad being knocked down and left unconscious on the road, and then suddenly Mam was dead and gone out of our lives. I hadn't settled where I was living in

Cherry Orchard, and I started to feel trapped again. When I had first moved out of home, before Mam died, I felt I was starting to get my life back. Deborah was growing up and didn't need as much minding, and I could see light at the end of the tunnel of being a single parent. Then, *Bang!* My mother was gone and my father needed to see me every day. Even though I loved this man dearly, I just felt I was sinking beneath the weight of other people's needs. He started to call me Mamie, and when I'd correct him, saying, 'But I'm Mary!', he'd reply, 'I know, but you just look like my sister.' So in the end I gave in and just answered to Mamie. Through bereavement and the pressure of life, I was slowly being dragged down into a black depression. It got so bad that I begged my GP to send me for counselling. I would recommend it to anyone who is dealing with difficulties in their life: go and talk about it to someone who is qualified. This was also the first time that I was put on antidepressant medication, which really helped me get through this dark time.

Thanks to the counselling, the medication and the passing of time, gradually my life started to brighten up again. But over the next few years we started to notice things that suggested Dad was going down the same road as Mam had gone down before him. His memory was starting to fade a little, and he was becoming melancholy. The doctors never diagnosed Alzheimer's, instead they just said that his memory was deteriorating due to old age. My sister, Betty, had gone to her solicitor and managed to get Dad some compensation out of his hit-and-run accident, so in 2000 we took him on a holiday to America. We chose Florida, to give him some sunshine and brightness. After we boarded the plane, Dad said, 'I think I'll go out to the deck for a walk.' I said to him, 'Dad, you open that door and you won't find any deck, I promise you!' I explained where we were and he broke his heart laughing. 'I knew I was on plane!' he said, but I don't think he did.

It was a long flight, so I was determined to make sure he exercised his limbs to keep the circulation going. I kept on at him to lift his legs and move his feet, and he found this very funny. Then I made him walk up and down the aisle of the plane, but we were mortified when he'd stop and start talking to the other passengers. Willie would slide down into his seat and groan, 'He's up there at someone.' I'd give him a dig in the arm and say, 'You go up this minute and get him. I can't leave the kids!' We had Deborah and Willie's son, Mark, with us and I was chief child-minder, which meant Willie had to be chief Dad-minder.

When we arrived at Atlanta, we had to take a connecting flight to Orlando and then a bus to our hotel. As we approached the city of Orlando, Dad announced loudly, 'This doesn't look a bit like Ballyfermot!' Poor Dad. Anyway, the hotel was lovely and the next morning we got him into the pool, where he floated around in a big, black rubber ring, singing, 'South of the border, down Mexico way ...' The Americans loved him. He was always in great form when he was in company, and nobody outside the family could tell there was anything wrong with him. He only got into difficulties when he was left alone. When that happened, he'd somehow lose himself in his thoughts and wouldn't remember anything, which made him frustrated and then aggressive.

I had bought a bottle of Bacardi in Dublin Airport because I knew this wasn't going to be a drinking holiday, but that Dad and I would enjoy having a sip of something of an evening. One night, Willie brought the kids over to the indoor swimming pool and I poured Dad and myself a small Bacardi. By the time Willie came back, we'd had about four each and Dad whispered to Willie in front of me, 'I would have gone with you to the pool, but I felt sorry for her. You know the way she doesn't have anybody. I didn't want to leave her in the house on her own.' He thought he was back in Ballyfermot, never mind about him feeling sorry for me! There I was, pouring him drinks, singing songs to him and making him laugh. I was only sitting in because of him, but Dad thought it was the other way around. I looked at Willie and laughed.

By then, Dad had become a terrible wanderer, just like my mother in her last years. We had to put a chair up against the door in the hotel room on that holiday, to make sure he didn't go walking in the middle of the night. In fact, over the next four years, Willie had to ring the Ballyfermot police on three occasions to come and help us find him after he'd gone missing in the neighbourhood. Willie would tell them that Dad had a touch of Alzheimer's, though we never knew if he did or not – it just made more sense than saying he suffered from melancholy. The thing was, though, that when he'd come to my house at Christmas, he would remember all my friends from my youth, even their names.

He was particularly fond of my close friend Lulu (her name is Carmel Power, but that's what we called her). Her son, David, actually built Dad his own chair after Mammy died, and he'd sit in every Christmas. Lulu would have us up for sandwiches, a few cans of Guinness and a sing-song, letting him sing away to his heart's content. Lulu's other son, Jonathan, spotted Dad wandering one day when he was out with his boss in their van. He didn't know that Dad had gone missing on us, but when he saw him walking around in circles in The Lawns park, Jonathan realised that help was needed. Thank God for Jonathan that day; he was only fifteen years old, but he knew that Dad was confused and he told his boss that they'd have to go to Cherry Orchard to get Mary Byrne. Fortunately, Daddy recognised Jonathan and allowed the teenager to help him into the van, and they drove him back home to Willie.

Dad never went back to his childhood, like my mother had done during her illness. When he was finally taken into hospital, he always knew who we were. The only thing was, he wanted to go back to where his father had lived. One time, he made his way to the church where he had married my mother – he actually walked miles, from Ballyfermot to

Kimmage, on his walking sticks. To this day, we don't know how he did it. That day he went into the local police station, asked them for a glass of water and told them he was lost. So he knew enough to know that he was lost. They asked him where he lived and he was able to tell them that, too. I think sometimes he felt trapped in his life and just wanted to get out and keep walking, but he kept to the areas he knew, the places he had grown up. Maybe he just wanted to see them again after all those years. He knew he was heading towards Kimmage that day, so I don't know if he really did have Alzheimer's.

In November 2002, the Corporation granted me a transfer from my house in Cherry Orchard to my present home in Ballyfermot, where I moved with Deborah and was now close to my old home again … and to Dad. As his health deteriorated, we got him a little wheelchair and I used to wheel him up to the County Bar on a Saturday night and sit with him. We'd just have a couple of drinks because I'd have to push him home again afterwards, but he loved those evenings out, and we grew even closer than we had always been. Now I'm so happy for that time we had together. I have to say, though, that he got very possessive and didn't like any guy coming up to talk to me in the pub. One time a fella I knew came up to say hello, but when he greeted my Dad, he received a very cool, 'Do you want something?' He replied, 'Ah no, I'm just a friend of Mary's.' I couldn't believe it when Daddy said, 'That's alright, stay that way!' He then turned his back on the poor fella and started talking to the people beside him.

Willie had been minding Dad for a few years by now, and he decided to put Dad into hospital for a week-long respite. He walked in there singing on a Saturday, but I was shocked by his condition when I went in to visit him on the Monday. He couldn't open his eyes, although he recognised my voice. He could hear me on the phone to a doctor and he mumbled, 'Oh, there's Mary!' He was on a lot of medication. The following week he was moved to a different part of the hospital, where he spent the next nine months. He could no longer walk and they had to put him in nappies. He never walked again and was in a wheelchair for the rest of his days. When he left there, he was moved to Cherry Orchard Hospital. When we visited, he mightn't always be awake, but mostly he just sat in the chair, eyes closed and humming to himself. I used to bring him in his favourite music to listen to, American singers like Al Jolson and Jim Reeves.

Dad eventually came out of Cherry Orchard and went to live with Willie again, in the family home. Deborah and I visited him almost every day. She really doted on him after my mother died. They would play cards for hours, with him propped up in bed, each accusing the other of cheating. In a way, I reckon my dad was the father figure in Deborah's life. He and Willie were the two men who had an influence on her as she grew up. I would go up to the house after work, and Willie would have my dinner ready for me. I went to work every morning, finished at two o'clock, met Deborah from school and we'd go to Willie's until about nine in the evening.

The end came in 2004. The night before Dad slipped into a coma, I was staying in the hospital with him. All of his children took turns to stay and hold his hand. He hadn't opened his eyes in a couple of days, and that night I was holding his hand and singing to him. He sighed heavily a few times, then opened his eyes and looked at me. I said, 'Are you alright, Da?' He had a big, beaming smile on his face, but he had great difficulty speaking, though he managed to whisper, 'Yeah, yeah!' It was the liveliest I had seen him in a while. Then I asked him if he wanted me to stay on and again he whispered, 'Yeah, yeah!' I bent over and kissed him; he did his best to kiss me back and keep breathing. 'Get some sleep, Da,' I told him. He asked me where Willie was and I said, 'He's at home, he'll be in to see you tomorrow.' He nodded happily and then he slipped into a coma for the next five days. That was the last conversation I had with him.

The whole family was gathered with him the night he died, thanks to one of the nurses advising me to ring them because she felt the end was near. Some of them had gone back home for the night. They all returned and we were with him for an hour before his breathing started to get shallow, as he began to drift. The nurse told us to say our goodbyes, so I leant into his ear and said, 'Mammy is waiting for you on the other side, Dad. You're a saint on this Earth. You did everything for your family. You've absolutely nothing to be afraid of. Be proud of who you are, you're a lovely man.' I gave him a big kiss and added, 'I'll see you some day.' He never flickered or responded in any way, but I know he heard me as they say that hearing is the last sense you lose. Then Betty bent over him and said her goodbye, and he took his last breath.

To this day, I still think my father was a saint. He put up with so much crap from us and when we were young, he worked so hard to try and give us the best life he could manage. Family always came first with my Dad. And I feel blessed that my daughter, Deborah, will go through life with wonderful memories of my father, so that his legacy lives on in the next generation.

11. Stage directions

I had never given it much thought, but singing had been part of my life from the start. We were a family who loved a sing-song, so I was often called on to give a blast of some old favourite, and when Dad was in his final years, it came naturally to me to sing to him as a comfort. It had always been there, a love of music and an ability to sing, but I'd never considered doing anything about it. It was so much part of who I was, it never occurred to me to see it as something that set me apart.

The first time I ever sang on stage was at a hen's party in a pub in Dublin's Stonybatter, when I was fifteen years of age. Of course, I shouldn't have even been in a pub at that age, but I looked about three years older than I was and no one ever asked any questions. My friends had to force me up onto the stage and I sang Tom Jones's, 'I'll Never Fall in Love Again'. When the song ended, I ran from the stage, a nervous wreck, and swore I'd never do that again. Even though I knew I had a singing voice, my chronic lack of self-confidence acted as a solid obstacle to me ever using it to my advantage, or even just enjoying it. It went beyond stage-fright – it wasn't just initial nerves that went away once I started to sing. This was a paralysing, nauseating reaction to having to stand up and sing in front of people. It was nerves on a chronic level, and it took a huge amount of effort for me to overcome them and sing out loud.

Growing up, I was a sensitive child and any kind of rejection, whether intended or not, would cut me to the core and make me curl up and go back into my shell. I must have been really traumatized by one particular incident as a school child because it's still a raw wound that hurts me today when I think about it, even though it happened over forty years ago. It was just after my Communion, so I was only about seven years old. Our school used to stage a play every year and when it came to my class's turn, the one they chose was *Snow White and the Seven Dwarfs*. We were all excited and our teacher made a huge fuss about it. She told us, 'This is going to be great because it's the first time this class has been asked to do something. So, I need a good singer to be Snow White, someone to be the evil witch and we also need seven dwarfs.' Our class would be the stars of the play, while the other classes would have smaller parts.

We were given the songs to learn, but I was already very familiar with *Snow White* because it had been on in the cinema and Mam had brought me to see it a few times. I would sit there, eyes wide, drinking it in, and every time I went, I enjoyed it even more. I knew all the songs and I particularly loved, 'Someday My Prince Will Come'. I knew I could both sing it and act it. So, when the teacher asked for people to put themselves forward for the part of Snow White, for the first time in my life I was first one to put up my hand. It turned out that there were four of us who wanted to be Snow White. One of the girls was lovely: she had long, jet-black hair and her mother had made her a perfect costume, which she wore to school on the day of the audition. I turned up in a clean, but old dress that was ripped from climbing over walls. We didn't get the chance to sing separately, we just sang together as a group. Now, I have to say, this girl didn't sing the best, as far as I could hear, but she looked an absolute vision in her gorgeous costume. The inevitable happened and the teacher picked her. I was absolutely gutted because I was sure I had sung so well that I'd get the main role. The other three girls were very upset, too; one of them actually sobbed, but I didn't cry. I consoled myself by thinking that if I wasn't to be Snow White, well, I'd be happy enough to be the wicked witch. Not alone did I not get that part, I wasn't even picked to be a feckin' dwarf! In the end I was allowed to help out backstage, but that was it.

That experience left me feeling totally rejected. It wasn't even so much about being a singer. It didn't occur to me at the time that I wanted to be a singer, or that I could be a singer. The only singers I was aware of then were the likes of Frank Sinatra or Gene Kelly, and they lived far away from Ballyfermot, on another planet altogether. It was really just a moment of rejection that scarred me, even though I knew it wasn't anything personal on the part of the teacher. People have told me over the years that I was stupid to be, and remain, so upset over being turned down for that *Snow White* play, but I'm afraid it did affect my confidence for many years after that. I might get up and sing in the years that followed, but I always felt that I was holding back, and I really do believe it was the result of the hurt caused by that episode. I felt that I just wasn't good enough to be considered for the part. Also, because the teacher picked that girl based on her appearance, I started to question my own looks. For one thing, my mother always cut my hair and it had to be as tight and short as she could get it because fleas and nits were rampant back then. Then there was the fact that while my audition dress was clean, the pocket was torn and Mam hadn't had the time to sew it on that morning. I also blamed my plastic sandals that I wore all year round: in summer they were cool, and in the winter I wore about five pairs of socks with them, but in all weathers they looked scuffed and cheap.

That unintended rejection by the teacher worked on the self-doubts I was already developing and made me look at myself and, for the first time, see faults, imagined or otherwise, that became the reason why I couldn't be Snow White. I just wasn't worthy enough, I decided. In the strange way that a thought can take hold, the reasons why I couldn't be Snow

White turned into the reasons why I couldn't be beautiful, or loved, or sing in front of an audience – it planted a seed that took root.

Another knock-back that stands out in my memory happened during one of my great trips to Oakwood farm, in Wicklow. One night they organised a singing competition and my lack of self-confidence didn't do me any favours when I got up to sing. I had to support myself against a chair because I was shaking so much as I sang 'I Asked My Love To Take A Walk'. I sang the song well, but with all the stage presence of a timid mouse. The girl who finally won the competition had stood up and sung, 'If I Could Write A Song', and though her singing was average, she brought the song to life by doing physical actions and giving a great performance. She definitely was more entertaining, and I lost out because of my nerves and lack of confidence: I was the singer, but she was the self-assured entertainer. Her prize was a beautiful silver chain with a stone in the centre. I didn't feel hard done by because I knew she had done such a great job in getting the song across to the audience. That was the final night of our stay in Wicklow and later, as I was packing my bag, do you know what that girl did? She came into the room and presented me with the chain, a moment I'll never forget. She said to me, 'You deserved to win, Mary, you were the best singer tonight.' What an absolutely beautiful gesture. As she was so genuine and so lovely, I accepted the chain and I still have it today. It's in my home in a jewellery box that also has sentimental value, as it was a present from my mother.

Whatever about falling to pieces on the public stage, when it came to singing at home, I had always been confident. I performed for my family regularly, especially at Christmas, and my mother loved to hear me sing. When Dana won the Eurovision Song Contest in 1970 with a song called 'All Kinds of Everything', the whole country celebrated. It was the very first time that Ireland had won the Eurovision; another decade would pass before Louis Walsh's then artiste, Johnny Logan, scooped it again for

Ireland with the Shay Healy song, 'What's Another Year'. In the wake of the Eurovision, Dana's 'All Kinds of Everything' became a big hit and we all loved it. I learned it off and could sing it word-perfect. Around that time my brother, Jimmy, bought a big reel-to-reel tape-recorder machine. I remember him arriving in one Saturday morning to our house with the contraption, which looked like a big box. Mam was frying rashers in the pan and Jimmy set up the box and was very excited about it. He spoke into it, 'One, two, three …' and out came the sound of his voice. I couldn't believe it. Turning to my mother he said, 'Come on, Mammy, sing a song.' And she sang 'Little Drummer Boy' and 'You're All The World To Me'. When Jimmy played it back, you could even hear the rashers sizzling away on the cooker.

Then it was my turn. I was sitting in the chair with my legs tucked underneath me and Jimmy asked if I wanted to sing a song into the machine. I said yes immediately and when he was ready, I started singing, *'Snowdrops and daffodils …',* which was, of course, Dana's winning song. It was the first time I had done anything like that and when we listened back to it, I thought I didn't sound too bad at all – apart from the moment when Jimmy stood on the cat and it let out a screech of pain. That was my very first recording, at the age of ten. Jimmy still has the tapes, but unfortunately the machine is broken.

Among those tapes is a recording of us all in the house one night – my sister, my brothers, their friend and my parents. They must have had a few bottles of stout, and they're singing a song called 'Whistling Jack'. You can hear the bottles being cracked open and then Uncle Willie must have fallen asleep because someone wakes him up and he says, 'Where's me teeth?' I wouldn't mind, only he hadn't even got false teeth! And then Tomo, the funny brother, tells the story about Uncle Willie coming home one night very drunk and walking into the railings at the playground, splitting his head open. Tomo tells it as if he was reading the news on the radio: *'Beep, Beep ... Here is the nine o'clock news ...'* He describes Willie walking into the bar of the Monkey Tree and my mother saying, 'Oh, he's like Jesus Christ in the bed!' because of all the blood pumping out of his head. My brother Willie is on that recording, too, but he was so shy that he would only sing if he could stand by himself in the hall. You can hear him singing the Rolf Harris song, 'Two Little Boys', and then there's a knock at the front door and he races through the rest of the song at breakneck speed, to finish it before he opens the door. It's hilarious.

Those tapes are golden memories of the happy times we had together as a family. I'd love to get them digitally remade, or whatever you can do these days with tapes, so I could hear those memories again. We didn't have video cameras in those days, so listening to those voices is just a treasure – it's my way of capturing the past. When we could play those tapes, before the machine broke, I used to sit listening to them, picturing Mam sitting in her chair, with Dad beside her. We'd all sit around, lights on, no television, and laugh and sing into Jimmy's tape-recorder. I really hope, one day, to hear them again.

So that was where it started for me, but I could never, ever have imagined where it would end up. My singing ambitions were limited to being able to stand up the pub and sing without vomiting or making a holy show of myself. Our local pub, The Lawns, became a well-known venue for cabaret and there was always a great sing-along on a Sunday night. In the early days, when I first socialised there, I often got up to sing a song if my name was called out, but it usually meant having to stand in the Ladies' toilets for an hour beforehand, trying to get a hold of my nerves. On the nights that my name wasn't called out, I would be so relieved. My friends were demons for giving in my name so that I'd have to get up and do a song. On those occasions when I did get up to sing, I'd almost wobble back to my seat, I'd be shaking that much.

I entered my first singing competition as an adult in The Lawns when I was twenty-one. Again, I was forced into it by my friends. It was torture because it was spread over six weeks – a bit like a local version of 'The X Factor'. Every Monday morning when I'd wake up, I'd have butterflies in my tummy thinking of what lay ahead of me at the end of the week. I didn't have the confidence, but somehow I managed to work through the nerves and my voice carried me through to the final, which I won. It was the first talent contest I'd ever won and I still have the lovely silver cup that they presented me with as the top prize.

After that, I became known locally as a singer and would be asked to sing for charity events. My nerves were still really bad, though, so I'd turn up for some but ring in sick for others. Not that I'd be lying, as when I got really nervous my voice would go completely. I'd have to ring the organizers of whatever event it was and say I had a sore throat and couldn't make it. That happened a lot. I convinced myself that I didn't like getting up to sing, and I certainly couldn't understand why people wanted me to do it in the first place because I didn't think I was a good entertainer.

When I had Deborah, at the age of twenty-seven, I gave up singing altogether, apart from a couple of times where I tried some cabaret. That was usually a disaster, again thanks to my nervousness. One of those rare nights was in a place called The Ringside, on Dublin's South Circular Road. I hadn't realised that I'd have to walk across a big, wide, open floor to get to the stage, and I honestly don't know how my legs carried me that far. In fact, my mind was in such a haze from the stress of it that I found myself standing on the stage, wondering how the hell I had gotten there because I couldn't remember the trek across the empty floor in front of the crowd. Then I wished my legs hadn't brought me to that spot because my mind went totally blank and I forgot all the words to my first song. I was mortified, especially as there was a live band accompanying me. I still get a shiver down my spine thinking back to that embarrassing incident.

Tomo, my brother, did a lot of singing and I when I went to see him perform, I would sit there wishing and wishing that I had his confidence to get up and do it. When I was about forty-five, around 2004, Tomo began singing along to backing tracks on discs – a modern one-man band. Meanwhile, I had started trying my hand at karaoke in Downey's pub, in Ballyfermot. A guy called Jim was the resident karaoke singer there and I'd get up and sing with him. He'd always tell me, 'You're bloody wasted here!' I'd just laugh. Then one night, Tomo suggested that I start learning the songs for his backing tracks, so that I could sing to the music. The first song I chose was Shirley Bassey's 'Never, Never, Never'.

When I was forty-seven, my friend, June O'Connor, started to goad me about taking up singing professionally. Every time I sang in the pub, she'd say to me, 'You sicken me, Mary Byrne! I hate you because of the talent you have, but you're wasting it.' Her nagging got so bad that I'd say to another pal, June's sister-in-law, Trish, 'I'm not going to Downey's tonight because June is driving me bloody mad!' But June would plead with me: 'I'm only saying this because I love you. You've got it and you're wasting it.' I'd just nod, 'Yeah, yeah, I know, you're right, I'll do something about it.' Inside my head, I was screaming at her to just button up and leave me alone.

One particular night, we went around to a club in Ballyfermot. There was a chap there called Pat McLoughlin, another guy who did karaoke. Behind my back, June asked Pat to call out my name to go up and sing. He had never heard me singing, but he nonetheless announced, 'Can we have Mary Byrne on the stage for a song'. I got up, shaking like a leaf, and sang 'Never, Never, Never' and 'Diamonds Are Forever'. When I finished, Pat was staring at me in shock. 'Jaysus, where did you come out of!' he blurted out. 'What the hell are you doing?' he asked me. I told him I wasn't doing anything, singing-wise. 'What a bloody waste of a voice,' he replied. 'Look, I'll give you a shot now and then, if you're interested.' I presumed he meant that I should go to wherever he was hosting karaoke and he'd get me up a few times.

One night, Pat rang me. 'Mary, I need someone down at The Barn, in Dolphin's Barn. Will you come down?' I agreed and asked the girls to come with me. I told them I was going down to do a spot of karaoke and we'd have some fun. When we walked in, there weren't too many people in the pub. Pat was sitting on his own in front of a big TV screen, watching Leona Lewis singing on 'The X Factor'. I walked up to him and said hello and asked, 'Who's with you tonight?' He looked at me and said, 'You are!' Jesus! He meant that I was going to be singing with him the entire night. I started to babble, 'No way! No way! No, Pat, I can't do it. I just can't!' I think I went into shock, while he tried to calm me down, 'Mary, you *can* do it. Of course you can. You don't have to talk, just sing the few songs. I'll do the calling up.' When he announced my name, Pat told everyone that it was my first time and I was very nervous. They all gave me a hearty round of applause. I started singing and won them over all by myself. I was still in bits on the stage, though, even after receiving this wonderful reaction from the audience.

By now, I was feeling persecuted by Tomo and June, as they were both constantly on my case about my voice and trying to go professional with it. They knew I could do it now, that I just needed to have more confidence. So, largely just to get them off my back, I went to Pat and told him I'd sing for him. I ended up following him and his karaoke session around venues for the next three months … and shook with fear every single time.

One night I was in The Lawns, chatting to the manager, Damien, and Pat told me to ask him if there was anything going there, because he was looking for more work. I mentioned it to Damien, who I always got on well with, and he decided to give us a shot that Friday night. That's where

I sang for the next two years. At some point Pat went on to do something else, and I hooked up with another guy who had a karaoke machine and sang with him. Then Tomo, now a Tom Jones impersonator performing as Tommy Lee Jones, started asking me to sing with him. I still got nervous before a show, but was nowhere near as bad as I used to be. In fact, I was starting to enjoy it.

Tomo asked me to go to Limerick with him one night, as part of a show being run by a fella called Anto, who does a fantastic Michael Jackson tribute act. Tomo wanted me to sing to backing tracks, but on the journey down I insisted that I wanted to sing Shirley Bassey, with live music. Tomo eventually gave in to me, but it turned out to be another feckin' disaster. Everything went wrong. I told the guy the key to play in and then I went off singing in a different one. The crowd was so drunk that they only heard the voice and decided they liked it. Anto, on the other hand, didn't. He told me out straight, 'You made a bollix of that!' and then said to Tomo, 'She's brutal!' I cried my eyes out, feeling that I had made a complete show of myself. To rub salt into the wound, I wasn't even given my full fee because of how bad I was.

I think it says a lot about how I was managing my nerves by this time that I didn't stop singing after that awful night and Anto's blunt criticism. In fact, following that night, I started to go out more frequently with Tomo. His show was a two-hour gig and during it, I would go on and do four songs, just to give him a bit of a break. Well, they say that from tiny acorns, oak trees grow, and it was like that for me and my singing: by doing these small shows in small places with low expectations, slowly my singing got stronger and stronger and my confidence grew. I didn't know where I was headed with it, but I knew, for the first time, that I loved singing for people and wanted to keep on doing it.

12. Ready to take a risk

Around this time, there were more important things in life to worry about as our family received the devastating news that my lovely brother-in-law, Liam, had been diagnosed with cancer. Liam had been complaining about a pain in his back for a couple of years, but the medical people kept telling him it was arthritis. Then, in April 2006, I received a phone call from my sister, Betty. She was hysterical and the only words I could make out were, 'Liam … cancer …' The rest of her conversation wasn't making any sense and she was obviously in shock. I said to her, 'Put down the phone, Betty, I'm going to get a taxi over to you.'

Deborah and myself went straight to their home, in Tallaght, where we found Betty and her three daughters, Diana, Brenda and Elaine, in a terrible state. Then Liam came down the stairs and when I looked up at him he simply said, 'Well, you heard my news. I'm just trying to get all my affairs in order.' He turned to Betty, who was beside herself with grief, and said, 'Look, Betty, stop crying, get over it.' I could see that Liam was trying to be strong for everyone, and it broke my heart. He said to me, very matter-of-factly, 'I'm going to die and I just have to accept it.' I don't know where the strength came from within me, but I turned to my sister and nieces and said firmly, 'Why have you got him dead and buried already? Liam is a strong man and miracles happen every day of the week. He could be with us for another ten years. So why don't you try to put some positive energy out into the universe.' I knew it was far easier for me to say that than for them to do it; Liam wasn't my husband or my father. But after they got over that first shock, that was eventually what they did. It brought myself and Betty closer because she could chat with me openly about it, and I would keep up the positivity, no matter what was going on. She started to think positively about it, too, giving Liam all kinds of vegetable juices to drink, which he did, though he hated them. He was on medication too, of course, but the cancer was spreading. Liam was now living his life one day at a time.

As my sister and her girls struggled with that devastating blow to their lives, Deborah and I gave them as much support as we could. Deborah was a wonderful child, and truly cared about all of her family. She never gave me an ounce of trouble during her teenage years. She never drank, never smoked and never hung around street corners; I'm very glad she didn't take after her mother! She was just a great kid who loved being with the family, loved her grandad and her Uncle Willie. She has always been a home-bird, again unlike her mother. And although, like every parent, I worried about her being taken advantage of by fellas, she was never taken in by any of them. She had plenty of offers, but preferred to play football with her cousin, Mark, and her good friend, Andrew McLoughlin.

From the start, Deborah and I shared a love of music and it's always been a bond for us. Her biggest passion is Westlife – they are the start and end of her world. The first time we saw them live, they were supporting Boyzone in some park and I hadn't a clue who they were, but she loved them from that moment onwards. The next time we saw them, they were playing their own gig, a small one, in another park, with bouncy castles laid on for the kids. We all went with her to see them, including my father, and we had to traipse through muck to get to the stage, as always seems to be the case at an outdoor concert in this part of the world. When Westlife started doing their big concerts, I would be dragged down to the black entrance gates reserved for performers at the Point Theatre (now The O₂) in Dublin, to hang around to see Shane, Nicky, Kian, Mark and Bryan arrive. This went on for years, in all kinds of weather, whether or not we had tickets to the actual concert; sometimes I couldn't afford the ticket price. Deborah was twelve or thirteen at the time and Shane was the only man for her, but she also loved Mark. Meanwhile, Nicky was my favourite. I thought he was very handsome and I loved his personality.

One time, when I was obviously a bit flush with money, I brought Deborah to see Westlife in concert at The Point two nights in a row. I had no tickets for the third night, but Deborah still dragged me back to those black gates again, with Laura, her friend, just to see the band go in. The things I used to do for that girl! But it was worth every drenching I got, standing out in the rain, to see her face light up at the sight of the lads. On the third night of this series of concerts, we stood at the gates from five in the evening and when it got near the time for the show to start, I found myself really wanting to go in and see the concert again. There were some German girls nearby who were selling their tickets, and one of them came up to me. I had €50 in my purse and I asked her how many tickets she was selling. She said she had two. I had no problem letting Deborah and Laura go in and waiting outside for them, so I agreed to buy the two, but then a second German girl came up with a third ticket. It wasn't near the two other seats, but it would still get me in the door. I gave the girls the €50, but I still owed another €25 for the third ticket. The second German girl accepted my silver bracelet as collateral and I promised to be back at the same spot the next day, with the rest of the money.

When we got inside, Deborah and Laura were sitting in the second row, while I was behind them, in the fourth. Laura's mother, Helen Daly (aka Juicy Lucy), a good friend of mine, rang my mobile, wondering where her daughter was. She was so jealous when she heard she was at the gig! We had another brilliant night and the next day we did go back to give the German girl the money, and get my bracelet back.

A while after that, Deborah set herself up on Facebook, and befriended a Westlife fan called Nicole Stafford. They became good friends and swapped phone numbers, but had never met. One night Deborah, Laura and myself were at yet another Westlife concert in The Point when my daughter's mobile rang. It was Nicole, who was also at the concert. We were in the third row and we discovered that Nicole was in the first row, so we met up with her for the first time. Since then, Deborah and Nicole have been the very best of friends. Nicole introduced Deborah to another pal, Fran, who knows Shane's mother, so Deborah got to know Shane's mother, too. They now exchange Christmas cards and postcards! So, these three Westlife fans are the best of friends today, and I'm so happy about that. They're great girls and the Staffords look after Deborah when I go away and treat her like a daughter.

I remember during those early Westlife days, when we were on our vigil outside The Point, there was another guy we always shouted out to. He was medium-sized with impish, boyish looks, a cheeky smile and was always dressed casually in jeans and a leather jacket. Everybody knew him as the manager of Boyzone and Westlife. This was long before the one and only Louis Walsh became a very famous judge on 'The X Factor'. But even then, he seemed like the happiest guy in the world and always had a friendly wave for the fans who supported his groups. We'd all call out, 'Hello, Louis!' and he'd laugh and wave at us. Little did he, or I, know how our paths were going to cross down the line!

I think it was those two things that really got me to take the final leap of faith towards a career in music: watching Liam fight to live and knowing how short life is; and having that bond with Deborah that made music so important and so much a part of our lives. I finally got my mojo as a singer while performing in The Shamrock Bar in Finglas, on the northside of Dublin. I was still singing on Friday nights in The Lawns, still going around with Pat the odd time and still performing with Tomo at his shows. Tomo had been doing gigs at the Shamrock for a year or so when he asked if I'd like to come over and do a bit with him. I sang a few times, and the people in the Shamrock used to come up to me afterwards and tell me I was brilliant. They were the ones who really built up my confidence, so much so that I agreed to take part in a televised national singing competition.

Michael Jackson impersonator Anto rang Tomo one Friday night to tip him off about auditions that were due to take place for the competition in one of the Jury's hotels in Dublin. It was being staged by TG4, the Irish language television station, and was a talent contest called 'Nollaig No. 1', or 'Christmas No. 1'. Tomo rang me on the Saturday morning and asked if I fancied going to auditions in town. 'Auditions for what?' I asked, and he told me. 'Come on,' Tomo pleaded, 'we might as well go and have a look.' Now, Anto still hadn't heard me sing karaoke at this point. His impression of me and my singing was limited to that disastrous night in Limerick. I was reluctant, but Tomo persuaded me and we went into town that evening, despite the fact that I was hungover, dying of a cold and had an ear infection. Tomo and I did our auditions, with me performing under the stage name Mary Lee, and then we got the bus back home, giggling like two kids.

A couple of weeks later we got a phone call to tell us that we were both through to the next round. I was in Tenerife with my friends when Tomo was next called to appear on the show. He didn't make it through that night, so I assumed I was going to suffer the same fate when my turn came some time later. To my surprise, I was put straight through to the next round and then went on to win the bloody contest! For my prize I got to record a song, which the record company hoped would be a big Christmas number one in the Irish charts.

My brother-in-law, Liam, was very excited about the whole event.

Three years on from his cancer diagnosis, Liam was bravely battling on and it was a miracle we still had him in our lives. Liam was so proud of me for getting to the final of 'Nollaig No 1'. The whole thing was a great distraction for him as he coped with what was going on in his own life. For the contest, I had wanted to sing one of my own favourites, like Shirley Bassey, but I was encouraged to do 'You'll Never Walk Alone'. At first I was a bit put out, but then I thought of Liam and realised that the song had a lovely meaning: you're not on your own, you'll never be on your own. After I recorded it, I gave Liam the very first copy and signed it for him. He loved it and played it every day.

After that huge achievement, I was sure Anto would apologise for calling me 'brutal', but he didn't. Tomo was so proud of me, though. He had been one of the people who gave me the support and encouragement I so badly needed to finally achieve something as a singer. June had been the first, then Pat, then Tomo and, lastly, the crowd at the Shamrock. This was my road to singing confidently on stage. Anto might have been right in Limerick, where I certainly didn't do well, but I had shown everyone now that I was good enough. Most importantly, I had shown myself. Winning 'Nollaig No. 1' was a huge boost to my confidence. If it hadn't been for that show, I really don't think I would have auditioned for 'The X Factor'. It was a hugely important moment in my life. I sang my heart out, but made sure not to look at the judges; I sang over their heads. That is what I did in 'Nollaig No. 1' and what I would later do, week after week, as I faced 'The X Factor' panel.

All my life, I have believed that our paths through life are laid out for us. Cliff Richard once said that when you hand yourself over to God, or to whatever power you believe in, and you say, 'Okay, put me on the right path, let me do what you want me to do', you can only be successful. This is what he believed personally, and he says he owes his career to it. I heard him say that years and years ago, but then I forgot it as I was going through my twenties and thirties. But when I hit my forties, I felt a strong turning towards my faith again. I said to God, and to Jesus, 'I don't think I can do this by myself. I know You're there and I beg You to put me on the right path. I feel I've wasted a lot of time up to now because I didn't believe in myself and I didn't put enough faith in You either, though I always knew You were there.' Remembering Cliff Richard's words, I repeated them to God: 'Here I am, here's my life, You do with me what You want.' Then I left it out there. All of a sudden, the paths I had been on just vanished away, leaving this one path right in front of me. I had to follow it, I simply had no choice in the matter. When I handed myself over to Jesus like that and told him that I trusted him completely with my life, I believe He looked and me and said, 'Okay, you're ready and you're showing me that you think you're ready now, so it's time.'

It wasn't time immediately, though, there was still work to be done. If I'm being honest, I was a bit disappointed after 'Nollaig No. 1'. TG4 is a small, Irish language channel and though I was meeting lots of people who had seen the programme and thought I was great, nothing really came of it. There wasn't enough money to put a CD out in the shops, so it was only available as a download. There wasn't enough money because not enough people had watched the show. When I made 'Siúil Leat (You'll Never Walk Alone)', I didn't really think it was going to go anywhere and, sure enough, it didn't. That said, it was a great experience to record in an actual studio, albeit one that was a small room in a house. I learned a lot. I learned that it was important to listen to people and to hear what they were telling me. When you're working with people who know what they're doing, however frustrating it is when they keep correcting you, you have to take it on board and trust them. It wasn't about me, it was all about making the record as good as it could be. The song got good reviews, but it was only downloaded nineteen times – in other words, a total feckin' flop! On the other hand, it was a complete success for me and my confidence. A few years earlier I wouldn't have believed I'd have the guts to go for the audition, let alone to sing in front of a television camera. It might have felt like a bit of an anti-climax, but it was a sign of great things to come, even though I didn't know that at the time.

It wasn't just singing confidence it gave me either. I had to give a lot of interviews to camera, and I'll never forget one of the show's producers telling me, 'You were born for this, you do it too well.' I hadn't a clue what he was talking about or whether I was doing anything particularly well or not. Apparently, though, instead of doing fifteen takes on my very first outing, it only took me four, and they were amazed at that, while I was oblivious to it. I am so grateful to TG4 and to that show, so grateful that Anto rang Tomo and that Tomo rang me about it. But, as I say, it came up after I had handed myself over to God, so I don't believe it was a coincidence. I believe that God had put me on the right path, at long last, because He knew I was finally ready for it. He sent the opportunities and said, 'Now, it's up to you to make the most of it.' I had tried for stardom earlier in my life, but I hadn't made it. I think the reason it didn't happen for me back then is because I wasn't ready for it, it wasn't the right time. I had to go through all those knocks and setbacks before I was ready for my moment. As my mother liked to say, 'If it's for you, it won't pass you by.' It was for me, but at the right time, not when I wanted it.

The first time I had tried was back in the late 1980s, when I auditioned for the British television show, 'Opportunity Knocks', which was hosted by the late Bob Monkhouse. A customer at The Lawns pub had put my name in for it, and the first thing I knew about it was when I got a letter in the post, giving me a date to turn up for my 'Opportunity Knocks' audition. My initial reaction, naturally, was, 'No way! You must be joking! Absolutely not!' My friend, Julie, egged me on to do it and even offered to come with me. After much cajoling by everybody, I eventually decided, what the hell, I'll give it a go. Julie and myself managed to scrape together the money for the ferry to Liverpool, where the show was held. In honour of the occasion I bought a brown suit to wear – a horrible, shapeless one at that! I don't know what I was thinking.

Needless to say, I died a thousand deaths before I ever got onto that stage. I was in a right state when we arrived at the audition – the sweat was running off me and I couldn't stop my body from shaking. I turned to Julie and said, 'I can't do this!' She fixed me with a look and said firmly, 'Yes, you can!' My friend Jimmy Storey, the Lord have mercy on him, had written out the music to Shirley Bassey's 'Never, Never, Never' and to a second song, Elkie Brooks's 'Don't Cry Out Loud'. Jimmy, who played the organ in The Lawns, kept telling me to sing the Elkie Brooks song, but I wasn't comfortable doing it, so I went with 'Never, Never, Never' instead.

Well, I sang 'Never, Never, Never' right through, from start to finish, at the top of my voice, with my eyes closed and head facing the ground. When I finished, the people standing around clapped like mad. I ran out the door. I just knew that I wouldn't be called back. Julie and I had watched a few of the other contestants and they knew how to act into the camera, to sing directly act it. These were people who were meant to be on television and I wasn't, not at that time in my life anyway. A little while later I got a letter in the post telling me that hundreds of people had auditioned and, unfortunately, I hadn't been successful – 'but fair play for trying', it added. Other people might have been disappointed, but I was incredibly relieved that I wouldn't have to go through all that again. In fact, I'd say if I had got through, I wouldn't have gone back to Liverpool anyway. I hadn't enjoyed the experience at all because I was so frightened the whole time.

So here I was, twenty years later, having another shot at it and again it seemed like it wasn't really going anywhere. When nothing happened after 'Nollaig No. 1', Betty and Liam's daughter, Elaine, suggested I should go for 'Britain's Got Talent'. '*What!*' I said, 'How can I go for that when I'm not British? I'm Irish.' My niece started laughing. 'But loads of different people go on it,' she insisted. 'No, get lost, I'm not doing it.' Being a cheeky devil, Elaine put my name in for it anyway. Just like before, a letter arrived at the house to tell me that I had an audition that October, for 'Britain's Got Talent'. I didn't go. I just didn't feel it was for me.

Elaine was disappointed that I didn't take up the offer, so I said to her, 'Look, I'm sorry I didn't go, but I'll tell you what, if 'The X Factor' ever comes here, I promise you I'll go for it.' Now, I said that because as far as I was concerned, that would never, ever happen; Simon Cowell had said in an interview that he would never come to Ireland. That's a safe promise to make, I thought to myself – it placates her, but gets me off the hook. The following year, it was announced that 'The X Factor' was coming to Dublin. 'Ah, for feck's sake!' I thought, knowing that Elaine would be on my case to keep my promise. Sure enough, she took it upon herself to send off an application form with my name on it.

I can't really explain why this was different, but it was. Maybe God was gently nudging me along towards it, but when the letter arrived to tell me I had an audition, I was determined to do it. I didn't really know what I was doing or what I was letting myself in for, but I was determined to go for it, whatever it was. I wanted them to hear me sing and I would be delighted if they said to me, 'We love your voice, but you're not for this show.' That would be enough for me, I thought, as I set out for the auditions.

13. Audition agonies

You have to be a little bit mad to do what I did next. Here I was, at the age of fifty, leaving my Ballyfermot home shortly after one o'clock one morning in May to go and queue up with a crowd of excited young kids in Ireland's historic Gaelic sports stadium, Croke Park, for the chance to appear on 'The X Factor'. I don't know what came over me at all, but, hey, you only live once. I went there with the voices of my friend, June, and my brother, Tomo, ringing in my head, telling me I could do it.

Deborah agreed to accompany her mother on this latest adventure, and we took our places in the Croke Park queue shortly before 2.00am. It would be five hours later before the cameras put in an appearance. I was sitting in a camping chair that Deborah had bought, and feeling wrecked. It was now seven o'clock and fresh as a daisy, I was not! The camera crew approached me and asked, 'So, who are you? What brings you here? Who are you with?' I tried to look awake and replied, 'I'm with my daughter.' They immediately turned to Deborah, assuming she was the one auditioning. 'No,' I interrupted, 'I'm going for it!' The guy looked very surprised, 'Oh, so you're going for it?' 'Yeah!' I said. 'Ah, fair play to you. How old are you?' 'Fifty,' I replied. I'm sure he thought this was going to be a great laugh. I shrugged and said, 'If I don't give it a try, I'll never know.' That was my first encounter with the 'X Factor' cameras.

The next stage was to queue in a big area where Dermot O'Leary, the show's presenter, and Louis Walsh came out to see the contestants. It was now midday. I was feeling incredibly tired and cranky, muttering to myself, 'Jaysus, just get this show on the road.' Three hours later we got inside the stadium and took our seats. Down below us, spread out all along the pitch, were lots of huts covered in green felt. I don't know how many people I watched coming out of those huts, some screaming for joy and jumping around, others looking very depressed. 'Oh, Jesus!' is all I remember thinking. I was exhausted, my arthritis was killing me and I was more than ready to go home to bed, but Deborah wouldn't let me. 'You've come this far, Ma, you can't just walk out.'

A friend of mine, Louise, who I worked with in Tesco, was going in after me. When it was my turn I said to her, 'Well, here goes nothing!' Louise laughed, 'I hope you do it, Mary.' I looked at her and shook my head wearily. 'To be honest, Louise, I'm so knackered, I don't care anymore.' Off I went and gave my name to the guy who met me and looked – it has to be said – less than impressed with the middle-aged woman slouching in front of him. I could almost hear him thinking, 'Oh, for fuck's sake!' Anyway, I started singing the Tom Jones hit, 'I Who Have Nothing', and everyone went quiet. I kept singing, but felt a bit panicked at the utter silence. When I stopped, the place erupted into applause. 'Who's that for?' I asked the guy. His reply was brief and to the point, '*You!*' I stared at him. 'Oh ...?' was all I could manage. 'Right, off you go, you're through to the next round.' He didn't ask me another thing. The crowd was still cheering as I left the stage. I went upstairs to another room, where I was told to come back the next morning, at seven o'clock.

I was up a cock crow again the next day and Deborah came with me again for a bit of support. Warren Dempsey, a young lad in his twenties from my road in Ballyfermot, had also got through to the next round; he's a brilliant singer. At about two o'clock in the afternoon, I was finally called in to do my song. 'About feckin' time,' I thought, yet again exhausted from hanging around since the sun had come up that day. I was greeted by a guy and girl and told them my name. The guy asked what I was going to sing for them, and I told him I'd do the same song I had done the previous day. So I took a deep breath and started, 'I ... I who have nothing ... I ...' Suddenly, I was cut short: 'Okay, you're through to the next round and I can't wait to see you again.' Well, that was something else!

The next round took place that very evening. We went off to get some food and a rest and returned to start queuing all over again, as well as filling in umpteen forms. It was about seven o'clock when I was called to see the last guy who would listen to me sing. This was when the filming started. I sang the same song again, then he asked me if I could sing a more modern number. The only other song I could think of was Alexandra Burke's version of the Leonard Cohen song, 'Hallelujah'. I told him this, adding, 'Well, I've just started learning it, but I'm not sure how well I know it.' He encouraged me to try it, so I sang a bit of it before I was told to stop with the words, 'That's fine, Mary!' When I finished my spot I was dying to get away, but as I began to edge towards the door, the 'X Factor' guy called out, 'Eh, hold on, there, Mary Byrne! You'll find out in a month's time whether you're through or not.' I was almost out the door when I said, 'Oh, fine, yes. Thank you. Bye now!' I just wanted to go home. Deborah and I were absolutely exhausted by this stage. We went straight home and slept for the next sixteen hours or so.

After that, it was back to my regular life on Till 40 at the Tesco store in Ballyfermot. When I told my friends what I'd done, they were all excited for me, but I played it down, honestly thinking that nothing would come of it. My work mates kept saying, 'Ah, you might get through, you never know.' The next few weeks went by and I heard nothing. When almost five weeks had passed since the auditions, I told myself that I hadn't made it. The guy had said I'd hear after a month, that there would be a phone call if I got through, probably a letter if I didn't. I resigned myself to the fact that I wouldn't be appearing on 'The X Factor' that year, or any other year for that matter. I was still delighted I had gone for it, though, and wasn't going to die wondering what might have been. The audition process had been an experience in itself and I had got lovely feedback from everyone about my voice, so I was feeling good about Mary Byrne at that moment.

I took a week's holiday from work and on the Friday, the last morning of my week off, I was lying in bed, thinking about getting up, when my phone rang. 'Hello?' I said. A girl with an English accent introduced herself, saying she was from 'The X Factor'. I think I gulped while saying, 'Er ... yes?' She said, 'I want to ask you a few things first before I say anything to you.' By now I had shot up in bed and as I sat, propped against the pillows, I completely forgot that if you got through, you got a phone call. I was just bewildered by her needing to ask me questions. She started asking me about my health and I told her that I had arthritis and was on anti-depressants. 'But I'm not mad!' I assured her. 'Well,' I added, 'I'm probably a little bit mad.' She laughed and said, 'Okay, I've something to tell you. Mary, you made it through to the judges.' I fell off the bed ... literally. No joking. I went to stand up, slipped and fell off the bed. Deborah heard an almighty crash and came racing up the stairs, 'What's wrong! Are you okay?' I was shouting like a wild woman, '*Aaarrgghh!!* I'm in 'The X Factor'. I'm through! I'm *in!*' It was crazy. I was crazy. I couldn't believe it, just couldn't believe it. Deborah helped me up off the floor. My backside was so sore, and my knees from the arthritis, but I didn't give two fecks – I was through to 'The X Factor'.

When I went back into work on Monday, the response was tremendous – and not just from my friends. All the customers queued up to congratulate me while they were in to get their shopping done. I was so taken aback by the goodwill I was shown, and how pleased people were for a local girl to get so far. It made me really want to do well, for myself and everyone who knew me and supported me. I felt like I'd set a ball rolling and it was gathering pace and there was no stopping it now. My head was in a spin with the whole thing.

When the day came to face the actual judges at the Dublin Convention Centre on Monday, 28 June, I brought a few people with me for support. There was my niece Brenda, with her husband Darren, and their three children, Diane, Niamh and Ciara. There was also Betty and my devoted brother-in-law, Liam, who sat through fourteen hours, in pain, because he was so determined to see me sing. Deborah's pal, young Andrew McLoughlin, also came with me. Deborah was there, of course, along with my friends, Caroline Callaghan, Caroline Foster and Patrick Hughes from Tesco. They came in, not realising they were going to have to sit there for fourteen hours. None of us did.

We got there at half-past ten in the morning and there was a great atmosphere. I was enjoying myself with my friends and family, and every so often I'd be told that I'd be interviewed shortly in front of the camera. The hours ticked by and nothing happened until about eight o'clock that evening. Then it was just a short talk, introducing myself and explaining why I was there. When I was finished, I was told it wouldn't be too much longer before I faced the judges and sang for them. I'd be performing in front of Simon Cowell, Louis Walsh, Katy Perry (standing in for Dannii Minogue) and Cheryl Cole.

People were coming and going and by that stage, the place seemed to be emptying out. I glanced at Liam and he looked so tired, and I knew he was in pain, 'Why don't you go on home?' I suggested. But he absolutely refused. There was no way he was missing me doing my bit. He and the rest of them were convinced that once I got on the stage and opened my mouth, I'd win over all the judges. Meanwhile, all I was hoping would happen was that Louis and Simon would tell me I had a good voice, but that the show just wasn't right for me. I couldn't think about anything more than that. It had been a long day and, just like the auditions, I was tired and impatient to get home.

They finally called my name at a quarter to midnight. We all piled into the backroom and Dermot O'Leary, who I had been looking forward to meeting, just put his hand on my back and pushed me through. After all those hours of waiting, suddenly it felt like I was being thrown onto the stage without any warning. Here I was, at last, facing the four judges. Simon was sitting there messing with his pen, while the lovely Louis started to ask me questions. I told him I was going to sing, 'I Who Have Nothing' and he said, 'Oh, that's a big song.' I laughed and told him, and everyone there, 'Yes, I know. I hope I do it justice!' I took a deep breath, and started to sing.

I never noticed the faces of the judges as I sang; I didn't look at them once. So I didn't see their first reactions until I watched the show on TV. Katy Perry kind of went, '*Oh my God!*' Cheryl Cole looked like she got goosebumps, while Simon just stared at me with an intense expression on his face. As I didn't see all this at the time, I was bowled over by their responses when I'd finished singing. I just could not believe what the likes of Simon Cowell, Louis Walsh, Cheryl Cole, and Katy Perry were saying to *me*. In the show that aired on television, they cut out the part where Simon said, 'You're the type of person I like, and you're the type of artiste I could work with.' I walked off that stage in a daze. I was through to Boot Camp ... and Simon Cowell had called me an artiste!

Deborah ran at me, screaming, 'Oh, Ma, I can't believe it!' Neither could I. Liam looked like somebody who didn't have a care in the world, he was so happy for me. His face was beaming with pride and delight. He said to me, 'When the music started, I could feel it under my feet and then I could hear your voice booming and there were shivers up and down my spine. I just felt so proud and I said to myself, if they don't put her through, I'll go and sort every one of them out.' And sure he could barely walk, God love him, but I believed him!

We finally got out of there at one in the morning because there were more forms to be filled out for Boot Camp – they must have cut down a whole forest to run that show. It had been a very long day, but my God, was it worth it.

When I went into work, everyone knew I had got through. The crowds in Tesco were huge, so much so that very little work was getting done. It was like Christmas Eve all day long with the amount of people that were filing in and out to congratulate me. While I was trying to serve customers, people were coming up to the till just to see me and talk to me. I had to do something, because it wasn't fair on the shop and the rest of the staff. Annie, my manager, called me into the office and I asked her if she could take me off my till and put me somewhere else. She shook her head, 'There's nowhere else I can put you, Mary.' Then she added, 'But I was talking to management and they're prepared to pay your wages while you're off at 'The X Factor', so you may as well start your leave now.' I was over the moon: this was a fantastic show of support from my employer, especially as I didn't have a cent to my name.

At that time, it was mainly Ballyfermot people who knew that I had got through to 'The X Factor'. Word had leaked out to the media that some supermarket worker from Ballyfermot had made it on to the TV show, but Louis Walsh was giving out false names and false locations to the radio stations and the newspapers who were trying to find out my identity and track me down. Louis was trying to keep the mystery going for as long as possible. It was a mystery to me that I had made it through in the first place, but by God I was going to give it my all. Bring on Boot Camp!

14. Surviving Boot Camp

Boot Camp was due to start in June and I was now booked on a flight over to London. When I got my airline ticket with a week to go, I believed then that it was really happening and that it wasn't just some kind of crazy dream. I was so excited at this incredible chance I'd managed to land for myself, so I didn't expect all the emotions that overwhelmed me when it came time to leave. It suddenly hit me, the enormity of what I was taking on and the fact that it would mean a lot of time away from Deborah. I had a bit of a wobble, then, at the thought of being without her. Boot Camp was only for a week, but I began to feel a bit guilty about the whole thing. Was the career I hoped to get from this worth leaving Deborah behind on her own, even though she was now a young woman? We were so close that leaving her was tearing at my heartstrings. The wobble passed, though, and the more I thought about it, the more I came to terms with what I was doing and accepted all that it would entail. I realised that it was going to benefit both of us, not just me. I was doing 'The X Factor' as much for Deborah's future as for mine. With that thought to keep me going, I packed my bags and boarded a plane for … God knows what!

Boot Camp turned out to be really bloody tough. I remember Louis Walsh giving an interview at the Camp and telling journalists, 'To survive in this business, you've got to be tough. All the contestants have got to go out there and deliver.' Simon Cowell's comments to the media were even more scary: 'I'm going to push them so much harder this year. I mean, seriously.' I felt a chill down my spine when I heard that. I was lucky to have got that far though, as I learned that around 200,000 had applied for that year's 'X Factor' and only 211 of us had made it through to Boot Camp.

It was a long slog of a week and I reckoned that I'd be gone as soon as it ended. On arrival, we were booked into the Premier Inn in Wembley, and told we had to check out the next morning, bringing our suitcases to Wembley Arena, where Boot Camp would take place. If we got through that day, we would be delivered back to the Premier Inn, booked in again for the night, packed up the following morning, checked out again and brought back, suitcases in hand, to Boot Camp. That alone was tiring and not a little nerve-racking, watching to see which contestants never came back to the hotel at night because they hadn't got through on the day. We were all just there on a day-to-day basis, so none of us could take anything for granted. I had to drag my heavy case for the half-hour journey to the Boot Camp, be there from eight in the morning, and wait to audition. Some days you didn't sing until twelve or one o'clock the next morning, which meant you were kept on tenterhooks for sixteen hours before you were even asked to sing. This was definitely a contest for young people, I thought to myself, because it required superhero levels of stamina.

There was an awful lot of waiting around, given that there were so many of us to perform every day. We were grouped together by gender, groups and age. At the start of the process, the girls were given Beyoncé's 'If I Was A Boy' to sing in groups, the boys got Michael Jackson's 'Man In The Mirror', while the actual male and female groups sang 'Nothing's Gonna Stop Us Now', by Starship. The Over-25s, which was my group, had to sing Lady Gaga's 'Poker Face'. I made it out of the bunch on my first day. There were now 108 of us left and we had to face more anxiety as the process of elimination continued.

While the pace they set was absolutely gruelling, I understood why it had to be so tough. We were all being forced to ask ourselves: is this what I really want? Do I have what it takes? The message was: if you haven't got the stamina and dedication, then leave now, because this is what it's going to be like from now on. At the time, I hated every single person putting us through that. It was only when I looked back later, after 'The X Factor' was over, that I realised what that week had been all about. They were being cruel to be kind. In fact, I soon discovered that the pressure piled on us in Boot Camp was just a taste of how tough it would be for those of us who made it through to the live show.

Each day I was convinced I wasn't going to be bunking down in the Premier Inn that night. During Boot Camp I struggled hard with a complex dance routine they gave us to do. 'I'm here to feckin' sing for you, not bloody dance,' I thought to myself as the choreographer, Brian Friedman, did his best to turn me into a female version of Fred Astaire, while my lack of confidence and arthritis ganged up to ensure that was never going to happen. But I kept going, refusing to be beaten by arthritis and determined to work through my lack of confidence. 'I'm not going to let myself down here,' I thought.

When we were first told that we'd be doing a two-hour dance class for this, I wanted to break my heart laughing, thinking, 'No way am I going to be able for that!' I was one of the oldest there, but then I told myself, 'Feck it! I'll just do my best.' So I stood at the back of the stage, hoping that I'd be alright. Out of the corner of my eye I noticed the camera crew setting up their equipment and facing it in my direction. 'Ah Jaysus, I don't believe this!' If I was a bit more savvy, I would have taken this as a good sign, that they wanted to follow me at this point, but I wasn't, and I didn't. Every time Brian Friedman asked the back line to move forward, I'd just edge back again. I did this for an hour and a half! They kept saying, 'move forward', and I kept moving backwards. Ninety minutes later, I knew the routine, but my fifty-year-old arthritic knees had started to swell. I asked one of the girls if I could sit down for a bit and she said, 'Of course.' Next thing I see Dermot O'Leary heading towards me, with the cameras following him, 'Mary, what's wrong with you, chicken?' 'Ah,' I said, 'I'm just having a rest. Me knees are in bits. I think they're trying to kill me on that stage.' He asked, 'So, are you finished now?' 'I am in me arse,' I told him, bold as brass. 'They're not getting rid of me that quick!' As he walked away, I heard Dermot say, 'She's a real tryer, fair play to her.'

I got myself back up on the stage and tried again, for another ten minutes, but my knees just wouldn't cooperate. One of the producers called me over and told me to take it easy and sit down for another while. So I sat down and watched the young kids being put through their paces. Believe me, they gave them some gruelling stuff to do. When that finished, there was another announcement that they were putting us in groups to dance. 'Oh for the love of God!' I thought. 'Please don't put me in a group.'

They called out a few names and the last one was mine. I seriously thought about not going back up, having no idea how I was going to summon up the energy and strength, but then the voice in my head told me, 'If you don't get up and do this, you're going to regret it.' That was enough to get me going. I walked up, and where did they put me only right in front of the group, making it impossible for me to hang back or hide. There were twelve of us on stage, in three lines of four, and I was in the first row. I spoke up before the music started, announcing, 'I don't remember the routine.' Louis Walsh was there watching us and he started laughing, so I said to him, 'What are you laughing at? This is all your bloody fault! I'm only doing this for you.'

The music started and I could remember the first few steps, and managed to get into it, despite my poor knees. Then I hadn't a clue what to do next and I just thought, 'Improvise!' That involved some shimmering and wobbling of my chest, but I think it was in time to the music. I happened to look down and now I spotted Simon Cowell and Louis, in stitches laughing at me. I didn't care. I was just happy that I had proved I was determined to do this. That was the only plan in my head at that point: show them I'm up for trying anything. A few minutes later and I was grateful to be allowed to sit back down again. While half of the contestants went home that day, I was still in, despite making a bags of the dancing. Afterwards, Brian Friedman said on camera, 'Mary didn't give up and I love that. You need that drive and ambition.'

Another day that went badly for me was when I was trying to pick a song to sing from a list of forty they had given us to perform individually. The only one that appealed to me was Leona Lewis' cover of Roberta Flack's, 'The First Time Ever I Saw Your Face'. Personally, I didn't like Leona's arrangement as much as Roberta Flack's or Shirley Bassey's. I asked them for the Shirley Bassey version instead, but they couldn't get it for me, so I was desperately trying to learn the Leona Lewis one. We had to sing our song in front of the choreographer, Brian Friedman, during the rehearsals. When it was my turn to perform in front of Brian, I froze. I managed to sing it through, but had to keep my eyes closed. I made mistakes, didn't sing the song right and just about blew it completely. I had to do a little interview afterwards, and I said that I knew I wasn't going through because of my performance.

When I got out from the interview, Joe, one of the researchers who looked after us – a lovely chap with whom I got on really well – came up and asked me, 'What can we do to make this better?' I told him, 'Get me Shirley Bassey's version.' God bless him! He made a few phone calls and they got back to us to say they had it. I leapt on Joe and kissed him to bits. I took it back to the hotel with me and played it non-stop, knowing that I had just two days before I'd be singing it at Boot Camp for Simon, Louis and Nicole Scherzinger. But I sang it great in the room, I thought.

Before we started singing for the judges, former Pussycat Dolls member Nicole Scherzinger said, 'This is where we separate the boys from the men and the pussycats from the dolls. Have fun and kick some butt!' Cher Lloyd was the first to perform, doing her version of Coldplay's 'Viva La Vida', with her own rap thrown into the mix. Another contestant, Chloe Victoria, sang 'Wishing On A Star', but she forgot the words. Matt Cardle performed 'The First Time Ever I Saw Your Face' and the judges liked him, although Simon said Matt needed to work on his confidence and self-belief. 'We have something in common,' I thought. And so it went, with contestants rising and falling on the big occasion.

Simon had told us before it kicked off that he wanted us all, before we sang, to make a statement about why we thought we should be there. All around me I could hear the other contestants reciting what they were going to say, and some of them were quite long and complicated. I decided I'd just tell them honestly that I deserved to be there because it was such a wonderful opportunity for me and that I felt there was a market for my voice. So, that's what I did when it was my turn, and Simon said, 'Short and sweet!' 'Well,' I replied, 'that's what you asked for.' He made a face and looked away as if to say, 'You cheeky devil!'

I started singing the song and sang the first verse really well, but then on the second, I came in too soon and lost the track. Simon called out for me to stop. He just said, 'Thank You'. I said, 'Thank you for stopping it,' and walked off. I saw the disappointment on Louis' face and I went outside and completely broke down. The film crew followed me as I sobbed my heart out. I pleaded with them not to, but of course, it was their job; they had to capture me in pieces because it made good television. Afterwards, the camera-man hugged me and told me he was so sorry for me. He was actually the same guy who had interviewed me back in Croke Park, at the first auditions.

In a way, I was very surprised by my own reaction. I hadn't really believed that I would get through Boot Camp anyway, but I think in that moment, when I thought it was over, I suddenly realised, with a huge shock, that I wanted to succeed at this more than anything else I had ever wanted in my life. I learned that I wasn't the only one who broke down that day, and that those contestants still got through. So then I realised it meant, thank God, that the judges weren't basing their decision on that one performance; they were taking in the whole of the past week. I was still in with a chance.

The next day we were going to be told if we had made it through to the judges' houses or not. That was one long, horrible day for everyone. At that stage only thirty-two acts would be going through, with each judge mentoring eight, an increase from six in the previous series. We had to wait until the following evening for the results. The day was taken up with bits and pieces, pottering around and really just waiting and waiting. The heat was tremendous, too, and all our nerves were on edge. You just couldn't relax at all. We did our best – we had a bit of a laugh and gossiped about who we thought was or wasn't going to get through. There was a lovely lad with me, a big guy from Scotland, called Steve. He said to me, 'I'll tell you now, Mary, who has got through.' He pointed to a few people and said, 'they're gone, but those are staying'. 'No, they're not!' I argued. Back and forth it went in every corner of the room. That was generally the tone of the day.

Eventually, the time arrived when we were going to be told if we'd made it or not. We were separated into different rooms. I glanced around my room and saw it was all the oldies. 'Ah, that's it,' I thought to myself, 'we're gone for definite.' Different groups were called in one by one, and they never came back. Finally, it was down to our group and one other. I was tired and worn out by the time they called us. It was about eleven o'clock at night and I couldn't have cared less what happened at that stage, as all I was looking forward to by then was bed. Everyone around me felt the same way. One minute we were excited and saying, 'Oh, I really want to get through', the next minute we were rubbing our eyes and saying, 'Kill me now!' There was no air-conditioning and the air was thick and heavy, which didn't help.

Suddenly, it was our turn to walk back out onto the stage and face the judges for probably the last time. We formed a nervous line. I looked at Louis, then at Simon Cowell, trying to figure out where I stood with them. They had started dealing with the people on the opposite end from where I was standing, so I couldn't catch their eyes. I remember the sad expression on Louis' face, and he was deliberately avoiding eye contact with me as I tried to get him to give me the nod as to whether I was in or out. He wouldn't, or couldn't, look at me, so I had to stop staring at him because it was making me even more nervous. That's when I decided in my head that I was out, and that Louis was dreading telling me.

A lot of people in our group were getting through, as the judges worked their way along the line. Then Louis handed the microphone to stand-in judge Nicole Scherzinger and put his head down. 'Oh Jesus!' I thought, 'he's going to make her say it to me.' She said, 'The next person going through is ...' – Well, it's certainly not me, I thought – '... MARY BYRNE!' It's fair to say that I forgot all about my arthritis, and all my exhaustion disappeared as I leapt in the air, while screaming at Louis Walsh that I loved him. He had put on such an act just to convince me I was going home. My heart was pounding and I was trying to take it all in. I had made it through to the judges' houses!

I raced down the steps, passing Dermot O'Leary, who shouted at me, 'What about your arthritis?' 'It's GONE!' I roared. I can tell you that I was punished for it the next day when my limbs were stiff and aching, but in that moment of elation, I didn't give a damn. What a wonderful feeling. I had made it! Eight of us had made it through in our category, which was now called Over-28s, and included John Adeleye, Wagner, Stephen

Above: Do we look like we have the X Factor? Fellow contestant Katie Waissel and myself clowning around backstage on the show.

Right: One Direction – young Niall Horan from Mullingar and myself having a laugh behind the scenes at 'The X Factor'.

Below: 'Mammy Bear' sandwiched between One Direction young fellas Zain Malik and Louis Tomlinson.

Above: This is My Life: Pouring all my emotion into another big song on 'The X Factor'.

Below: Good man, Louis: My mentor encourages the crowd to go crazy for me in the 'X Factor' studio.

Above: Deborah is flying without wings here as she meets her idols, the gorgeous guys in Westlife.

Below: I've had many hair-raising experiences, but this wasn't one of them. John and Edward, aka Jedward, are two young gentlemen. The other lady here is the legendary Maureen Grant, who has run Maureen's Bar in Dublin's Olympia Theatre for over sixty years and has a wealth of great stories to tell.

Next! Back at Till 40 in Tesco, Ballyfermot, on the day of my 'X Factor' homecoming. It was great to be surrounded by my friends and work colleagues who supported me. It was another emotional day for me.

Right: Cheers! Relaxing backstage after giving a good performance.

Left: As if performing as the special guest on Neil Diamond's show wasn't exciting enough, my record company presented me with a platinum disc for sales of my first album, *Mine & Yours*, backstage that same night.

Above: Pleased to meet you Ma'am: It was lovely to get a personal moment with Queen Elizabeth II on her historic visit to Ireland.

Below: Singing for the Queen, but I forgot the words of the U2 song, 'All I Want is You' – not that she noticed!

I don't believe it! My surprise as Neil Diamond turns up at my dressing room before the show at Aviva Stadium, Dublin, and then gives me a big bear hug as my daughter, Deborah, looks on. Billy, who does my hair and make-up, is completely awestruck in the background as I chat with my new best friend, Neil.

Above: Where's the crowd? Pictured during rehearsals at the Neil Diamond concert in Aviva Stadium. Don't I look pleased to be there – it was even more exciting when 40,000 music fans turned up for the show!

Left: Our 'Miracle Baby': Deborah becomes a godmother to my niece Brenda's little son, Dara, who was born four months premature and won the battle to survive. I just adore him. Also pictured is Dara's godfather, my niece Elaine's partner, Alan Gittons.

Hunter, Justin Vanderhyde, Storm Lee, Yuli Minguel and Elesha Moses.

That night, all of us who had got through went back to the hotel and celebrated with a few beers. I didn't have too much to drink because I was so tired. All I had was one glass of wine, and then I just had to sleep. For a little while I could relax again. I was through for now and I was going back home to Dublin, to see Deborah and my friends and family. It felt like ages since I had seen any of them. I flew out of Heathrow the following day and from the airport I went straight home to Ballyfermot. When I told them I had made it, there was great celebration, though Deborah didn't react as much as the others because, as she said, 'I just had a feeling you were going to get through.' 'You liar!' I joked, but I believed her. She doesn't say a lot, but when she does have a view, you know it's genuine. When Deborah compliments you, she's being absolutely honest.

A few weeks later I got a phone call from Helen, one of the 'X Factor' researchers. She asked me how excited I was and so forth, then she asked, 'If you were to get a mentor, who would you prefer it to be? What about Simon?' I told her the truth, 'I find Simon a bit intimidating, though I'd be fine if he was my mentor. But I probably wouldn't choose him myself.' Simon Cowell just has this aura about him – when he walks into a room, you know he has arrived. There's just something about him that makes you feel you wouldn't want to cross him. He's not big in stature, but he certainly makes up for it with the presence he has. (Now that I know him better, he doesn't bother me at all. I can have a good laugh with him. We're practically the same age, when you think about it!) I said to Helen, 'If I really had a choice, the one I'd pick would be Louis Walsh.' She asked me why and I said, 'Because I just feel Louis really gets me, and not because we're both Irish. He knows the type of music I like to sing and he likes it too.'

I had watched 'The X Factor' for six years and had always liked Louis

Walsh because he showed a real compassion for the contestants. I remember him crying because he had to tell someone they were going home. I felt that he wore his heart on his sleeve, but could be a real bitch, too. That's what I liked that about him: he could be very soft, yet was a hard nut when he had to be.

A few weeks later I flew to London for a four-day trip, to meet people at Sony Music record company. All of the acts were brought to the Sony offices, where we were given the list of songs we were going to be singing at the judges' houses. I looked at my list and blurted out, 'But I don't know any of these!' The girl told me that this was 'what your mentor had sent down for you'. 'That's Simon Cowell!' I thought to myself. 'He's trying to sabotage me!' Only two people, out of our whole group of eight, got songs they knew and were comfortable singing. Storm hadn't a clue about his songs, neither did John Adeleye; whereas Dutch woman Yuli got two songs that she loved and already knew by heart. My Scottish friend, Steve, didn't know how he was going to handle his selection. We both read each other's list and I wished I was singing his songs, while he wished he had mine. He had two Shirley Bassey songs, including the modern one, 'Get This Party Started', while I got Coldplay and Whitney Houston. I wasn't a fan of hers and had never really listened to her music.

The following day we were told to pack our bags because we were going to the airport to meet our mentor. I now felt I was getting Louis Walsh, despite thinking for a brief moment it might be Simon when I got my selection of songs. I said it to the others in my group that I'd bet them a fiver we had Louis. They assumed that I was disappointed because it meant flying back to Ireland, rather than jetting off to where the other judges lived, like Simon's fancy mansion in Los Angeles that we had seen in the glossy magazines. 'I don't care at all,' I told them. 'I'd be more relaxed doing this in my own country.'

At the airport we were left standing together at a point where we could have been departing for a variety of different destinations, just to keep us in the dark a bit longer. The 'oldies' asked the researchers how long we were going away for, and we were told three days. At that point I knew we were going to Ireland and so did Storm, who was standing beside me, because it was such a short trip.

We flew to Shannon Airport and when we got out of the plane, the sun was splitting the stones. It was just the most glorious weather – one of those all-too-rare summer days you get every now and then in Ireland. A bus arrived to take us to Limerick, where we did a bit of filming. Even though I'd had that terrible experience singing in Limerick a few years previously, I absolutely loved all the scenic spots they took us to and couldn't stop taking photos. The television cameras followed us everywhere, which did become a bit annoying after a few hours. We were also very hungry, having only had a bread roll since early that morning. At one point the bus pulled in to another scenic spot and there was a couple enjoying a picnic. Wagner asked me to go over and ask them for a sandwich, but I refused. Someone else came up and put a camera in my face and I snapped, out of hunger and boredom, 'I've a pain in me face between that camera there and this one here', and with that I whipped up my top, flashed my bra, then walked off back to the bus, leaving them all stunned behind me. Then they burst out laughing, the cameraman saying, 'I ... I just can't believe she did that!' 'Well, there you go,' I shouted, 'that's what I do when I get bored!' I think some of the others had filmed it on their cameras and the feckers later put it up on the Internet for the whole world to see. Ah well!

The bus continued on its way and a few miles down the road we were told we were going to a posh place called Adare Manor. It turned out to be a nineteenth-century manor house on the banks of the River Maigue, and is now a world famous five-star hotel, on an 840-acre estate near the gorgeous village of Adare in County Limerick. I had heard of it and knew of it as a hotel where the rich and famous stayed. President Bill Clinton was a guest there during his visit to Ireland in 1998, but, needless to say, I could never have afforded to set foot through the door, so I had never even seen it before. When the bus pulled into the driveway, the place took my breath away because, as President Clinton might say, 'It's awesome.' We weren't brought into the manor house, however. Instead, we pulled into a laneway on the estate. 'The story of my life,' I laughed to myself as I realised we weren't going to be staying in the actual hotel. Then the 'X Factor' crew, who were shadowing us, passed us by and we learned that we were just letting them go on ahead, so they could film our approach.

We 'arrived' again, got off the bus and began to walk until we rounded a corner and had our first proper sight of the Manor. Oh my God! It was beautiful. The day was so perfect, and now standing in front of this house, with the river running through the grounds, I turned to John Adeleye and said, 'It's like being in the South of France'. He agreed. We had never seen anything like it before. We went inside and the staff fell over themselves to look after us. They couldn't have been nicer, and they took a special shine to the Irish girl, of course. They were thrilled that an Irish person had gotten this far in such a big competition.

Next, we were brought over to the bungalows where we would be staying. They were gorgeous, too. I had two double beds in my room; I didn't know which one to sleep in. Of course, this wasn't a holiday. We were allowed to settle in that day, but the next morning we were flung into rehearsals and told we'd be meeting our mentor later that day. Obviously, we said we knew full well who our mentor was. When the crew saw how confident we were in our assumption, they warned us how unpredictable the show was: 'You all think it's Louis because we're in Ireland, but it could well be Simon Cowell, or Cheryl Cole.' Cheryl hadn't been well after being struck down with malaria on a foreign holiday, so maybe she could only travel to Ireland? We began to wonder if we possibly had been tricked into thinking we were getting Louis … and were about to get the shock of our lives.

We were sent to wait outside, in a line, for our mentor. We walked down some steps and at the bottom was a small table with a bottle of champagne and glasses on it, along with a letter. I opened it, and all it said was: WELCOME TO ADARE MANOR, CAN'T WAIT TO MEET YOU ALL. ENJOY YOUR STAY. SEE YOU IN AN HOUR.

I still have that card at home. We opened the champagne and clinked glasses, in a state of pure excitement. The cameras were there and recording us chattering amongst ourselves, wondering if we were right about our mentor. Once again the waiting went on a bit and we started to get a little impatient: why didn't they just bring the mentor out already? The next thing, a little man walks out of the house. My heart leapt for joy, it was the one and only … LOUIS WALSH! Thanks be to God! We all went wild. Afterwards he said to me, '*You!* Did you, by any chance, ask for me?' 'Yeeaaah!' I replied. And that's why he had been given to us, because I wanted him, while he would have much preferred to be working with the groups! Well, I, for one, was delighted to have him, never mind about what he wanted. My wish had come true.

Louis told us that he had a surprise for us and almost out of nowhere, this woman suddenly appeared in front of us – the wonderful Sharon Osbourne. You could have killed me then and there and I would have died happy. I've always loved Sharon, and she didn't disappoint in person. She was the nicest, kindest lady you could ever hope to meet, and I do mean lady. We all hit it off with her: she was as kind and as firm with every single one of us. Her and Louis have such a close bond, they banter off one another, and I think it's such a terrible shame that they're not sitting side by side on that panel anymore. We were all in awe of her at the start, but then we couldn't believe how down-to-earth she was.

Furthermore, she looked completely fabulous in the flesh.

Afterwards, Louis confessed how much Sharon was taken with me and she told him not to let me go. I was thrilled at that. I did get a chance to have a talk with her, but our conversation got distorted in the media. What happened was, I had sung my first song for her and Louis and had made a bloody mess of it. Well, to be honest, I made a mess out of every song I sang for them. I don't know why they had so much faith in me; I was constantly letting my nerves get the better of me. Louis took a big chance with me and to this day, I don't know why. Anyway, I messed up the Coldplay song, 'Fix You', and then I messed up a Whitney Houston song, which was off her new album and I still don't even remember the title of it. The two of them sat and stared at me in disbelief, and I could see that Louis had tears in his eyes.

Sharon met me as I was heading outside to meet John Adeleye; we were going for a drink. I genuinely thought I was gone after the poor performances. She called out to me, 'Mary!' and I ran over and gave her a big hug. We chatted about our daughters, and she also told me that she saw lot of herself in me, which was a massive compliment and confirmation, because I felt the same way. Like me, she had struggled with weight all her life, along with the ups-and-downs of having children and so on. She was delighted that I was taking this chance at my age, proving that once you hit fifty, it didn't mean you were an extinct dinosaur. The people from the newspapers were lurking in the background and they must have heard bits and pieces of our conversation, because they came up with the story that I was having a nervous breakdown and Sharon had to talk me out of it. No such thing happened, although maybe they just heard me talking about making a mess of my song and wondering if I should go home. 'Don't you dare speak like that!' had been Sharon's instant reaction. 'This is a tough experience. People don't realise how hard it is, so don't be knocking yourself!' But that was all we said to each other. When I read the sob story in the paper, I had a good laugh at it.

We had a day and a night to wait through before we'd find out if we had made it to the next level or not, so I had lots of time to resign myself to the fact that I hadn't made it, and I was fine with that. They had to put the best contestants through, and that just hadn't been my best performance. I knew a couple of the other girls, including Yuli, had done really well, so I accepted that my 'X Factor' adventure was over. That night, we were called upstairs. Dermot was there, waiting with us too. John went in before me and came out expressionless. I couldn't tell if he was through or not before I was brought in. I had to wait a bit longer, though: I was shifted back out of the room because I had come in too early.

I was genuinely surprised by some of the ones who didn't get through, like Yuli and Steve from Scotland. It seems the producers wanted not only a good singer but someone with a good life story. This was all very new to me. I had to wait for a while until being brought back upstairs again, to be told my fate. I opened the door and walked inside. There was a huge fire blazing in the room and the entire film crew was there. There were two big armchairs, and Louis was sitting in one. I sat down in the other armchair and – thank goodness they didn't show this later – I spoke up first. 'Before you start, Louis, I just wanted to say that you have given me such a wonderful opportunity. I'm so grateful. Now, you have a job to do that you don't want to do,' I said, trying to be as upbeat about it as possible. 'I know I haven't made it through. You're not to feel bad about it because I'm happy with what I've done.'

Louis looked at me for a while and then started. 'Well, Mary ...' He paused for ages and I said, 'Will you just tell me, Louis, I'm not going to burst into tears.' He spoke again, 'I mean, you aren't the sort of pop star we were looking for.' I nodded, 'I know, I know! You don't have to tell me because I know that.' I'm sure the poor man was wishing that I'd just shut up and let him get on with it, but I wouldn't because I was nervous and couldn't stop yapping. 'So, anyway,' he said, 'I've made a decision and it wasn't easy. I just want to tell that I'm going to have to ...' Pause. '...take you to the next round.' *AARRGGHH!* Well, I jumped up, grabbed him, I actually lifted him into the air and kissed the face off him. He was crying, I was crying. It was hugely emotional.

Wagner went in after me. I was brought down to the very end of the room to be interviewed, and I couldn't stay still; I was like a two-year-old. I was dancing around, telling the cameraman I had got through. Then I had a moment of panic and told him to stop filming. 'Hang on a minute,' I said. 'I made a hames of my two songs. How in God's name am I going to be able to get up at a live show and sing in front of everyone?' He grinned at me. 'Don't you dare think about that now, Mary!' he told me. I promised not to think about it, but I couldn't stop myself. How was I going to do it, week after week, when I had messed up so badly on my two songs for Sharon and Louis? One of the producers came over to calm me down: 'Mary, you only had two days to learn two songs you had never heard before. Now, come on, you kept the melody, you just got mixed up with words.' When he put it like that, I began to see the sense of it. It was true. I had known neither of those songs but had managed, after a couple of days, to sing at least half of the both of them. It was a great achievement, and I was now one of the twelve finalists going through to the live stage of 'The X Factor'.

The next day I was brought in a Mercedes to Betty and Liam's home in Tallaght, where Deborah was staying. I had spoken to them on the phone, but somehow I had managed not to tell them anything. Everyone was at the house when I got out of the car. I thanked the driver for driving me all the way from Limerick and waved as he drove off.

My nieces were on top of me in an instant, 'Will you hurry up and tell us!' I took a deep breath and said, 'I didn't make it.' They were all lovely. 'Ah, Mary, don't worry about it, sure it doesn't matter.' I couldn't keep up the pretence for more than a couple of seconds before I exploded laughing and told them my amazing news. Then they went wild with excitement and attacked me, 'You bitch! You got through!' I was slapped on the back I don't know how many times; I was covered in bruises afterwards. Then I had to swear them all to secrecy because no one was meant to know yet.

As Tesco were paying me for my time off, I had to ring my boss and tell her I was through to the live show. She knew she couldn't tell anyone except management, but they were absolutely delighted for me. God love her, my boss, Anne, she drove up later on that day with a huge bunch of flowers from the Tesco head office, threw them at me, and then jumped in her car and was gone before any of the neighbours noticed anything.

The newspapers were going mad to find out if I had made it through to 'The X Factor', but I couldn't tell anyone. It would be easy enough for them to track me down in Ballyfermot, so my only option was to get away. My sister, Betty, made me disappear by inviting me to stay at her house, along with my small army of dogs and cats. Nobody knew me there, and that's where I stayed until it was time to go over to London, two weeks later, and face the music on live television, in front of millions of people.

15. The X Factor'

In the last week of September, I flew out of Dublin Airport with butterflies doing acrobatics in my tummy. That was nothing to do with the flight taking off; I was thinking about the great unknown that lay ahead of me, wondering how I was going to perform on live television and dreading the thought that I might make a show of myself. 'Think positive, Mary,' I told myself as Ireland disappeared out of sight down below.

There was a car waiting to pick me up at Heathrow for the trip to a hotel, where I would spend two nights with the other 'X Factor' contestants. We were told that they hadn't finished decorating the 'X Factor' house, so we couldn't move in right away. I thought this was hilarious as they had had a whole bleedin' year to get it sorted! On the morning of the third day, a fleet of cars came to pick us up for the transfer to the house and everyone was rushing around with bags, chatting madly and really excited about the next stage of this grand adventure. There were now sixteen finalists in the group as Wagner, Paije Richardson, Treyc Cohen and Diva Fever had been added to the contest as wild cards, having failed to make it through the earlier judging process. Then there was Matt Cardle, Nicolo Festa, Aidan Grimshaw, Rebecca Ferguson, Cher Lloyd, Katie Waissel, John Adeleye, Storm Lee, Belle Amie, F.Y.D, One Direction and myself. The house was obviously going to be a big barn of a place, I thought.

As the convoy of cars made its way up a very exclusive road, I couldn't help admiring all the big mansions behind massive gates. We were definitely on millionaires' row, I remember thinking. Then the cars slowed down at the end of the leafy road and I realised we were actually stopping at one of those mansions. We couldn't see the house at first because it was shielded by lots of big trees. The cars didn't take us up to the entrance; instead, we all had to get out some distance back and walk up to it, so that the 'X Factor' crew could film our arrival.

I must admit that I was disappointed when I saw the size of the house from the outside when it finally came into view. 'How the hell are we all going to fit in here?' I said. But when we went through the entrance door, we realised that the exterior was deceptive because it was absolutely huge inside. It really was a mansion and far removed from my little two-bed Corporation house back in Ballyfermot. The downstairs area was enormous, with two big living rooms that had a giant TV set in each one; there was a piano room and a massive kitchen. There was also a bedroom on this floor, while upstairs there were six very large bedrooms and four bathrooms. The place was as big as a hotel. It was absolutely stunning. Not everyone got a bed, though, and poor old Wagner ended up sleeping on a couch. The house had a beautiful garden with a large water feature, like a waterfall, and there were fields and countryside in the background. And in the distance I could see Wembley Arena, the venue for the 'X Factor' live show. The house and garden was very private and exclusive. I felt like a millionaire myself at that moment.

We barely had time to settle in before being whisked off to the studios in Wembley Arena, to begin rehearsing for our very first 'X Factor' live show on Saturday, 9 October. When Louis Walsh handed me the song he had chosen for the scariest moment of my life, when I would sing it live on TV for the first time for the four judges and the millions of people tuning in around Britain and Ireland, I flew into a state of panic. The song he gave me was Christina Aguilera's version of James Brown's, 'It's A Man's Man's Man's World', which I was told she had performed at the Grammy Awards. I wasn't familiar with the song. The butterflies in my stomach were doing somersaults at the thoughts of having to master it and perform it confidently. I was a million miles away from my comfort zone with this song. In fact, I had never even considered singing the original version during my karaoke years. I didn't even know the words and until fellow contestant Paije Richardson had sung it at his audition, I hadn't heard it for years. '*Help!*' I thought as I imagined the disaster that lay ahead for me, just as I'd finally been granted my big moment to shine.

'I can't sing this song, there's no way I can do this,' I said to anyone who would listen. Everyone around me was trying to reassure me that it would be alright on the night and not to worry, as I had two weeks to learn it. Oh God, what had I let myself in for? Then I met the vocal coach, Yvie Burnett, and the 'X Factor' music director, Nigel Wright, and I felt a bit more relaxed about taking on the song. They are the best in the business at what they do and as the three of us were around the same age, we clicked immediately.

The two weeks of preparation went by in a flash as I worked on my opening number and before I knew it, it was Friday, the day before the live show. We were up at seven that morning and taken straight to the studio to rehearse, and everyone was stressed off their heads. I was seriously getting cold feet at this stage. My confidence went through the floor as the nerves took over during the rehearsals, so while on a break, I rang Deborah in a bit of a state and told her I didn't think I could go through with it, and that I might just come home.

Deborah was having none of it. 'Don't you start!' she wailed. 'After all we've gone through for this? Don't you dare come home yet!' Holy Moses, which one is the mother here? I thought. Deborah was right, of course. It would have been stupid to throw in the towel having gone that far. It would also have been one of the biggest mistakes of my life. I agreed to stay, but, not surprisingly, I didn't sleep a wink that night and felt exhausted when I woke up on Saturday morning, still sick with nerves. I don't think any of us slept that Friday night – we were tense, nervous and, yes, very excited. By the time we got to the studios, the air was crackling with the tension we were generating.

The Saturday rehearsals began after breakfast, at 8.00am, and it was a dress rehearsal too, so for the first time we got to see what we'd be wearing that night. The outfits were chosen for us by the 'X Factor' team. I was told that fashion companies would send in their clothes, hoping to get them showcased by the contestants to an audience of millions. I couldn't believe it when they showed me my first outfit: a black trouser suit. If I had been nervous about singing in front of thousands of people that night, I now went into a fright over my clothes. 'I can't wear that!' I howled. 'The trousers are too baggy. I'm a big girl and they're going to make me look even bigger.'

Actually, I loved Ann Harvey, the company that had sent in the clothes for me; I wore their jeans all the time. They were so generous to me throughout the show, letting me keep lots of outfits, from the jumpsuits to the jeans and a poncho. People always asked me about those jumpsuits. Now, they were an item of clothing I would never have gone near before, because of my size, but I was pleasantly surprised when I put on that first one for the dress rehearsal and found it to be really comfortable. In the end, I consented to the trouser suit and when I was dressed, everyone started telling me that I looked great, so I began to feel good about myself. Then they did my hair. Suffering Jesus! When they dragged every single hair back off my face, I hated it. I thought I looked very severe, like I was about to play the wicked witch in *Snow White*. But there's a reason for everything they do, and the first one was that Louis wanted to give me the 'Diva look'. He wanted plain old Mary Byrne to look like a star. The second reason was that I sweat terribly from my head. Even though my hair would be washed and pampered, in the TV studios I could feel the sweat on my head rolling down the back of my neck. It's the only part of me that perspires, but it's hugely embarrassing; sweat beads on your forehead is not a good look. With my hair styled this way, it definitely helped me to stay cool under the lights. I faltered here and there during the dress rehearsals, but overall it went well for me. Now all I had to do was repeat the performance live on TV!

I would have loved it if Deborah could have been with me in London for that first show. That would have been a massive boost to my confidence, knowing that my daughter was sitting there in the audience, watching me and urging me on. But Deborah had developed a terrible fear of flying after 9/11. She had watched those planes crash into the Twin Towers in New York and had become so traumatised by it, she refused to get on one. I was glad to know that she would be sitting in front of the telly, watching at home, but I did miss not having her there. I did have lots of family support in the studio that night, though. My sister, Betty, was there, along with Liam and their daughters, Diana and Brenda, and Diana's son, Sean, and Brenda's daughter, Diane; their third daughter, my niece, Elaine, couldn't make it because she was working. Knowing that they were out there, among the crowd, was a huge boost. Six years on from his shock diagnosis, it was great to have Liam with us and still in my corner. I thought, well, if Liam can sit suffering with me, the least I can do is go out there, face every challenge and push forward. His determination and courage were rubbing off on me.

As the countdown began to the moment when I'd take the stage, I was in the dressing-room having my make-up touched up. I had to stop myself hyperventilating. I was so nervous, but I was with a great bunch of people who worked in the make-up and wardrobe departments. They knew how to make you feel at home and give you the right words of encouragement. I became good friends with those people who worked with me, including Liz, the head of make-up. She's small, funny, but quite stern and very focused when she's busy. All of the contestants were nervous, just like me, but I think Liz took special pity on me that night, and she gave me a wonderful pep-talk that I only half believed. 'You're going to be great. You'll knock them dead!' she said.

Two songs from my turn, I was called out to wait backstage. I was standing there, my nerves shot by now, continually asking myself, 'How in God's name am I going to do this?' Then I did what I always did in a crisis: I blessed myself and said a little prayer. 'Please, Jesus, be with me. If I go tonight, well and good, but just give me the voice. Don't let me forget the words, or the melody, just let me do this for everyone at home. And please walk onto the stage with me.' I also asked my Mam and Dad to walk out on stage with me, too, and any of my other friends and relatives who had passed over. So that first night, as I waited there in the wings, I really felt I had a crowd around me and that they were lined up and ready to do something fierce if anyone said a bad word to me. 'You upset her, Simon Cowell, and we'll flatten you!'

Suddenly, I heard the music to introduce me and they were playing the little film about my journey to the competition. It was time.

Someone led me up the stairs. I swear to God, every single negative feeling and nerve that had ever stopped me from singing in the past came back a hundred-fold during those last few steps to the stage. This time, though, I was determined they weren't going to get the better of me. They were there, but I wasn't about to give in to them. Just before I walked out, Yvie Burnett said to me, 'Put a rocket up it! Give it all you have and just lift them off the stage with you.'

I was shaking from head to toe. When I stepped out onto the stage, the video clip of me was still playing to build up the excitement. I grasped the microphone to stop my hands from shaking, looked down at Louis, and then scanned the audience, trying desperately to find Betty, Liam and all the gang among the strangers. It took a few seconds to spot them, but once I did, I felt the family coming around me and the nerves started to recede. Then the first notes of my music started, 'It's a Man's Man's Man's World', and it was weird – the nerves simply disappeared and pure adrenaline kicked in instead. I heard Yvie's words in my head, and I gave it everything I had. The words of the song came easily and I started telling the story with actions. I couldn't believe what I was doing. I was feeling those words, feeling every slight I'd ever endured at the hands of a man and every bit of love I'd ever offered up, regardless of whether it was returned or not. All the bits of my life jumbled together and what came from that was a sense of being at one with the words and the feeling behind the song. It was like magic.

When I finished and the applause started, I had time to notice everything. I could see Dermot O'Leary at the side of the stage. I could see the four judges. I could see the smiling faces in the crowd. Dannii Minogue was the first judge to address me and she opened her mouth to speak, but she stalled because the applause was so loud. That made me feel very emotional, which made me panic a little. They let the crowd go on and I found out later that, at three minutes, it was the longest standing ovation anyone had ever gotten on the show. During those three minutes I saw Dannii trying to talk, and I saw Simon looking down at her to see why she wasn't giving her comments yet. When she finally could speak, Dannii was so generous with her words, telling me, and the millions watching, 'I can only say that that is one of the best vocal performances on the show. It was fabulous. And you know what Simon says about there being a new wave of pop star – you're *it*. It would be an absolute crime if you went back to your day job. This needs to be your day job.'

Louis' expression was a gem. I saw the triumph in his face and knew that I hadn't let him down. He looked at Simon as if to say, 'Up yours!' I had let him down at Boot Camp and again at Adare Manor, but I had finally pulled it off, when it really mattered. 'Oh my God!' Louis declared, 'Mary, the Tesco lady from Dublin, has become a Diva!'

I felt so proud of myself. I had done myself, my family and my friends proud. I hope I never forget that feeling, because it was wonderful. Like Cheryl Cole said in her comments, 'It's like you waited to sing that your whole life.' She was right; I had. The next highlight of that evening was Simon's reaction to me. He said he hadn't thought I was good enough, but now he had changed his mind. Later I learned that I had got the highest public vote as well. It was unforgettable. None of the shows after that, no matter how brilliant some of them were, ever equalled how I felt and the reaction to that first performance. To see all those complete and utter strangers shouting my name and clapping madly for me was such an experience and a thrill that I didn't want to leave the stage. If I had been given the boot that night, I wouldn't have cared because, thanks to that crowd, I already felt like a winner. This was my moment.

After the show, I went back with the others to the 'X Factor' house with a private sense of victory. I realised then that the nerves would come, that I couldn't stop them, but that they'd never take me over and push me under again. I had won the battle. This was where I was supposed to be. I felt I was born to sing on that stage. If I had to describe how I felt standing there, I would say that it was like I had finally come home. This is what God had meant for me all along. I should've been there years ago, but I had let everything else get in the way. Now, finally, I was there, I was focused and I was going to make it count.

16. Behind the scenes

There was the 'X Factor' that everyone saw on their televisions every week, and then there was the 'X Factor' that goes on behind the cameras. The media loved nothing better than to get a 'scoop' on the behind-the-cameras bit, but they didn't always get it right and I found that amusing whenever I was at the centre of some story.

One of the things they loved to report about me was how poor Mary Byrne couldn't cope with all the noisy boys and girls in the 'X Factor' house. That was completely untrue. I had lived on a kibbutz for a year, shared houses during my working life and loved the company of people, so it was never going to be a problem for me. Louis did give me a break at his hotel when I was feeling the pressure of being on the show, so I suppose that's where the stories came from about me not being able to cope with my fellow contestants in the house. But I can honestly tell you that I didn't have a problem with anybody in that house. For one thing, we spent very little time in the house, and for another, all those young lads and girls – and the older ones as well – had nothing but respect for me, and I mean that from the bottom of my heart. The young girl band, Belle Amie, were absolutely lovely to me, especially Rebecca Creighton, the Irish girl from Tallaght, who found me crying one morning and asked me what was wrong. When I explained about missing Deborah and her hugs and kisses, every one of those girls in Belle Amie made it a part of their routine to come up and give me a hug every day. Then One Direction, which also featured a young Irish kid, Niall Horan from Mullingar, Co. Westmeath, heard about it and they started hugging me every day, too. Mind you, young Harry Styles from One Direction would also moon me every so often, but I got used to that.

Storm Lee and John Adeleye were absolute gentlemen to me in the house and while we were struggling on the show. If it wasn't for the two of them, I wouldn't have got through the group-dance sessions. They would stand either side of me and hold my hand. The three of us had a great bond. When Storm, whose real name is Lee Gardner, left in week two after receiving the fewest votes for his performance of Bruce Springsteen's 'Born To Run', John took over the role of looking after 'Mammy Bear', as he called me. I have a huge soft spot for John. His mother must be so proud of him because he's just a lovely, lovely chap. In his day job he looks after people with Alzheimer's and sings to them. Before he left I asked him to record himself singing a Nat King Cole song for me, because he has a wonderful voice.

Italian student Nicolo Festa was the first one to go on the live show, which was a shame because I loved him. He was a very nice guy, though he could be a moody little fecker, but we hit it off instantly. I thought FYD were also lovely lads, but they went out in the first week of the live show, too. For the couple of weeks they were there, they looked after me as well.

When I first met young Aidan Grimshaw, from North Shore, Blackpool, I found him to be something of a strange lad. I only got to know him properly on the post-show tour, and it was then I realised he was a gem, and a heartbreaker, I'm sure. Essex lad Matt Cardle was always very courteous to me. He had his run-ins with Katie Waissel, but he never showed me anything but the height of respect throughout the show and the tour afterwards. He called me 'Mayser' and I was his cigarette supplier. Both he and Aidan constantly asked me for cigarettes, though what I loved about Aidan was that later, when we were on tour and he had the opportunity, he would get me packs of cigarettes in return. I'd say, 'No, I don't want twenty!' but he'd make me take them, explaining that he might have to ask me for cigarettes again. To me, that's the sign of a nice lad. During the show, I wouldn't have seen anyone go without a cigarette, if they wanted one, because I knew how much stress everyone was feeling.

I was always honest with little Cher Lloyd, but there wasn't the big ruckus between us that some people claimed in the media. Cher was a bit of a madam on the show and could come across a bit big-headed at times. She wanted success so badly for her family, and I can understand that. She wanted to make a better life for herself and there's nothing wrong with that, but she made the mistake of blowing things out of proportion, and people didn't like the diva act. Having said that, I thought she was a nice kid. She's extremely talented and I'm very fond of her. Certainly, there were times when she lost her head and I'd have to say to her, 'You're not the only one in this house, get a grip on yourself!' But that would happen when everyone was knackered and stressed. The other big thing that people tended to forget or overlook was how young she was – she had only turned seventeen when she appeared on 'The X Factor'. She was full of confidence when she was on stage, but off stage it could be a completely different story. What I saw in Cher was a young girl battling with low self-esteem and lack of confidence. The papers made her out to be a little bitch, but that just isn't right. During the post-show tour it came home to me how young she was. She has problems, just like the rest of us, and she's doing her best to deal with them. I hope she has great success in her career. I'll never forget when she told me, 'I want this for me, but I want it more for my family!' I really admired her for wanting to make her parents proud of her.

I have to admit that I didn't like Katie Waissel, from Harefield in West

London, when I first met her, but I've grown to love her since then. In Boot Camp, I had seen her from a distance and heard a lot of people talking about her, and I took what they said at face-value and didn't form my own opinion. I judged the book by the cover and I shouldn't have done that. I remember when Storm came into Boot Camp late. Katie knew him from the auditions and was happy to see him, but the thing was that his arrival into the camp was being filmed, and it didn't look good to me when she started screaming and ran and jumped into his arms. It looked like she was trying to steal the limelight. How wrong I was! When I got to know Katie, just as we graduated from Boot Camp to the next stage, I found that I liked her a lot. I met up with her again when I went over to start preparing for the live show and we were staying in a hotel for a couple of nights before moving into the contestants' house. For some reason, the two of us were the first to be brought to the hotel. We checked in, then she turned to me and said, 'I'd love a pint!' I nodded, 'So would I!' We put our bags into our rooms and met back downstairs, and all the while I was wondering how I was going to put up with her. But we sat outside, had one pint each and a couple of cigarettes, and as I listened to her, I saw her vulnerability. This, I felt, was the real Katie, and I found myself liking her a lot. As the weeks went on, I grew to love her like a daughter. Yes, she is pushy, but I realised that it was just that she wanted it so much, she didn't know how to play it and ended up appearing all 'camera-camera' mad.

The fact is that Katie doesn't need to be like that because I've heard some of the songs from her album and she is one talented girl. I don't understand why she's not getting the right breaks at the moment. At the same time, she is the type of person who would do anything for you. My heart went out to her the week the story broke in the tabloids alleging that her 81-year-old grandmother worked as an escort. Katie was already having a rough week, so the 'X Factor' team waited until after the show to tell her. I was in a room nearby and I suddenly heard someone wailing, 'Oh my God! I don't believe this!' I remember thinking, 'Oh, it's just Katie again', but I didn't know about the story.

When we got back to the house that night, I went outside for a cigarette and she came out and asked me, 'Did you hear?' I said, 'No, hear what?' 'My grandmother has come out and said she's a prostitute.' I was so shocked that I started laughing. In fact, I was doubled up, barely able to get the words out: 'Your granny is a *what*?' Katie was a bit hurt and said, 'It's well for you, to be able to laugh.' But then when she saw I was in stitches, she began to smile in spite of herself. 'Katie,' I puffed, 'there has to be an element of fun to this. The papers have put you through the mill, and this is just the icing on the cake for them. It can't get any worse than this.' So she did laugh with me, but then cried afterwards. She had had no idea about her grandmother's life and went into shock, as any young girl would do. That night, she sat in my room for ages. There wasn't a lot I could do for her, except be there and listen. The more I saw her being flung into the lion's den, the more I wanted to help her. Today, I still text Katie and we talk on the phone. I love that young one to pieces and she will always be in my life now.

I always got on well with Rebecca Ferguson. She is so elegant and from day one, she reminded me of the beautiful Hollywood actress Audrey Hepburn. I loved the way she dressed and how she carried herself with such poise and style. I always thought she had a great voice, too. She's also a mother to two beautiful kids. We got on well, but Rebecca is very quiet. Sometimes I would find myself questioning if someone could really be that shy. At the same time, she was capable of flying off the handle and telling you exactly what she thought of you, although that was rare. She would annoy me when she was glued to her Blackberry when I was trying to have a conversation with her, but then again, she was young and, like me, had never had much in her life up to that point, so this was all new and exciting for her.

I got on brilliantly with Londoner Paije Richardson. There's something about him that makes you want to cuddle him when you see him. He was very funny and had a real softness about him. Before 'The X Factor' he was an extra in the *Harry Potter* films, but he can't make up his mind what he wants – whether to pursue singing or acting. I fell head over heels in love with him; he was like the son I never had. He used to stick by me, and I think that's a lovely trait to see in a young man. He treated me like his mother, but made me laugh as well. He used to show me the songs he was writing, and I have nothing but good hopes for him. I love him to bits!

I also got on great with Treyc Cohen, while Diva Fever were a howl. I got very close to those two lads, Craig and Joe. They were two of the nicest guys you could ever meet and they deserved a lot more than they got. They had talent, big hearts and a lovely gentleness about them.

Despite what you might have heard through the media, Wagner and myself got on well together in the house and on the show … and he never had any interest in me romantically. The papers put out a story that I didn't like Wagner, but nothing could be further from the truth. There was also that story about him barging in on me when I was half-dressed and me being very upset by this. I think there were headlines like, *Wagner Walks In On A Naked Mary Byrne!* The truth is, he did come into my room one evening when I was in my bra and trousers, but it was a genuine mistake on his part.

As I mentioned, when we moved out of the hotel and into the 'X Factor' house, there was no room for him at first, so he had to sleep on the couch. Then he got Storm and John's room when they were voted off. My room was facing theirs, with a bathroom in between. On one of the precious few times we had been allowed time off, Wagner had gone for a lie down. It was his first night in that bedroom. I had a shower and was getting dressed to go down and get something to eat. I was sitting there and just about to put on my jumper when Wagner came out of his room and went into the bathroom. I heard the bathroom door open and close, and then instead of turning right, to his room, he took a left, and my door was open. He got as much of a fright as I did to find me sitting there in my bra. He shouted and I shouted because we startled each other, and then he ran back to his room. Mind you, he would have got a bigger fright if I'd been sitting there starkers!

I knew it was a genuine mistake and that Wagner had just been a bit disorientated in the house, but I told some of the others about it later when I went downstairs, playing it for laughs, and a completely exaggerated account landed in the newspapers. It was someone in the house who gave the story to them. They said that Wagner had been carpeted by 'X Factor' bosses for 'barging in on a naked Mary Byrne'. One report was hilarious, stating that my scream was 'one of the highest-pitched notes ever heard on the 'X Factor'!' The honest truth is that Wagner never tried to do anything 'funny' on me. It was a mistake – he had literally taken the wrong turn, and he continued to apologise to me about it for ages afterwards.

When I first met Wagner, I didn't know how to take him. He's a hard man to get to know. I think he's a bit like Marmite – you either love him or hate him. I became very fond of him over time, although he did get on my nerves sometimes, as I'm sure I got on his. I think he saw me as his only friend in the house because we were the same age and I understood him. Wagner is twice divorced and has a young son who he loves to bits, and we talked a lot about parenting. That's why he wanted to be a success on the 'X Factor', for his son, and I identified with that and admired him for it. So, yeah, he had his moments and, yeah, he liked young women – what man doesn't? The dancers were young, gorgeous and wearing tights, so of course he enjoyed that. Apart from that, he was a nice guy: he held doors open for me; if I walked into a room, he'd make sure I had a seat; if I asked someone for a glass a water, he'd go get it for me. He was nowhere near as bad as the papers made him out to be. And in terms of romance between us, well, Wagner likes his women tall, slim and young and he likes his friends short, fat … and Irish!

The young kids on the show didn't really 'get' him. As his English wasn't great – he's originally from Brazil – there were times when he'd say something and it might come out sounding aggressive. The kids would look at me and ask, 'What's he saying?' and I would say to him, 'Wagner, do you mean this …?' He'd reply, 'Yes, yes, yes!' Usually what he meant bore little resemblance to what he had actually said. As a result, he accidentally got their backs up, but they gave as good as they got and, being kids, they did sometimes set out to provoke him. They would call him names and play pranks, but they were just kids. The funny thing is that during the 'X Factor' Live Tour, they all got on great. The tour was nothing like when we lived in the house together.

Away from the cameras, we weren't pampered pop stars in the 'X Factor' house. If there were clothes to be washed or ironed, we had to do it ourselves, using the washing machines and spin-dryers in the house. There was no catering laid on for us when we relaxing there, so we had to organise our own food as well. Most of the time we bought in takeaways, but I did try to stay a little bit healthy for the show by getting tuna salads from the supermarket. Sainsbury's had done an online deal with 'X Factor' and every Wednesday or Thursday their staff would come into the house and cook up a meal for us, giving all the finalists a lesson in how to do it. This was filmed for the Sainsbury's and 'X Factor' websites and shown during the nine weeks of the live show. In fact, we were filmed 24/7 as there was an 'X Factor' film crew in the house with us all of the time as well. You had to go and sit on the loo for a bit of privacy!

All of these experiences brought the housemates together, but we always knew – or certainly, I always knew – that the house wasn't real. It was for the cameras and it made for good television, but when you put people together like that, you're creating a false situation and letting it spark. So I always viewed anything that went on in the house as a bit of a distraction, and nothing more. We definitely got to know each better, and in a more real way, later on, during the post-show tour.

There were perks attached to being on 'X Factor', of course, and one of those was a night out at the Pride of Britain Awards in early November, at London's exclusive Grosvenor House Hotel in Mayfair. It was there that I finally got to meet one of my - and Deborah's - singing idols, Tom Jones. I was sitting down at the end of the room, watching the ceremony at this very posh affair, and I didn't even know Tom Jones was there until he arrived onstage to give out an award. A little later he walked by me and I jumped up and ran, not before kicking off my shoes, screaming 'Mr Jones! Mr Jones!' His son, Mark, who manages him, saw this mad woman in hot pursuit and his initial reaction was to protect his father. 'Keep moving, Dad!' he said. But then he glanced at me and said, 'Oh, hang on, Dad. Stop! Stop!' He had recognised me from the 'X Factor', thank God, and proceeded to introduce me to his amazing father. It was only for a few seconds, but it was the most magical moment for me. Tom Jones put his two hands on my face, and I gazed up into those beautiful eyes that I had gazed at for years and years, but only in pictures, as his son explained, 'This is the girl who sang your song on the 'X Factor'.' I couldn't believe it when Tom Jones said, 'You sang my song better than me.' He was such a lovely man. I really wanted to fling my arms around him, but I was afraid his son would have to drag me off him and throw me to the ground.

That was a great night. I also got to meet Paul O'Grady, Barbara Windsor and Irish boxing legend Barry McGuigan, who actually came over to talk to me! I had watched a lot of his matches and I even knew the one song he had released, 'Somebody To Call My Girl'. Barry knelt down by my chair and told me that he and the whole country was so proud of me. 'I wish you all the best, and if you don't win it, it's a fix!' he added. I'll never forget him saying that to me. Later, Deborah was so jealous when I told her about the people I met that night … and not just Tom Jones, whose singing she's loved since she was in the womb. Deborah is also a huge Paul O'Grady fan, as I am myself. I just think he's just so warm and honest.

That was an incredible night off, but otherwise it was all go. With so much to learn and rehearse, we actually spent more time in the 'X Factor' studio at Wembley than we did in the house. Most of the time we left the house early in the morning and didn't get back until late at night, then all we'd want to do was sleep because the day had been so stressful and exhausting. There was always some kind of practical joke going on among the contestants and crew in the studio during the week days, and that helped to ease the tension. I remember one day, when we were rehearsing, a contestant came out on stage and nobody knew who it was. This singer had a moustache and a big wig. 'Who the hell are you?' one of the crew shouted. 'It's me, Katie!' came the reply. Katie had gone out in disguise for a laugh. You needed those light moments to take your mind off the serious job of getting your performance right for the weekend. On Saturday morning – the day of the show – we'd be in at eight o'clock and you wouldn't have a minute to spare for the rest of that day in the build-up to going live on TV. I did have a laugh with the make-up girls and the hairdressers, who were always trying out new things with me to turn me into a diva. Louis would pop his head around the door and I'd have a bit of a laugh with him, too. Many a time I stood in the hall around the dressing rooms chatting with Dannii as she held her gorgeous little baby son in her arms. She was just like every other mother. 'Oh, he kept me up all last night,' she told me one time.

In terms of the judges, well, I feel to this day that I got lucky when the

'X Factor' gave me Louis Walsh as my mentor because he totally understood me as a person, as a singer and, despite his fame and personal success, he never lost sight of how life-changing the show could be for me. Having said that, I got on well with, and liked, the other judges, too. I felt sorry for Cheryl Cole because I knew she had gone through the break-up with her husband, Ashley, and I know only too well what it's like to lose someone you love. I could relate to that young girl. I think most people just see her beauty and her gorgeous figure, but she's a lovely person, too, and I got on very well with her. She always came over and asked me how I was and touched me on the arm. I agree with the English media when they call her 'The Nation's Sweetheart', because that's what she is.

Dannii Minogue was Dannii: she said what she thought, no more and no less. I found her very nice and I liked and admired her honesty. I thought she was a great judge and a really lovely person. Like Cheryl, she was very warm and would hug me when she saw me. Her baby boy is just stunning, like his mother. I also met her sister, Kylie, and she's like a little doll, very pretty, beautiful figure and bubbly personality and very down-to-earth, just like Cheryl and Dannii were, too.

As for Mr Simon Cowell, what can I say? I apparently called him an arrogant man in some interview, and of course he is, but that doesn't take away from the fact that's he's also a nice guy. He's a real gentleman, and I also find him quite handsome. I was intimidated when I first met him, though. I felt like I was starting a new job and the boss looked a bit fierce, but he's not actually like that in reality. Now, I'm not going to pretend that I got to know him very well, but from what I did get to know of him, I can honestly say he is a very gentle and kind man. He and Louis were always having great craic with one another and enjoying the whole thing.

For me, week one was the most special week of the whole 'X Factor', but by week two, after another standing ovation for my performance of

Dusty Springfield's 'You Don't Have to Say You Love Me', I really felt I was getting the hang of the 'X Factor' lark. That song had long been a favourite of mine, and I was thrilled when Louis chose it for me, even though I was more familiar with the long version. I experienced a bit of difficulty trying to cut it down to fit the allotted TV time for the performance. Nigel Wright was a perfectionist and noticed things that nobody else did. One time, during rehearsals, I sang a song and was a tiny bit off on my timing. No one spotted it, except for Nigel, who made me sing it right through again.

Yvie Burnett, the vocal coach, would stand in front of me and count me in, so I'd have to start when she told me. Yvie is a darling and has become a good friend of mine. I think she's gorgeous, and I'm jealous of her long legs. She has long, blonde hair and the prettiest face, and she looks a good ten years younger than she is. I would love to look like her. Every one of the contestants loved her because she was so kind and approachable.

Nigel, on the other hand, could be a little frightening when you first met him. He has a big build and a bit of a beard and looks far tougher than he actually is. Underneath that hard exterior is a man with a good heart. He has the same kind of aura that Simon Cowell has, in fact. When I later recorded my album with him, I remember him getting annoyed on the first day and I was so grateful that I already knew him – otherwise I'd have been terrified of him. I would have forgotten about the album and ran away from him! He doesn't take any crap, but it's for the good of the record. I loved him just as much as I loved Yvie, and I was honoured to meet both their spouses and children. They looked after me as if I was one of their own. If it wasn't for them, I would have been more homesick. As it was, I was starting to struggle to keep myself going in the midst of all the 'X Factor' craziness, and the toll it was taking on me was beginning to show.

17. Taking the lows with the highs

As the weeks went on, I had some good nights on the show, and some bad ones. One of the good ones was singing 'I Who Have Nothing', after getting it changed from Louis' original song choice, 'Ain't No Mountain High Enough', which I couldn't master and the struggle had reduced me to tears. But I had a terrible performance down the line in November, the night I sang, 'There You'll Be', because I wasn't comfortable with the song and was feeling really worn out.

There had been a lot of trauma in my family before and during my time in the 'X Factor', which I didn't reveal while I was on the show. This was another reason why I was sometimes very emotional when the going got tough, although I also drew on those battles to give me the strength to keep going. There was my gorgeous brother-in-law Liam's courageous fight with cancer, which I had talked about. But also, just before I went for the 'X Factor' auditions, Liam and Betty's daughter, my lovely niece Brenda, almost lost the baby she was expecting.

When she was just three months' pregnant, Brenda lost her waters and was told that it was unlikely the baby would be born alive. Two months later, in April, Brenda was taken into the Coombe maternity hospital and her baby boy was delivered by Caesarean section. He had a Grade 4 bleed in his brain, which is a stroke to an older person, and she was told there was no hope for him. He had actually died upon being removed from the womb, but the doctors had resuscitated him. Brenda had pneumonia and was in a terrible state, while her child was at death's door. The baby's lungs weren't developed, he was on a breathing apparatus and hooked up to all kinds of medical devices. We were all sick with worry and everyone was praying hard for a miracle. As the days passed, he got stronger and then the doctors said he was out of danger. The doctors told Brenda they didn't know where he was getting the strength from, that he just kept fighting. It was a pure miracle.

Brenda called her little miracle baby Dara, which means 'the strong one'. The other strange thing is that Dara is like my own father in so many ways. He has the same big ears and shovel hands – well, they are big for his size. Brenda has a memory of feeling my father's presence in the hospital when she was really bad one night. She remembers him saying to her, 'Everything is going to be okay.' Today, Dara is like a little man that was here in this world before. He's like his daddy, Darren, but so like my own father as well. I believe people come back in certain ways, just to show you that they have never really left. My father had a habit of purring through his lips when he was walking or cycling, and that was the first thing Dara did when he started to make sounds. Brenda says she used to wake up in the morning to find Dara staring at the wall, talking and making that sound with his lips. It's our belief that my Mam and Dad were there with Dara all through his fight. And he is a little fighter. He was born to be in this world and was determined to be in this world.

I was away in London on the 'X Factor' when Dara came home, so I missed all that excitement. He was still hooked up to a big machine when he was discharged, but he had come a long way. Dara weighed just over a pound when he was delivered and was only the size of an adult's hand, but you wouldn't know it today. He's very bright and quick to pick up everything that you say and is adored by his three beautiful sisters, Ciara, Niamh and Diane. The funny thing is, Dara is fascinated by the song, 'I Who Have Nothing'. His Mammy and Daddy sing it to him to calm him down when they're changing his nappy. He looks up and smiles and claps his hands. It's just that one song that has that effect on him. He's such a cute little kid, always smiling and never crying unless he's hungry or teething. My daughter, Deborah, is his godmother and I just adore him.

All that worry over Dara and Liam, along with my pining for Deborah, left me feeling very low many times while I was away in London at 'X Factor'. I must admit that a lot of the bad nights on the show also had to do with not being fit and healthy, in that I lacked the stamina needed to survive week after week under that pressure and coping with that workload. It was a great adventure for the younger ones, but it was tough on me, now a fifty-one-year-old mother, to be away from my daughter and our home. On top of all that I was struggling with depression again.

Depression had hit me badly around the age of forty-five, when the menopause kicked in. I knew something was wrong because I'd always been very regular, but then it all went haywire and my periods didn't come for months on end. One thing I did know for certain was that I wasn't pregnant, because there was nothing going on in that department! When I went to my GP, he told me that, at forty-five, I was too young for the menopause. I pointed out that I hadn't had a period in months, but he still insisted it was too early for me to be going through the change, so he wouldn't send me to be checked out at the time.

I didn't know that the menopause could cause depression, but three years later I was in a bad way. I was feeling very low and melancholic. I thought about the past a lot and was kind of living in a state of nostalgia the whole time. Certain smells would remind me of my mother or father, and I would end up sitting for ages, roaring crying, for no real reason. Then I'd get very moody and wouldn't be able to sleep. I'd think of my mother and start crying and not be able to stop. I don't think I ever dealt properly with the grief after the deaths of my parents. I remember that Mam still missed her parents a good thirty years after they had died, so I don't think we ever finish the grieving process. It just becomes part of our life, that we miss those who have left us. That said, it's not good when grief becomes a debilitating problem, as it was for me.

After I had been off sick from Tesco for six weeks, my doctor finally decided to have me tested, to see if I was starting the menopause. The results came back that, yes, it was a possibility that I was starting it. This was no surprise to me since I hadn't had a period in a year by that stage. They say you know your body better than anyone else, and I think that's true. My doctor spoke to me about HRT, telling me to read up on it and to make my own decision about whether or not I wanted to take it. So I did what he told me and read about it. I didn't like the fact that there were side-effects and I didn't like the way you could still have a period. I was finished with them and had no need for them anymore. In a way, it was very freeing not to have periods, but now I had this depression, mood swings and sweats to deal with!

Then a problem with my thyroid was discovered, and that can cause depression too. It's no wonder that I had got so down and didn't care whether I was here or not. I wouldn't say I was suicidal, but if I hadn't gotten help when I did, God knows what would have happened. I remember days in Tesco when I didn't want to be there because I wanted to be sitting at home, crying. It was a killer to have to get up, get dressed and go do my job that I actually loved. And there were plenty of days when it was too much, even though I had difficulty persuading the medical people how bad it felt. When I had first gone to a doctor for a sick note, he told me sternly that I had to get back to work and just sort myself out.

I went back to the GP and told him I didn't want to go on HRT, but that I couldn't cope with how depressed I felt. We had a good talk and he asked me, 'What about a mild anti-depressant, just for a while?' By God, it was the best thing he ever gave me and I'm still on them. I function just like a normal person, the mood swings have gone and the sweats have eased. My better diet is a benefit, too. Now the next thing I've to do is give up the cigarettes, as that should be an all-round help. I hope to have kicked my ciggie habit by the time this book is written. It did take a while for the anti-depressants to kick in – they say it can take anywhere from six weeks to six months before you start to feel a real benefit. I certainly felt a lot better in six months, but it was another six months before I really felt a whole lot better … and six months more before I felt normal again.

So why, five years later, when I was enjoying the opportunity of a lifetime, did I get struck down by depression again? I think it was a result of the utter exhaustion produced by the demands of being on 'The X Factor'. I got low and emotional, and I really believe that if I hadn't been on those tablets, I wouldn't have lasted my entire run on the show. For me, they were a lifesaver.

The medical care on the 'X Factor' was great and because I was a bit of a wreck, they paid for me to go and see a lovely doctor in London. I told her that at home I was being monitored for thyroid and diabetes, as my father's father had died from diabetes. She had me checked for both. I was cleared for diabetes, but my thyroid came back extra low, and she said that this explained my chronic tiredness compared to the other contestants. I couldn't believe how over-tired I had been feeling, but now at least I knew why. That doctor put me on medication for the problem.

They did go to great lengths to take care of us. One week, I got a Vitamin B injection, as did Matt Cardle. We both needed it because we weren't well and our energy was gone. I was as high as a kite afterwards, but I sang my song and got through the show feeling fabulous. Matt and I were both raring to go after the injection, full of energy and enthusiasm, but then we were both dying two days later when the effects wore off.

Naturally, the 'X Factor' team don't want anyone to be sick because it affects the live shows, so anyone feeling off-colour is sent off to see a doctor immediately, even if it's just a cold. I think it would be much more sensible to make sure that the contestants have the rest they need, preventing them from becoming rundown in the first place. It would save 'X Factor' a fortune on medical fees. There was simply no let-up on the pressure. We were constantly knackered, constantly learning and, I have to say, we all got cranky and nearly killed one another at different times, just because we were so tired. Even the nicest, loveliest people got on my nerves until I wanted to scream at them, 'Get out of my bloody face, I've got problems too, you know!' But I wouldn't have meant it – it was just a build-up of months of stress and tiredness.

Now, this might sound a bit crabby, but I'll just put my tuppence-worth on the table anyway. People think 'The X Factor' is an easy thing to do, but I'm here to tell you that it's far from easy. I heard that Elton John made a comment about people going for 'quick fixes' by doing shows like 'The X Factor', that they don't do their time and learn the ropes by grafting on the pub and club circuit. I agree with him, to a certain extent. I mean, I did all of that myself, but the younger contestants wouldn't have gone through that learning experience. But I couldn't help feeling that if Elton came in and saw what we went through during the ten weeks of the show, young and old, he'd understand that those weeks were nearly equal to years of singing in front of small audiences in pubs and clubs. He'd understand that it wasn't an easy task for *any* of us. Physically, the younger contestants probably coped better than the older ones, but at the same time, I felt that the older ones, who had more experience and common sense, were mentally and emotionally better able to handle the pressure than the younger kids.

Many of the kids on the show treated me like their substitute mammy. I felt I could be useful to them, and be there for them when they came to talk to me and tell me their worries about not making it. I'd try to tell them not to take it too seriously, that all they could do was try their best. 'It's different for the likes of me,' I'd tell them, 'I'm old and worn, while you're young with all your life and years of opportunities still ahead of you. I don't have all those years left.' God bless them but they'd say, 'Oh, Mary, you're not old!'

If you asked me now would I change anything about what I experienced during the 'X Factor', I'd say no, but I might have given you a different answer as I was going through it. Some critics talk about how horrible the 'X Factor' is and have been highly critical of the judges for their sometimes harsh comments to and about contestants. But I went through all that when I started out singing in pubs. There were nights when I had to sing to a crowd of drinkers who thought I was crap; and there were the nights when I sang to maybe three or four people, feeling like a fool. I experienced rejection and people laughing at me. That night in Limerick sticks in my mind to this day. And it happened all over again oon the 'X Factor', but I had to keep telling myself, 'If it's meant to be, it's meant to be.'

Louis Walsh was a huge support to me throughout everything. I don't think I would have stuck it out if it wasn't for him taking care of me. Towards the end he would book me into his hotel, when he was flying back to Ireland, to give me time to myself, away from the 'X Factor' house. Not that there was much time for me to relax – it could often be eleven o'clock at night before I'd get back to the hotel room, but then I would enjoy the peace and quiet. Taxis arrived at seven the next morning, so I had to make the most of every minute I had to sleep and chill out in my lovely hotel room that Louis had personally paid for. He was such a dote to me, so generous. Nonetheless, there were times during the nine weeks I was on the live show that the workload just overwhelmed me …

and one day I snapped.

I remember we had been working non-stop for maybe four or five weeks and it was starting to get me down. I was extremely tired, and at this point I didn't realise that the thyroid gland was affecting me, too. Emotionally, I was all over the place and very worried about the new song Louis had given me for that weekend's performance. It was American country singer Faith Hill's tearjerker, 'There You'll Be', from the movie, *Pearl Harbor*. I had never heard it before, I didn't know the melody and I didn't have the luxury of a two-week preparation before I'd be singing it live. Instead, I had a day-and-a-half to learn the melody and then work on learning the words, and I was in rotten form because it was a bloody tough time for me. By then I had hit my lowest point on the show, around my birthday, on 3 November, when I turned fifty-one. I hadn't seen Deborah for weeks in the lead-up to it. I rang her on the day of my birthday and ended up bawling my eyes out down the phone. Yes, I was working on my birthday and I was working the following day, but I still shouldn't have been crying over it. I know now that I was just worn out in every way, but at the time it felt like I was going a bit mad and throwing a new song at me that I couldn't sing was the final straw.

Simon was always very busy with the amazing career he now has around the world, so we didn't see much of him, but he was available to sort out any problems. I went to see him upstairs in his office, or 'in the gods', as I used to tell him, on more than one occasion. I remember one time nobody was getting the songs they wanted. There was murder over Rebecca's songs; she was turning into a bit of a diva and demanding different songs, which was totally out of character for her. Treyc and myself were also unhappy with the song choices we were being offered, so the three of us kicked up murder and demanded to see Simon. I remember sitting outside his office shaking because we were going in to see SIMON COWELL. When I got in there and sat down, he was just another man to me. After I laid into Simon, I remember him laughing and saying, 'Remind me never to take on a fifty-year-old woman who has a brain.' We got on well. It's funny now to look back on it. It was like I was back in the days of being a shop steward in the factory and just like those times, I was left to do the talking all by myself. As a result I earned the nickname of 'The Moaner'. It's fair to say that I did moan at everyone, including all those lovely people I was so fond of, but it was just that I was so bloody tired, so bloody bored and I wasn't getting the songs I wanted.

After all that worry and mayhem, when I went out onto the stage that Saturday night and sang 'There You'll Be', I wasn't myself at all. I told myself that I didn't care if I went home, that I wasn't going to worry about mistakes or anything else because I'd had enough. I remember singing the song and there was one note in particular that was off. I looked down at Louis' face and thought, 'I can't do this to him'. So I brought myself back, still feeling crap, but sang the rest of the song to the best of my ability. Louis knew how down I was feeling. When I finished, Simon asked me, 'What happened tonight?' I told him I was tired and missing my daughter. Somehow, I got through it and got to stay on for another week. What I didn't say was the truth: that I was at breaking-point and if something didn't change soon, I wasn't going to be able to hold it together.

When I told Simon that I missed my daughter, it was a huge understatement. The biggest torture for me as I struggled to keep up my spirits every week on 'The X Factor' was being separated from Deborah. It really, really got to me, especially on days when I was feeling fragile and vulnerable and unable for the demands of the competition. On those days there would be tears and I'd think to myself, is this really worth it? I know I was being a soft auld eejit, but Deborah is everything to me. It was such a shame, I kept thinking, that she couldn't come to the shows because of her fear of flying. But I understood where she was coming from, and I knew it must have been really bad to keep her away from the 'X Factor'.

My mood didn't get any better when I was given an Elton John song called 'Can You Feel The Love Tonight?', from that wonderful movie, *The Lion King*, to sing on week six, 13 November. I didn't want to sing it. Yvie, God bless her, was doing her best to teach it to me, and I was desperately following her lead, but I was singing it in her voice and it just didn't suit me. It never sounded like it was coming from within me. That was really getting to me and getting me down, making everything seem worse than it actually was.

I wasn't alone in feeling like this – at that stage we were all experiencing problems, due to mental fatigue. The little waif Cher was having breakdowns all over the place. God love her, every time I looked at her, she was crying. Like the rest of us, she was utterly worn out, and she got herself worked up to fever-pitch every week, fearing she was definitely going to be knocked out. Meanwhile, I couldn't believe I was still there; it's not that I didn't care whether I was kicked out or not, it's just I felt ready to go. I was sure that this next one was going to be my last live show. In fact, such was my belief in this that I had already asked one of the producers to book my flight home. They told me not to make a decision until I had spoken to my daughter. I think they were afraid that if the public didn't vote me off that weekend, I was going to do a runner anyway.

So I rang Deborah when I was alone in my dressing room. When I heard her voice, all the front I'd been keeping up for everyone else melted away and I told her that I'd had enough. She said I sounded tired. 'Yeah, I am,' I sighed. 'Sure, you saw me on the show last week and I was in bits. I feel the same this week. I wasn't even with you on my birthday.' She could tell that I wasn't putting on an act.

'Well, it's up to you, Mam,' she said after a short silence. 'Do what you have to do. If you want to come home, come home, but don't say to me in a week's time that you shouldn't have left or I'll just tell you to feck off.' Right, no sympathy there, then. She went on, 'You've put yourself through this just to walk off the show, and let me down by showing me you're a quitter. That means I can be a quitter too in my life.' Wow! This girl has really grown up, I thought, and I felt so proud of her. 'Okay, okay,' I said backing down, 'I just miss you. I'll have a think about it, but I wish you were here.'

What I didn't know was that the low point I was at was soon going to turn into a massive high point: Deborah had already made plans to come over to 'The X Factor' that Saturday night with her uncle Willie, his son, Mark, and her two Westlife-fan friends, Nicole and Fran. Willie had asked me for five tickets, but had given me the names of five other people he claimed were coming over to the show, to throw me off the scent. When the five of them landed at Heathrow Airport that Saturday morning, Willie called me and said, 'I've a surprise for you. I was told to tell you before we get there.' 'What is it?' I asked. 'Deborah's here!' Well, I livened up completely. I was a new woman. We met briefly before I had to sing and if I'd won 'The X Factor', I wouldn't have been happier than I was at that moment. It was like getting an electric charge and I went out on stage buzzing, knowing that Deborah was there in the audience. It made a huge difference. I sang 'Can You Feel The Love Tonight?' and though I didn't give a fantastic performance, it was a lot better than if Deborah hadn't been there. The words of the song meant something to me since she was sitting there, having braved her fear for me.

Now, I say 'for *me*', but I might just remind you that this was also the night that Westlife was the star attraction on the show. You can make up your own mind! In any case, I was just glad she was there, near me. Later, Deborah told me that she had been a bit scared on the plane during take-off, but once they were in the air and her friends were yapping away to her, with Willie and Mark sitting behind her, she felt a bit more relaxed; though the fear didn't leave her completely. I felt so honoured that she had faced down her phobia in order to support me and see the adventure through to the end.

After the show, we all gathered in Louis' dressing room, where Deborah got to meet the lads from Westlife. Of course, they all knew her by this stage. I was a very understanding mother, I have to say. There I was, at one end of the room, and there was my daughter, who I had been pining over for weeks, at the opposite end of the room, chatting with the gorgeous lads, Shane, Nicky, Kian and Mark, and oblivious to everyone else. But I understood. Willie and Mark were delighted to meet them, too, especially fifteen-year-old Mark. And as if Westlife wasn't enough, he also got to meet Robbie Williams and the rest of Take That; he couldn't believe his luck.

Lovely Shane Filan's wife, Gillian, a gorgeous, petite, blonde young woman, was chatting away to me, telling me, 'We've been watching the show and I have to say the way you lit up tonight, knowing that Deborah was in the audience, was just brilliant.' I told Gillian, who just oozes warmth and friendliness, that it had meant the world to me having Deborah there in the audience watching me perform, and that I had felt so proud to be up there representing the both of us. 'So,' she said, 'it would make you feel better if she was here again?' 'Ah, yeah, of course it would,' I nodded, 'but I can't expect her to come again. She paid for this out of her own savings and we wouldn't have the money for her to travel back and forth.' With that, she said, 'Oh don't worry about that. I'll talk to Shane.' I looked at her in shock. 'Ah no, Gillian, that's not what I meant!' She asked for Deborah's mobile number and I gave it to her, and then forgot all about it.

That night, Deborah also got to meet Robbie and the lads from Take That. I remember going through the corridors, being only half-made-up for the show, when I noticed this gorgeous, tall fella coming towards me.

I nearly fell over when I realised it was Robbie Williams, and nearly dropped on the spot when he said, upon seeing me, 'Oh, Mary!' Robbie Williams knew *me*! I gave him a big hug and he whispered in my ear, 'I champion you one hundred per cent.' I don't think I'll ever forget that as long as I live. I couldn't stop kissing him and I'm sure he was thinking, 'Will someone get this one off me!' He was just beautiful, much better-looking in real life, and I would never have guessed he was so tall, and his eyes were incredible. There was something very special about him, he had a real gentleness about him. He introduced me to the beautiful young woman standing next to him as his wife. I didn't know he was married, and I'm sure she would have given me a clatter except for my age, as I couldn't stop mauling her husband!

Robbie asked me where I was going, and I told him I was going outside to have a fag. 'Where do you go around here for a cigarette?' he asked, being a smoker himself. 'Come on, follow me!' I told him, and he did. We went outside and hid behind some portacabins to light up. As we started talking, he said to me, 'Fair play to you for doing this show!' 'You know what,' I said to him, 'when I watch you on stage, as fantastic as you are, I always felt there was a loneliness about you.' He looked at me and said, 'You know what, when I watch you on stage, there's a loneliness about you.' I asked him out straight, 'When you're on stage, and there are crowds screaming your name, do you ever feel an emptiness?' He said yes and I asked, 'What fills it for you?' He replied, 'When I'm singing.' I agreed, 'Same here!' 'I knew I had a connection with you,' said Robbie Williams to me. He went on to explain, 'Thousands of people could tell me I'm brilliant and one person could tell me I'm shit, and that one person will be the one I listen to.' I knew exactly what he meant, and gave him another hug.

Robbie had always been my favourite one in Take That. They had come on the scene when Deborah was very young, but we quickly became big fans of their music. I loved Gary Barlow, too, but Robbie, with his cheeky little face and funny ways, was the star of the group as far as I was concerned. I was quite sad when he left, but I had watched him grow up, go through a fantastic solo career and as he stood outside with me that evening, hiding behing the portacabins, I felt very honoured to be in his company. I remember turning to his wife, Ayda, and saying, 'Please look after him. He seems to be very happy with you and he needs someone to take care of him.' She said, 'Yes, I know he does.' Then the both of them invited me to stay in their house should I ever visit Los Angeles. I told them I had been there years before and would love to return, this time hopefully as a singer. 'Come stay with us when you get to LA,' Robbie said. 'Just find out where I am and come stay in our house.' I thought that was so lovely of him. Maybe one of these days I'll get the chance to take him up on the offer.

It had been a fantastic boost seeing Deborah, Willie and Mark. It made me feel a lot stronger than I had felt for a while, and I was thrilled for Deborah that she had been able to share in the 'X Factor' experience with me – never mind meeting Westlife and Take That and, of course, the gorgeous Robbie. All too soon it was time for her to go back to Dublin, while I had the following week's performance to worry about as I waited to find out what feckin' new song they were going to give me.

When I heard that week seven of the show had 'The Beatles' as its theme, I was still worried. I love The Beatles, but I was hoping that Louis would pick one of their songs that I could actually sing, and not give me one that he would see as a challenge for me. When he told me the song was 'Something', I gave him a big hug; I was so relieved. It's a song I've always loved and it has also been covered by my idol, Shirley Bassey, so it was perfect for me. 'I can do a good job on that!' I howled. When Yvie started working on it with me, I could see in her eyes that she was confident about this one.

The following Saturday night, 20 November, I was getting my hair done backstage before the show when one of the researchers told me that Louis wanted to talk to me in his dressing room. It was getting very close to the time for the show to start and I was as nervous as a virgin on her first night – well, at least back in the days when they used to be nervous. So I said to the assistant, 'But I have to get my hair done!' She was having none of my tantrums. 'Just go down to him for a minute,' she said.

I went down, feeling a bit sulky at the interruption, and tapped at the door, like I always did. When it opened I said, 'Yes, Louis?' I looked into the room, and there stood Deborah. I screamed and jumped on her, half afraid she was only a mirage – I had to get a hold of her to know she was really there. It turned out that Westlife had paid for her and Nicole, her friend, to fly over and stay in a hotel. I was gobsmacked. Don't get me wrong, I always knew they were decent guys, but hats off to Shane's darling of a wife, Gillian, for being the lady that she is. It was all her idea. She's a mother, and she knew what it meant to me. She knew how lonely it would be to be away from your child. When I spoke to Gillian, to thank her, she simply said, 'It was the least we could do, since Deborah follows Westlife everywhere.'

When I later went out on stage to perform 'Something', the diva came out in me big time. I was full of confidence, oozed attitude and enjoyed every moment of the performance. As I waited to go on stage I heard Simon Cowell saying in the pre-recorded video build-up, 'Mary is not in this to come second. Mary is in this to win, believe me!' That made me feel good as I hit the stage. When I finished, I just knew by the reaction of the audience that it had gone down well with them, too. Then I saw Louis clapping like a little demon, with a big, happy, smiley face on him. Afterwards, Dannii Minogue, the first judge to comment, said, 'That was up there with your best, best performance,' adding, 'You need to have that confidence every time you perform, though.' Cheryl said, 'You sing with such experience, it's because you've lived life.' Simon was great, too, saying, 'As annoying as this is, Louis did choose absolutely the right song. You sang much better than last week. And, I'll tell you what, you've definitely got your confidence back,' to which Louis chanted, 'Mary's got her mojo back!'

Deborah's visit was the best surprise of the whole 'X Factor', closely followed by my previously shy daughter being brought up on stage during the 'Xtra Factor' show, which follows the main one. I was being interviewed by the presenter, Connie Haq, and she asked me about Deborah being in the audience that night. I went to point her out but couldn't find her, and the next thing I knew she was standing beside me. It was lovely having her onstage with me, and I believe it made a few mothers cry, seeing the relationship I have with her, which is something I feel truly blessed by. Now, I have to admit that I was shocked to find my daughter on the stage beside me because this wasn't the Deborah I knew. She had always been so quiet and shy, but it seemed that the 'X Factor' was bringing her out of herself, just like it was doing wonders for my self-confidence. The experience was changing my daughter before my eyes. Before the 'X Factor', Deborah had depended on me for everything, but now she had made huge strides towards being more independent and more active about taking care of herself.

Seeing how the 'X Factor' was benefiting Deborah's life fired me up with the motivation I needed to carry on. I was going to see this through to the end, as far as I could take it.

18. The End

After a two-month run on the 'X Factor' – which was about seven weeks longer than I thought I'd get – I found myself fighting for survival and pitched against the other golden oldie in the competition, my friend Wagner. I felt it was inevitable, as the competition reached the final stages, that I was getting close to going home. In fact, I was sure that Sunday night, 28 November, was going to be the moment, but I was determined not to give up without a fight.

The song chosen for me by Louis that week was 'All I Want Is You' by U2, as it was a rock music-themed show. It had been a great week in the build-up to that performance as the 'X Factor' single, 'Heroes', for Britain's injured troops charity, had been released and we were taken into a record store to see it on display. I was so proud to be part of that single, which would go on to become a UK number one hit. I remember Dannii saying in the video interviews for my spot that night, 'Mary needs something intensely personal to bring this song to life.' I then said in my interview, 'It's a song about somebody who just wants somebody and that relates to a particular time in my life, with Deborah's father. All I wanted was him. You see, he's the only real love I ever had.'

I felt I did a great performance that night and the audience went wild. 'Mary, it has happened again, they are loving you,' Dannii said. 'You rocked it out, it had so much emotion, I loved the performance,' Cheryl told me and the 15 million or more people watching, before adding,

'That's what I absolutely love about you, you genuinely connect with everything you sing and we can feel it.' Simon loved it, too: 'This is what happens, Louis, when you choose a song that is a good song. I don't know why you didn't do this weeks ago. It's so much better than the Shirley Bassey stuff.' Louis dismissed Simon, saying to me, 'You sing your heart out every week. I know you love Shirley Bassey and Tom Jones because that's what inspires you.'

However, when the results of the public vote came in the following night, Sunday, I was in the bottom three, with Katie and Wagner. The three of us were left standing together in a huddle on the stage as Dermot O'Leary prepared to announce who was leaving the competition. I had my fingers crossed painfully behind my back, but had my 'oh dear, that's okay' face at the ready. The first name called was Katie Waissel, and I couldn't believe it, to be honest. She had performed well. As Katie had the lowest vote, she was eliminated, then Wagner and myself had to sing for our lives in a showdown. My song was the Shirley Bassey classic, 'This is My Life', and it seemed very fitting that I might be leaving on a song like that.

I hadn't gone on 'The X Factor' to win, because I had never believed I could win, but I had done it to prove something to myself. My God, had I proved it, again and again, that I could do it. My confidence had soared like never before and I felt the woman who had emerged throughout 'X Factor' was someone I should have been years ago, but wasn't until now. That didn't make me sad, though – it was better that the diva inside got out late, rather than never. In a way, you could say I was born again on 'The X Factor', and I will always be grateful to the show for that. It wasn't that I thought I wasn't good enough to win, but I knew in my heart of hearts that it was a young person's show and that I'd have to go eventually, but I honestly didn't mind. I had done what I had come to do, and had gone further in the show than I had ever imagined I could. That night, I was ready to give them a blast of Bassey that they'd never forget, and bow out gracefully.

Even though I was bracing myself for my departure, I still had a competitive spirit and I knew by the nerves I was experiencing that day that I wanted to go on for at least one more show. When it was my turn to sing, I gave it all I had and sang my heart out. In the sing-off, I obviously did want to come out on top because I got so nervous that I went into the same verse twice, but I somehow managed to cover it up. Wagner performed what was another great song for him, Nat King Cole's 'Unforgettable', and it was unforgettable and he's an unforgettable character. I was sure he'd done enough to get past me, but then as I stood there on stage, with my knees shaking, I heard Louis, Dannii and finally Cheryl saying that Mary Byrne was the one they were saving that night. It was such a huge relief. Wagner was very gracious in defeat, which was no surprise to me having got to know the man, and I loved his comment to Dermot later when he said, 'I'm happy. I just want to get home to my cat.'

I was through to the semi-final, along with Rebecca, Matt, Cher and One Direction. 'Mary Byrne is in the semi-final of 'The X Factor'.' I had to keep repeating those words out loud to convince myself that they were true. It really was unbelievable that 'The Tesco lady from Dublin', as Louis Walsh had described me, was having such an incredible run on the biggest show in Britain. And it wasn't over yet, although I wasn't kidding myself that I had a chance of winning.

Nevertheless, Louis was behind me, urging me on. 'You can still win the competition, but you need to go out there fighting,' he told me. 'This is your moment. If you get it right, then you're in the final.' I remember saying in the video-piece played before my performance, 'There are going to be five people fighting like mad this week and I have to be one of those people. No more standing back and being nice, saying I'm not in competition because I am in competition. I have to put on a performance that people will say, "Yeah, she deserves to be in the final."' The first song was chosen by Louis and it was The Jackson 5 hit, 'Never Can Say Goodbye'. Hopefully, I wouldn't be saying goodbye, but instinct told me that's what would be happening. As the contestants were allowed to select the second song themselves, I decided on Barbra Streisand's 'The Way We Were'.

The day of the semi-final, I was in a car with Cher, on our way to Wembley for rehearsals. She was very upset, as she was completely convinced that she was going to end up in the bottom two and be in danger of leaving that night. I was a bit worried for her and tried my best to convince her that it would be me, not her, who would be going home. The more I thought about it, the more convinced I was of this. Wagner was gone, and I had been in the bottom two with him the previous week. I turned to Cher and joked, 'Cher, if you don't shut up crying, I'm going to give you a slap!'

'But I'm just so nervous,' she sobbed.

'I'm nervous, too!' I said. 'Look, if it comes down to me and you in the bottom two, who do you think is going to go through?'

'You!' she sniffed.

'No, ye little wagon,' I laughed, 'it's going to be you, of course. It's a young person's show, so stop worrying. Either way, it probably will be me and you in the bottom two, but at the end of the day, no matter how well I do, or you don't, *you* are going to go through because it's a young person's show.'

Having said that, if it was a young person's show, what was I doing still in it? I was consoling her, but who knew what might happen? I don't know if, deep down, I still held out a tiny hope of being in the final, but it certainly wasn't at the forefront of my mind at the time. Rebecca, Matt and One Direction were hugely popular with the public and with the judges, so it was going to be an exciting night on the show – and a nerve-racking one for all of us!

Louis pumped me up before the performance, telling me, 'You have to get out there and own that stage and look amazing and feel amazing. I want you to be in the final.' He had chosen 'Never Can Say Goodbye' for me because it was one of his favourite pop disco diva songs, and he felt I had the voice for it. Brian Friedman then set to work on the choreography for the army of colourful dancers who were going to be on stage with me. When the moment came to perform it live, I felt a surge of confidence and I don't think I could have performed it any better. The judges loved it. 'That was you at your best,' Dannii said.

The reason I chose 'The Way We Were' as my second song is because it was my mother's favourite song. Mam used to get me to sing it to her. I hadn't sung it for fifteen years, but it was so personal to me that I thought it would be a great tribute to my mother. I hadn't thought it through, though, because I broke down crying at the end of the song as it was such an emotional moment. 'Mary, that was a beautiful performance and you look absolutely gorgeous, I don't know why you're crying,' Dannii said, and I then explained the connection with my mother. Cheryl was then cheering me up, saying, 'You came into this competition working on a checkout and your life has now changed forever. You're going to have an amazing platform, there's nothing to be sad about because this is an amazing time in your life.' Even Simon was hugely complimentary, telling me, 'This is not a time for tears, you should be proud. It was a much better version than the first song. You are a good singer. It ['X Factor'] is about finding the next big pop star and whatever happens [tonight], and I genuinely mean this, you are going to sell records, you are going to have concerts. Let me tell you, Mary, you are not going back to the Tesco checkout, sweetheart.' Louis said, 'You are an amazing role model for so many women out there.' I had to stop myself crying again.

Cher did American rapper B.o.B's 'Nothin' On You' as her first song and, again, the judges loved her. Simon Cowell said, 'You represent every teenager who's got a dream, who wants to do what you're doing, and I think if you didn't make the final after everything you've done, it would be a complete and utter travesty.'

As we both suspected, Cher and I did end up in the bottom two and for the first time in a semi-final, the decision on who would go through wouldn't be decided by the public vote. It was decided before the show that there would be a sing-off and the judges alone would choose who would go through to the final from the bottom two.

I knew they would select a young contestant, but I was ready to go and I wanted to go out with a bang. They had given me the same song that I had started the competition with, 'It's A Man's Man's Man's World' and I thought to myself, 'Right, this is *my* final. I'm going to win this last performance.' And I did, at least in my mind. Cher cried through her song, Britney Spears's 'Everytime', and didn't perform it to her full potential. I'm not a rap fan, but when Cher first sang 'Stay', she sent shivers down all our spines. In other words, she was quite capable of knocking me for six, but she didn't do it in the semi-final. As we stood in front of the judges, either side of Dermot O'Leary, Cher was very emotional because, I suppose, she felt her future depended on what was going to happen next.

Then it came to the judges' decision and, naturally, Louis picked me as he was my mentor. But Dannii and Cheryl, who was Cher's mentor, gave her their votes. Then it was all down to Simon, who said to me, 'I have supported you from the beginning. I think that you have been a great contestant and tonight proved what a good singer you are.' The he added, 'I see one of you who can walk away from this competition with pride and a future and change their lives.' He was referring to me because he was about to send me home … and send Cher on to the final, which is what happened seconds later. Cher came over to me and cried, 'I'm sorry!' and I said to her, 'I told you not to be worrying!' You can see me saying that to her on the recording. I hugged her and whispered, 'Cher, you're through. Now relax and enjoy yourself. I'm happy to be going home, honestly I am.' 'Are you sure?' she said through tears. 'Positive!' I replied, with as big a smile as I could manage.

Later, the two of us were once again in the car together, on the way back to the house, and she was still crying. 'Now, Cher, I'm going to feckin' kill you if you don't stop,' I bellowed. I could always make her laugh when I spoke to her like that.

I'm very glad today that Cher made it to the final, but I'd be lying if I said there wasn't a part of me that wanted to go through that night for Louis, and for the people who were voting for me. Although this was for my family and me, I did look down from the stage at the Louismeister sitting there, all tensed up in the judge's seat as I performed week after week, and I wanted so badly to do well for him. He had been more than a mentor to me, he had been a rock throughout the competition, there for me at the low points and the high points, and I would have loved to have given him a final to remember. It wasn't to be, but I'm glad we got that far, especially as no one really believed 'the Tesco lady from Dublin' had it in her at all!

I could see why Simon loved Louis, it's because the Mayo man is the best company ever, full of fun and divilment. He would have you in stitches laughing at his antics. There was one particularly hilarious incident during the 'X Factor', at Hallowe'en, when we were asked to wear costumes for the festive event. A huge hairpiece, which felt like it was made of porcelain, was brought in for me to wear. I was told it was worth three grand! It had a massive orange rose and a black hairband, and the whole thing went right over the head. It was huge and it was bloody heavy. They asked me to wear it in the dress rehearsal, but I could hardly move with it on my head. I didn't like it from the moment I laid eyes on it. I had said to Louis before the rehearsal to watch out for the headdress, that I didn't want to wear it. 'What? What?' he said, looking baffled. 'Watch the bloody headdress!' I hissed. After I sang my song, Dermot O'Leary, who was in convulsions with laughter, came up to do his bit, where we pretended the judges were sitting there, but I knew Louis was watching. 'That's a lovely piece you have there, Mary,' said Dermot, while I muttered out the side of my mouth that it was effin' killing me.

I went backstage and Louis met me in the hallway. He grabbed the hairpiece and legged it, with someone shouting after him, 'Careful! That cost three grand!' 'I don't give a shit!' he roared back. Then he hid it and held it for ransom, refusing to give it to anyone. 'Put a flower in her hair, or stick a pair of horns on her, but she's not wearing that thing!' he declared, still refusing to divulge the whereabouts of the precious goddamn hairpiece. They threatened to go to Simon and tell on him. 'Do what you want,' Louis shrugged, 'but she's not wearing it.' And I didn't, thank God. He refused to hand it over until the show was over. I was so grateful to him. The piece was gorgeous, but better suited to a dummy or a model, not me. That was the week Simon Cowell called me 'a Horny Little Devil!' He laughed when I told him later, 'I am, I just don't get it very often.'

I still laugh when I think of those funny moments with Louis Walsh. I just love him to bits. Even though he's no longer my mentor, I want to have a career that Louis would be proud of. I dream of him being able to say to me, in years to come, 'Fair play to you, Mary! You took it for what it was, grabbed it with both hands, and made something out of it. You delivered on all my expectations of you. My trust in you was well worth it.' To hear that from a man I respect, admire and love as much as Louis would make me very happy indeed. He is probably the very best memory I've taken away with me from the 'X Factor' experience, and that's placing him very highly, I can tell you, because the whole thing was such an incredible adventure. I had met inspiring people, I had learned to rely on myself and my own ability and I had caught a glimpse of a future I really wanted to live. That night, as I accepted the fact that my 'X Factor' journey was at an end, I was hoping and wishing that it wasn't the end at all.

19. From reality TV to reality

The week after I went out of 'The X Factor', I sneaked home for a check-up with my own GP. Only my family knew about that visit, so there was no one on the streets. As I was being driven up the Ballyfermot Road, it was my first experience of the local support I had been enjoying during the competition: there were posters of me festooned all over the neighbourhood. The County Bar was displaying a huge picture of me, as were Downey's pub and Tim Young's. My own Tesco store had banners everywhere. I stared out at it all, unable to take it in. I was so overwhelmed that I sobbed my eyes out in the back of the car, and really regretted not having made the final for those people.

When you're in 'X Factor', you're sealed off from everything and it just doesn't register how many people are supporting you back home. I did get some sense of it through my weekly Monday phone call from 'The Mooney Show', on RTÉ Radio 1, but not the whole picture. Derek Mooney, Brenda Donohue and their team took a great interest in my 'X Factor' shenanigans and interviewed me live on air every Monday afternoon. They rang me once while they were doing an outside broadcast and I could hear the Irish audience cheering for me. People also rang in to the show to tell me that they were loving what I was doing on the 'X Factor'. One caller was the actor Frank Kelly, who plays Father Jack in 'Father Ted'. He even suggested that I should sing a song called 'If You Go Away', although that never happened. It was a wonderful feeling to know that this great star of theatre and television was following me on the 'X Factor' and had phoned in to a radio station to suggest a song for me!

I would get phone calls telling me about the busloads coming in to look at Till 40, my checkout till in Tesco, and I'd hear tales about the small fortune Downey's pub was making every weekend from all my supporters, but it all just seemed so far away from me and didn't sink in. The weekly live shows sort of isolate you from the rest of the world, so I really had no idea just how much the 'X Factor' escapades had gripped the Irish nation and, particularly, my own people in Ballyfermot.

It really hit home then how everything I had achieved had been the result of help from all quarters. I had been lifted up on their shoulders. All through the contest, the backing I had received from Tesco, and from my work pals there, was just incredible. Every weekend, in Downey's pub, they threw 'X Factor' parties and cheered everything I did. I remember my friend, Joanna, ringing me and saying that if I didn't leave the 'X Factor' soon, they'd all end up in hospital suffering from liver failure. Every Saturday and Sunday they'd go to Downey's at four o'clock in the afternoon because if they left it any later, they wouldn't be able to get a seat in the pub due to the crowds. They did that for nine weeks in a row!

Whenever I could, I mentioned Tesco on the show because everyone there was just fantastic to me and I really couldn't have done it without their help and support. The management were right behind me every step of the way, paying my wages while I was off in London trying to live the dream. That was a massive help to me because otherwise, I'd have been very stuck in terms of money. I don't think I could have afforded to take advantage of the opportunity provided by 'The X Factor' if I'd been worried about finding money to pay the bills. You don't get paid for being on 'The X Factor', and a lot of the other contestants had to give up their jobs in order to go for the Boot Camp week. So I really can't thank

Tesco enough for backing me in this way. Now, I want to make it clear that Tesco never, ever asked me to mention them at any time during the 'X Factor' as a condition of my wages being paid. I spoke about them of my own accord. After all, I had worked with them for eleven years and loved my job and the people there.

It was funny how Tesco became such a part of my 'X Factor' identity – it just reflects how much I feel about the place. Till 40 had been my till at Tesco in Ballyfermot for the past six years. I had started out in the Bakery section, but when I was moved to the tills, I found my niche in the world! When I went onto Till 40, I began to attract my own regular customers who'd stop and chat with me, and I just loved all that banter with the great people of the Ballyfermot area. I was an awful one for singing when I was sitting there, waiting for a customer. Frank Sinatra was a favourite, and I'd start up singing one of his songs and maybe a customer would come up and sing along with me, and we'd have great craic. Other people would come up to tell me about their arthritis after I complained, loudly, about mine. And that was the way it went – after a while I had a huge amount of people who would purposely come through my till, including the students from Ballyfermot College, which was just beside Tesco. I'd slag them off and they'd slag me back. They started getting on my queue, even if it was very long and they only had an hour for their lunch. I'd be singing to them and they'd jokingly tell me to hurry up. 'Shut up!' I'd shout at them. 'If you don't like it, go to another till!'

I quickly became the 'Tesco lady' on the show and as I carried on through the different rounds and ended up on the live show, the staff started to put signs up around Till 40, declaring it to be 'Mary's Till', along with a photograph of me and an arrow pointing down to it. As bizarre as this seems, Till 40 became a bit of a shrine to me in my absence. I didn't know this during the show, of course, but when I came home and saw it for myself, I couldn't believe it. At some stage they had put a big board up at the back of the till, so that people could sign it. So many turned up to stick their names on it that they had to clean it off every couple of days, so eventually they brought in two big books, and people signed them instead. I still have those books at home. There are signatures and messages from people who travelled from Galway, Donegal, Clare, Cork, Limerick, Wexford and a load of other places around Ireland. They came up to Dublin just to see Till 40. Some of them wrote that their children had tormented them to make the trip to Dublin to see 'Mary's till'. I also recently heard that a crowd came over on the boat from England one day, got a bus to Ballyfermot, came in, looked at Till 40, took photographs, then went back to get the boat home again. I was bewildered by this, wondering why anyone would want to travel across the sea from England to see a supermarket till, but at the same time, I was absolutely overwhelmed by the support that was there for me.

Most of my friends were Tesco colleagues and I was very proud to mention them in the media whenever I got the opportunity. Joanna Barry had been my manager, and for years she had listened to me through all my ups and downs. I often came in depressed and had plenty of difficulties over the years, but Joanna and Jim Minahan, who had been my boss years earlier, always went out of their way to help me out as best they could, assuring me that I was a good worker. They saw me through my first depression after Mam died, when I had to take time off work, but they always stood by me and gave me so many chances. Any other job would have gotten rid of me. Joanna, in particular, was always there to listen and help me out in any way she could. She had to put up with me at my worst. I also got great support from store manager Annie Dowling, who came in shortly before I went for the auditions. I couldn't thank them enough for their help and backing, which came all the way from the top.

It wasn't just the staff and management who got me through the bad days, though, the customers were bloody brilliant, too. More often than not someone would ask how I was and I'd moan, 'Ah, I feel a bit down today.' I was very open, so they knew all about me and they often enquired after my mental health. Not that there were lots of bad days, because there weren't, but the thing was that the customers would reach out and touch me on the hand on days they'd see I was feeling down, and I loved them for their kindness. It was only when I came back that I realised just how proud of me they were throughout the 'X Factor'. Patrick Hughes, who works on the desk at Tesco, would ring me and tell me that all my customers were coming in, wanting to know how I was and requesting that their best wishes be passed on to me in London.

Even though I had seen the level of support on the quiet drive down the Ballyfermot Road on my secret visit home, it still didn't prepare me for my official homecoming. There was talk that the Lord Mayor of Dublin was going to organise it, but in the end it was the staff of Tesco who made all the arrangements, including telling as many people as they could, with just four days' notice. I flew into Dublin Airport on 14 December, and I didn't know what to expect as I arrived back to my home town. The first reaction I got was from the staff at the airport, who all clapped me as I made my way through arrivals. Then when I reached Ballyfermot and came down the road in the car, I just couldn't believe the crowds that had turned up to welcome me. I was so shocked by the number of people, especially considering the fact that I hadn't even won the bloody 'X Factor' for them. It was very emotional for me, seeing all these people I had worked with, drank with, grown up with, all turning out and saying, 'Well done, Mary, you did us proud!' In their eyes, I was winner. It was one of the happiest and proudest moments of my life, a truly magnificent feeling. I cried my eyes out, but then I pulled myself together and gave everyone a song. I sang 'This Is A Man's Man's Man's World' on a makeshift stage, and right then I felt like the happiest woman in the world.

So it was back to reality – sort of. I thought the 'X Factor' would vanish like a wisp of smoke and I'd be back to normal, but the show had started my life rolling in a different direction and I was only too eager to roll with it. All the same, it was very strange to move from the 'X Factor' stage and life back to Ballyfermot and 'normality'. People used to say to me that I wouldn't remember all the low points and the painful times I had experienced while on the 'X Factor' once it was all over, but I insisted at the time that I'd never forget them. They were right, though, or for a while at any rate. It was a bit like childbirth: you forget all the pain involved with the celebration of a new life. I came off the show believing that I was glad to be out of the pressure chamber and that I wouldn't miss it at all. But I did. I missed it terribly. I had lived in a bubble for ten weeks, with all my needs being taken care of by the fantastic 'X Factor' team, who made sure I was safe and well looked after. I didn't have to worry about anything, except my performance. Now, I will say I had a lot of apologising to do to those lovely people, because I was irritable and snapped a lot as I tried to cope with the demands of the show. But once it was all over, I could see clearly how much they had done for me and, yes, how much they meant to me.

One very positive side-effect of the stress of doing the 'X Factor' live shows was that I ended up in much better shape by the end of it. I actually went down almost two dress sizes while I was doing the touring show. I had to strive to be healthy in my eating because of the stamina and energy required to give my best week after week. We lived on sandwiches most of the time, which obviously wasn't good, but whenever I got the chance to go to the supermarket, I'd stock up on fruit. I found myself eating a lot of strawberries and grapes, for some reason. I never weighed myself, but I think I lost about a stone-and-a-half, and I have kept it off and am still wearing the smaller size clothes. The reason for it, I suppose, is that I'm much happier in myself now because I'm doing something I truly love.

I'm also aware of being in the public eye, though not overly so. I mean, I wouldn't make a point of slimming down just because people know who I am, but I can't deny that I feel healthier with the bit of weight gone off me. I also feel better these days, with regards to the arthritis. Eating healthier foods can be a bit boring at times, but I have to admit I feel more awake and energetic. I don't suffer from a bloated belly and I'm not yawning my brains out for no reason, and I love that.

I felt a bit stuck between worlds at this time – I had to do the dishes and pay the bills and take care of my daughter, but I was also getting exciting phone calls to talk about gigs and opportunities and the bright future. The two halves of me were having to live together for the first time, and it felt strange. But I was still determined to do all I could to make the most of everything stemming from 'The X Factor'.

The first gig I got after leaving the show was a guest appearance and performance at London nightclub, GAY. I had emerged from the 'X Factor' to discover, to my delight, that I was now something of a gay icon. This was largely down to the fact that I had come clean about my lesbian relationship, which seemed to strike a chord with people.

I hadn't planned to divulge that bit of my life, but before you agree to do it, the bosses of 'X Factor' warn you that if you have any skeletons in your cupboard, they might be exposed by the media when you are thrown into the spotlight. I read the form they gave us and one of the questions asked if there was 'anything you'd be embarrassed about if it became known, and would it upset your family?' Now, my family knew about my ex-girlfriend and I certainly wasn't embarrassed about it, but I had never told Deborah and I didn't know how she would react to it or deal with it if the story became a headline in some newspaper. I asked the producers if I could hold off signing the form until I made a phone call – this was after going through Boot Camp and before I went on to the live show. They told me that I didn't have to sign the form there and then, that I could bring it home with me and then bring it back to them. So, I went home and told Deborah about my colourful past.

Her immediate reaction was, 'I always knew you were a dyke!' and then she burst out laughing. She was absolutely brilliant in the way she instantly accepted what I was telling her. She didn't want to know any details about it because as far as she was concerned, it was something that happened before she was born and it was my own life then. She just accepted it as my past. She has a great brain like that. She's not a bit like me, who'd want to know the ins-and-outs of the whole thing.

Once I was happy that Deborah was happy with it, I signed the form and handed it in to the 'X Factor' team. I never said anything more about it, but then somebody rang a newspaper and claimed to be my best friend and said that I was a lesbian. A lovely lady from the paper rang me and said, 'Mary, I've an article here. Now, our editor is gay and she thinks this is a lovely story.' She took a breath and said, 'Were you a lesbian?' I knew there was no point denying it, so I replied, 'No, I wasn't gay, but I did have a lesbian relationship.' She said, 'Oh, I think that's brilliant!' The newspaper went ahead and printed the story, but there wasn't any fuss until the gay scene picked up on it, and they were so damned proud that this woman, who sings the way they love, had a lesbian relationship in the closet. It made me more popular with the gay community, which led to the invitation to perform at GAY.

I appeared at the club on the Saturday night of the 'X Factor' final, and had an absolute ball. Afterwards, all the young guys queued up to meet me. The club was packed and the owner, Jeremy Joseph, had to get security guards to stand around me as the young men waited in an area called The Departure Lounge to meet and be photographed with me. To be honest, I hadn't wanted to do the show that night because it started at midnight and I was still exhausted from the 'X Factor' run, but I was so glad that I hadn't turned it down because I really enjoyed meeting those people, hearing many of their personal stories and learning how much I meant to them.

Jeremy Joseph was feeding me brandies to beat the band as I sat and talked with the fans, and I ended up getting quite well-oiled before the night was out. But as drunk as I might have been over the course of that night, I found the whole experience hugely touching. One guy told me that he had been writing stories for a long time and getting nowhere, so he gave up doing it. When I came along on 'The X Factor' and said 'never give up on the dream', he decided to try again. He said that, thanks to me, he went forward with more belief in his work and in himself, and ended up getting his stories published, having insisted to one publisher: 'I'm not leaving here today until you read at least two of them.' He said that watching me on the show motivated him to do something with his own life. So many of those who came up to me for a photograph and a chat had a story like that, saying that I had fired them up with encouragement to chase what they wanted in life. I thought I was out on my own, but it seemed that my struggle and have–a–go attitude was actually helping other people to change their lives. I loved the idea that 'The X Factor' could have such a positive effect on its viewers, and that night gave me a lot to think about and feel grateful for afterwards.

While the transition from 'X Factor' world to 'normal' world was a bit strange, I came away from the show feeling in much better condition physically and emotionally and ready to take on the world. Thankfully, I was going to have professional support in trying to do that, as the 'X Factor' had set me up with a management team through an English company called Modest Management. My personal manager in that company is a lovely chap called Will Talbot, who also manages the 'X Factor' ultimate winner, Matt Cardle. With Will's help and my own new-found confidence, I was determined to build a brand new career as a singer and entertainer.

20. A New Beginning

Other than waking up and spotting the doll and pram Santa had brought me as a child, I can't recall being more excited than I was that Christmas after the 'X Factor'. It was then, as I relaxed in my Ballyfermot home, that I got the chance to look back on the year and think, 'Wow! I finally achieved something amazing in my life.'

Poor old Deborah – my other amazing achievement, as people who know her always tell me – had to organise everything that Christmas because, for the first time in her life, I wasn't around. Deborah had bought all the presents and decorated the tree, but we nearly ended up with no Christmas dinner because she didn't have time to get the turkey and ham. Annie, the manager down at Tesco, came to the rescue with a complimentary turkey and ham for us … and one for all my family! Even though there's only the two of us, I love my Christmas dinner with Deborah. Afterwards, we got our popcorn, put on *White Christmas*, and sang along to all the songs because that's what we do every year; it's our family tradition.

It had been a hectic few months on 'The X Factor', but my life was about to get even busier. The day after St Stephen's Day, I got a call from my lovely manager, Will, to tell me that all the arrangements had been made for the recording of my first album, *Mine & Yours*. Next, I got a call from music producer Nigel Wright, the musical director of 'The X Factor', who said he couldn't wait for me to come over to his studios and pick out my songs. On top of this, I had been given the schedule for an 'X Factor' live tour of the UK and Ireland, which I was told would kick off in Birmingham on 19 February and run through to Cardiff on 10 April, with shows in Dublin and Belfast, which I really looked forward to as they were going to be another sort of homecoming. It felt like everything was now happening so fast.

I didn't think I would get to make an album so quickly. A few weeks before leaving the show, I had received a call from an Irish record label, saying they'd love to do an album with me. I got very excited, and I remember Nigel Wright asking me why I was in such good form. I told him I had got an offer to make an album, and I nearly fell on the floor when he immediately said, 'I'll match that offer!' Naturally I said 'Alright', but I didn't really believe anything would happen. Of course, what I didn't know was that Louis and Simon had already decided I was doing an album with Nigel.

I remember talking about it with Louis in his dressing room on the night of the semi-final. Even though I hadn't made it to the final, Louis was as upbeat and optimistic as ever: 'Well, you're definitely going to get your album. We'll get it all sorted out for you.' I can't tell you how thrilled I was at the prospect of seeing my own CD on the shelves in record stores. That would definitely be another massive dream coming to life – another one I would never have thought possible.

Normally, only the 'X Factor' winner gets a crack at making an album, but the 2010 competition was the first time they gave record deals to five artists and groups from the semi-final and final. This is another reason why I think that year's 'X Factor' was meant for me, because it gave me an opportunity I probably wouldn't have got in any other year. So, my album had been talked about long before I was knocked out of the show. I remember the Sunday night, after I lost out to Cher, Simon came up to me and said, 'I'm sorry you're going, but you have your album.' He genuinely meant that I wasn't to worry and that my album was guaranteed, despite not having made it to the final. A journalist within earshot overheard this, picked it up wrong and did a story claiming that Simon apologised to me for changing the voting system with regard to the bottom two that weekend, by taking it from the public vote. That wasn't what Simon was referring to at the time.

When it came to selecting the songs, I was allowed to choose some of my favourites, with the remainder of the tracks being chosen by Louis and Nigel. I went over to London to record it, and I was happily reunited with Nigel and Yvie Burnett, meaning I was in the best possible hands. The three of us got on really well together and shared the same sense of humour. Whenever we sneaked out for a quick tipple, we'd laugh over the same things and I got to know them both as friends.

It was a bit intimidating at first, going into the recording studio. Before I went in, I was sitting across the table from Nigel and feeling a little nervous, but he and Yvie quickly put me at my ease. As I considered them to be my friends, I wasn't as nervous as I might have been with experts I didn't know. I hadn't a clue about the technology, of course. I'd see them pushing buttons and switches, and fixing the mic this and then that way, but it was all alien to me. All I knew was that I had everything I needed in my recording area, including water, hot tea and honey. There was a chair for me so I could sit down if I wanted to. Everything was for my benefit, so that I was comfortable and relaxed.

One day in the recording studio, the three of us were sitting together and Yvie asked me if I knew what Nigel had done to date. I asked her what she meant and she said, 'Do you know who he's worked with?' Nigel piped up, 'Of course she does,' and then was surprised to hear me say, 'Em, no I don't.' 'Do you not?' he asked. I shook my head. 'All the better for working with me,' he nodded. 'You didn't just take to me because I was a big producer.' Next thing, I'm listening to the names of the people he had worked his magic on, including Barbra Streisand, Madonna, Shirley Bassey ... I mean, he has worked with the very best of the best. I sat there with my jaw hitting the ground and gasped, 'I don't believe you!' Then I went to his house and saw all his photos of the legends he has produced. I was mortified not to have known all that, but it made me even more excited about doing the album with him.

Even before I discovered what a big-shot producer he was, I was already absolutely thrilled that Nigel was going to be my producer. On the 'X Factor', I could hear the quality in his productions – I don't mean any disrespect to anyone else, but Nigel really is a perfectionist. He researches you and really listens to the singer. There was just something different about his arrangements. He wanted the song to sound like the song, and he also wanted to suit the singer.

He told me a bit about working with Madonna on *Evita*. She used to have the lights dimmed and candles lit in the studio when she was recording, to get the right mood. This gave him the idea to do the same with me. For the first hour I just sang away, but when the candles were lit, there was a totally different feeling in the room. He turned out the lights and said, 'Now, act the song! Don't just sing it, act it. Pretend you're on the stage performing it.' This was particularly effective when I sang the U2 song, 'All I Want Is You', which sounded flat when I first sang it. After he told me to act it, it came out much better. I was learning all the time. Yvie was there to tell me when not to belt it out, or to pull my voice back, that sort of thing. I have only them to thank for the fact that when I do gigs now, I know how to breathe and therefore can sing better. I used to force my voice, but I don't do that anymore. I learned that I had a 'head voice', which is a softer voice; Yvie taught me how to do that. Now when I listen to songs like 'Galileo' and 'I Just Call You Mine' on my album, I can't believe that I can sing like that.

I remember well the day I heard the album played back to me for the first time after finishing my three weeks of recording. It was the first week in February 2011, and I was about to fly home to pack for the 'X Factor' tour. Yvie, Nigel and myself went up to the studio in Nigel's house, to hear the results of our hard work. Nigel's home is a lovely house with a swimming pool, but it's not a mansion. It has a homely feel and is the sort of place you could relax in. You wouldn't be afraid to tap your ash somewhere because his wife likes to smoke, too. His wife was very down-to-earth and made me feel at home straight away. They've two little dogs, and I always think that there's something nice about people who keep animals. Their home is located about ninety minutes from London, past Heathrow Airport, nearly in the countryside, in a beautiful area. You see the studio before you see the house, and it's equally comfortable and a very professional set-up.

We'd been there before, to do some recording, and usually when we'd finish a session, Nigel's wife would come over with two bottles of wine for a celebration. On this night, though, when they brought me up to play the finished album, she arrived with two bottles of champagne. As I sat back with my glass of bubbly and a smile from ear to ear, I couldn't believe how well the album sounded. I felt very proud of myself and was giddy with the anticipation of releasing it and letting everyone hear it. Afterwards, I asked Nigel if he'd had to make many changes to the sound, using all the technology that was beyond me. He said he hadn't had to do much, aside from a couple of things. He didn't have to alter the likes of 'Galileo', which is a slow song, because it was just my voice. Nor did he have to touch the Tom Jones song, 'I Who Have Nothing' or The Beatles' track, 'Something'. There were no changes at all made to those songs, they are just my natural voice. I was quite proud of that, but have to put it down to the coaching and tuition of Nigel and Yvie as much as to myself.

Once the album was 'in the can', as they like to say, it was time to gear up for the 'X Factor' tour, which I was warned would be a busy time. Well, that was an understatement! We played all over England, Scotland, Wales and, of course, Ireland. You name it, we played there during three crazy months on the road. It was another whirlwind of an experience. We did sixteen shows in just over one week at the start, and that really was exhausting. Some days we did two shows because there was a matinee, plus we had to meet all the competition winners. Needless to say, I was soon struggling to keep up the pace, but so were the younger performers. In spite of our best efforts, everyone got rundown during the tour.

Eventually, I was forced to take time off, on doctor's orders. I couldn't do the shows in Belfast because I ended up in bed for three days with a very heavy cold, which ruined my voice. I was so upset by that because I had met some of the fans when we arrived at the hotel, and they'd been so excited, saying that they were dying to see me on stage. Even though it was tough at the time, I am so glad I was part of that tour. I loved meeting the people who turned up to see us and I got to practice all the things Yvie and Nigel had taught me in the studio, until I felt my performance was stronger than ever. It was a life experience that I wouldn't have missed for the world.

I missed about six of the fifty-four shows we did on that tour, but three of those absences were due to promotional work for my album, as Sony Music got set to release it. The day the charts came out, I was singing in Sony's studios for fans who had won a Mother's Day competition. When I finished the performance, a Sony executive handed me a bunch of flowers and told me that they were going to tell me how my album had done. Oh God! I thought, I hope this is not going to be embarrassing. Nigel Wright had said to me that if it got into the Top 15, it would be a great result. Personally, I thought I'd be lucky to get into the Top 40. The man from Sony announced that it had gone in at number six in the British album charts, *and* it had gone to number one in Ireland, knocking Adele off the top spot. That was a fabulous moment that I'll never forget. It may never happen again, but what matters is that I achieved so much more than I would ever have believed. I'm just so happy about it. I'm not greedy. I mean, we all want success and lots of number ones, but it won't break my heart if it doesn't happen again, because when it did happen, it was worth it. It was worth every tear, every arthritic pain on that show, even missing Deborah so terribly – it was worth everything to see that album do so well.

The album's success really made me feel that I was truly embarked on a new career – the new beginning I'd hoped for had come to pass. The thing about the music industry, though, is that when one door opens, a load of other doors seem to open at the same time – you can never tell who'll hear something you've done and decide you're capable of something else. That's been the really brilliant thing about this 'new life' – it just keeps getting better!

I was enjoying a quiet afternoon at home in Ballyfermot when Will Talbot, my manager, phoned with some incredible news. He was absolutely beside himself with excitement as he said a sentence I certainly never expected to hear in the whole of my lifetime: 'Mary, you have been requested to sing for the Queen of England on the 19th of May, in Dublin.' Will, being an Englishman, albeit of Irish descent, is a huge fan of the Royals and he thought this was the greatest thing ever. I should have instantly responded, 'Not on your Nelly', just to give him a fright, but I was so excited myself that I just blurted out, 'Oh my God, that's great!' Apart from the fact that Queen Elizabeth always reminds me of my mother, it was a huge honour to be included as part of such an historic occasion. Queen Elizabeth II was coming to Ireland for the very first time, at the invitation of the Irish President, Mary McAleese, and I was going to sing for her. There's not enough times you can say something like that to yourself to make it sink in – it just remains incredible!

When it was officially announced, however, I discovered that there were a few nasty comments on Facebook, calling me a traitor and so forth, which made me feel a bit nervous. I thought to myself, 'Now, what do I do here? I don't have any political feelings about this. I know about my country's past and I admire my countrymen and women who fought and died for us, but I just feel that all of this went on so long ago.' I hadn't lived through the Troubles up North, so I felt I'd no right to comment on them. I believed that the majority of people who lived in the North wanted peace. So I said to myself, 'I'm not going to go down that road. If you want to threaten me, threaten me, but I'm not going to listen to you.'

As far as I was concerned, they were cranks, but it did unnerve me because I didn't want any trouble or shadows hanging over me. The way I saw it, here was a lovely eighty-five-year-old lady who was known, with her husband, all over world and it was an honour for our country to stand tall and welcome her as a head of state. And for me personally, it was a huge honour to be asked to represent my country in front of these icons of modern life. The statement I made, when asked about it, was that while we don't have to forget our past, we don't have to live in it either. We don't have to carry it all the time because the world is very small and life is very short and that would be a heavy burden. I said I believed that peace was the way forward, but I wasn't going to speak for other people who had different experiences. I had made my peace with my own decision, and I was happy with that.

For me, singing for the Queen was a unique opportunity to be televised globally, which made it a smart career move, too. I was also delighted to meet President Mary McAleese, but I must admit that my big moment was meeting veteran presenter Gay Byrne. When I saw him sitting in the audience while I was doing sound-checks that afternoon, in the build-up to the performance, I actually shook with excitement. The Queen was one level of excitement, but Gay Byrne was a whole different level for me because I worship the man. For people outside Ireland not familiar with him, let me tell you that Gay Byrne was our royalty, and still is today. He hosted the most popular TV show in Ireland, 'The Late Late Show', for nearly forty years. He was our Oprah, our Terry Wogan and our Michael Parkinson all rolled into one. I grew up with him, we all did.

When I spotted Gay during the sound-checks at the Convention Centre in Dublin, I went up to him, legs trembling, and said, 'I have to hug you!' I'd never met him before in my life, but I felt compelled to do it. He said, 'Of course,' and I did. I felt that I had known him all my life, which I had, because I had watched him on television and listened to him on the radio from as early as I could remember. My mother had idolised him, too, so he'd been like another member of the family – always in the house via the radio or TV.

It was fascinating to see the royal visit from the 'inside'. We had been brought into our dressing rooms in the Convention Centre very early and security was very tight; you couldn't leave the building again once you had been brought inside. Outside, the Gardaí (Irish police force) were doing a great job on the streets, and I felt a sense of pride looking at them in their smart uniforms, making sure that nobody came to any harm. It was sad that we needed 8,000 guards for such a visit, but I walked with my head held high thinking, these are *our* guys. They just looked so smart, you know, they looked the part. From my dressing room I could see snipers on the roofs of surrounding buildings. I couldn't believe that. I mean it was exciting, in one way, but sad at the same time that they had to be there.

Standing backstage with my manager, Will, before the performance, I was very nervous and kept saying to him, 'I have to have a cigarette!' At one stage there was a complete shut-down in the building because it was close to the Queen's arrival and no one could go outside. 'Oh God! Don't ever tell me I can't go have a cigarette!' I wailed. I went down to the officers on duty and they weren't letting anyone through the security cordon, but I had a chat with them and they very kindly let me out for a quick, and badly needed, smoke. When I came back in, I heard Westlife rehearsing, as they were also among the list of entertainers that night, which included Riverdance, The Chieftains and the Dublin Gospel Choir. The Westlife lads gave me a big hug and it struck me that they didn't seem a bit nervous, whereas I had the jitters. When I mentioned this to them, they said it was because they'd been doing it so long. But then Nicky Byrne confessed, 'Ah, yeah, I am a bit nervous. I think when you stop being nervous, you may just forget about it.' That helped to put me at ease.

During my rehearsal I sang 'All I Want Is You' brilliantly three times. But when I was sitting on the side of the stage watching the Queen and everyone stream in, the nerves hit me big time. By the time it was my turn to sing for the Queen, the President and the rest of the 2,000-strong crowd, I couldn't remember the words of the bloomin' song, which had been given a slightly different arrangement. I sang the first verse perfectly, but I got a complete blank for the second verse and had to make up the words as I was singing. The orchestra knew, the three backing singers knew and I knew that I was in trouble and and ad libbing desperately, but if anyone else noticed, they were too polite to say it to me afterwards. Louis Walsh was in the audience and I'm sure he was wondering what the hell I was singing. I was supposed to give the backing girls a chance to sing a few *oohs*, but that didn't happen. Thank God for the RTÉ orchestra and their conductor, who realised what was going on and guided the musicians to stay with me instead of me staying with them. I was in bits, but at least I held myself together and got through it. I think I was singing the right words, but just not in the right order, but it probably made sense to anyone who didn't know the song. Just as well the Queen isn't – I assume – a U2 fan! Louis texted me later to say I did very well, but I'm sure he was just being polite. He would know full well that I had messed up.

I went back out on stage at the end for the finale, where we were to be formally introduced to the Queen. I was standing beside two guys from The Chieftains, while along the line were Westlife and the other performers, including the dancers from *Riverdance*. I spotted the little white head coming up the stairs in the middle of a huge crowd of security people. Everyone was clapping and she spoke a few words to most of the performers, but then she stopped in front of me. Strangely, I wasn't nervous. I just couldn't stop thinking about how much she reminded me of my Mam. 'Your life has changed, hasn't it?' Queen Elizabeth said to me. I didn't know what else to say other than, 'Yes, Ma'am!' I didn't bow, but it wasn't a conscious thing, it just never entered my head. 'And what's next for you now?' she asked. I told her a bit of what I was doing, then she said to me, 'You've a great voice, I have to say that.' So I asked her, 'Do you watch the 'X Factor' show, Ma'am?' 'Oh no,' she replied, 'that's too late for me on a Saturday night.' However, I'm sure she said she might get to see it on the Sunday, or at some other time. She didn't say she disliked the show and she didn't say that she didn't watch it, so it's left to your own imagination.

I thought the Queen was lovely and very kind to me. She shook my hand and I thought she had quite a firm grip for such an elderly lady. Prince Philip came up to me next and said very loudly, 'Well, what's next for you, Ma'am?' So I told him my latest exciting bit of news: that I was going to be the special guest performer at Neil Diamond's Dublin concert the following month. He got very excited and said, 'Hah! Jolly nice fellow, that Neil Diamond,' and with that he turned to the crowd, leaving me wondering if he was finished with me.

The audience stood up and began to clap wildly. I could see in her face that the Queen was really touched by the warm reception she had received. I've watched her on many occasions down through the years, and I've never seen her smile so much at public engagements. I watched her entire Irish visit on television and thought she looked so relaxed and happy. I was so proud of the wonderful reception she enjoyed in Ireland, and proudly stunned to be part of it. What do you after you've met the Queen, I wondered, is it possible to top that? It turned out that it was, thanks to the 'jolly nice fellow', Neil Diamond, and an unexpected 'angel'.

21. Flying high

When I got the news about the Neil Diamond support gig, I couldn't speak for a good five minutes – which is a long time for me, I can tell you. I mean, Neil Diamond! I had listened to him for years, sung along with him, cried along to his songs, and now here I was being asked how I'd feel about being the special guest at his Dublin concerts in June 2011. How did I feel? Like I'd grown wings and floated off up into the sky, is how I was feeling. I couldn't believe this was actually my life.

While I was experiencing the brilliant side of success and a bit of fame, I was reminded that there is a dark side to the world of celebrity because of what was happening to my friend, Louis Walsh. As I was on my way home one evening from rehearsals for the Neil Diamond concert that weekend, I got a phone call from a journalist. 'Isn't it terrible what happened to poor old Louis?' the female reporter said to me. I had no idea what she was talking about and my first thought was that he'd been in an accident. 'What happened to him?' I asked in a panic. 'Have you not read the papers, Mary?' she asked. I had been rehearsing, so I hadn't seen a newspaper or been told anything about Louis. When I said this, the reporter told me that Louis had been accused of sexually assaulting some guy in the toilets of a Dublin nightclub. I couldn't believe my ears – it sounded ridiculous.

My instant response was, 'Louis Walsh is not that type of man.' She said to me, 'I believe he's devastated.'

'Well, of course he is!' I said. 'Wouldn't anyone be? How dare anyone say that about Louis!'

I hung up and texted Louis immediately, telling him I'd just heard about the story and assuring him that anybody who knew him would know that it wasn't true and that it would soon blow over.

Louis sent back a simple reply: 'Thanks, Mary. I'm sick to the stomach.'

I could understand that. Louis is a very generous man with his time and doesn't have any security. Whenever fans approach him, he always makes a point of stopping and chatting to them. I was so upset that any individual would try to destroy his character like that. I know that over the course of the following days, poor Louis went through hell. It would be another week before his name would be cleared by the Gardaí (police). Despite the retraction, it was still shocking for Louis that someone could make a false allegation and try to tarnish his good name.

Like Louis, I'm a very open person, but that acted as a warning to me that I should never let my guard down totally and that I'd have to be very careful about who I was talking to and what I was saying. Now, I would never allow myself to be alone in a room with a stranger because you just don't know what they'll come out with. I mean, I was always a bit wary anyway, just from watching stars on the telly talking about being stalked or whatever, so I knew that stuff went on. But for it to happen to Louis Walsh, knowing the kind of guy he is, I thought to myself: is this what people do to individuals who are open and trusting?

So, there is a bad side that goes with fame. In fact, there are a lot of bad sides to celebrity, like the fact that it doesn't last very long. You have to be savvy, grip onto it while it's there and enjoy it, while looking after your reputation and everything you're earning, so you're not left with nothing when your star wanes. I took a lesson from Louis' dreadful predicament, but I didn't let it hamper my enjoyment of all that was going on around me. How could I, when I was about to be involved in the performance of a lifetime?

On a beautiful, sunny Saturday evening in June, I stood on stage in Dublin's magnificent Aviva Stadium and thanked Caroline Downey-Desmond, from the Irish promoters MCD, for giving me the opportunity to share a stage with one of my all-time favourite singers, Neil Diamond. The American singing legend had performed concerts in Ireland for decades, but I had never been able to afford the ticket price for any of his shows, so I had worshipped from afar. On that night, then, not only was it my first time to see him singing live, this lady from the checkout till in Tesco was actually sharing the bill with Neil Diamond as a singer. If I had seen this in a movie I would have said, 'That's a bit far-fetched!'

Louis Walsh had told me that it was his friend, Caroline, who made it all possible for me. He said he had played only a very small part in getting me this incredible gig. That's why it was so important to me to thank Caroline publicly, on stage. I also said that I had someone else to thank for the amazing opportunity I had received at this stage of my life: Louis Walsh. At the mention of his name, the 40,000-strong crowd gave him the loudest, warmest cheer imaginable. At that point, the allegation against Louis had not been dropped, but it was obvious that not one person in that stadium believed the story. I knew by the response of the crowd that Louis was regarded as a national treasure and that none of us would let him be put down like that. Someone texted Louis to say that I had thanked him publicly and that the crowd had stood up at the mention of his name and gone wild in support of him. Louis then sent me a lovely text, saying he had been feeling very low, but hearing that had given him a bit of a boost and he couldn't thank me enough.

That really was a fairytale evening for me because as I sang on stage, Neil Diamond was standing just a couple of feet away from me, behind a curtain, watching my performance. He had promised to come and see me perform, and Neil Diamond is a man who keeps his promise. He stayed for a couple of songs before disappearing to prepare for his own show. I had to pinch myself to believe that I was standing on stage with Neil Diamond. While I always made sure that Deborah got to see Boyzone or Westlife or whoever she wanted to see, I had never been able to justify spending money on tickets for myself. Being part of his show was a very surreal feeling, like an out-of-body experience. I was in the spotlight, all dressed up like a diva and singing to a crowd of people who were singing along with me and enjoying every moment. As soon as I stood on that stage, I felt it was where I belonged. People told me it should have been nerve-racking, but it wasn't. I was quite proud, for myself and for my country. I was representing my country on this stage with this huge American singer who was a legend, and that night I felt I was up to the challenge.

What probably played a big role in helping me to hold my composure and keep my nerves in check was the fact that I had met Neil Diamond backstage that evening, before the show, and had been charmed by him. The first thing I had noticed in the corridors around the dressing rooms were notes up on the walls saying, 'Quiet'. Apparently, Neil is one of these guys who likes to rest once he has done his sound-check, so we tiptoed around and whispered to one another. After my own sound-check, I was on my way to get something to eat in the canteen, when an instantly recognisable person walked by me. It was the man himself. I could only stare, with my mouth open, until Deborah pointed out the obvious: 'There's Neil Diamond, Ma!'

'Sssshhh,' I hissed at her. I couldn't eat what I had in front of me, I was that nervous, and I ended up having to throw it away.

I went back into my dressing room, to get ready. There was a knock on the door. Billy, who does my hair and make-up for shows, went to answer it. He turned and started gesturing frantically at me. 'What? What?' I asked, my heart in my mouth. The next thing I knew, Neil Diamond was gliding into my dressing room and saying, 'Hi, how are you?' He threw his arms around me and gave me the biggest bear hug, as if he had known me for years. He shook hands with Billy, who was completely awestruck. As we spoke, I said, 'Do I call you Mr Diamond?' He laughed, 'Call me Neil, for God's sake!' He then proceeded to tell me that he had heard all about my story, adding, 'I wish you the very best of luck in life!' I thanked him and confessed that I was very nervous about the show. 'No,' he said, 'don't be nervous. These are your people that you're going out to sing for. Just sing from your heart, the way you did on the show, and they'll love you. Remember, now, you wouldn't be here if they didn't want you.' He looked over to Deborah and I blurted out, 'That's my daughter, Deborah. She's only here to see you, Neil!' He laughed and said to her, 'Now, you just watch your Mom on stage, don't mind about me!' She was absolutely delighted with herself and busy taking photos of her Mam hugging Neil Diamond.

He made me feel so relaxed. When I got the call to go to the stage, I stood to the side, amongst all the wires, and I was nervous, but then it occurred to me how mortifying it would be if I tripped over a wire, so I calmed my nerves by focusing on not falling flat on my face as I walked out in front of the crowd. I strode slowly out onto the stage and for some reason, all my nerves disappeared and were replaced by adrenaline, and I just became a performer. During the sound check that day, the stadium was empty except for the security team and the stewards. It was actually more daunting then, with me trying to imagine how I would sing to the crowd that would fill it later on that evening. When all the people were actually in front of me, it wasn't as scary. I could see that they were enjoying my performance, which helped me to enjoy myself too.

Neil had warned me to enjoy myself because it would go by so quickly, and he was right. I couldn't believe how fast the time went. I did my best to take in everything. There were a couple of women in the front row who'd obviously had a few bevvies that evening, and they were screaming my name. When I sang the U2 song, 'All I Want Is You', there was a fantastic reaction. Nearly every song that I started got huge applause. I called out, 'Where's my family sitting?' and the whole audience stood up. So suddenly my family was everyone standing in front of me. Meanwhile, my real family were roaring and waving banners, but I couldn't see them. My brother, Jimmy, was there, as was Willie, my nieces, and Betty and my darling brother-in-law, Liam, who was determined to enjoy my big moment despite his pain and discomfort. There was a crowd there who were all wearing the same T-shirts, with a letter on each one, and it spelt TEXAS when they stood together. They stood up for me, too. I mean, they came all the way from Texas to see Neil Diamond, but they gave me a brilliant reception as well.

Everything went like a dream that night, including the Irish weather, which you can never depend on when you do an outdoor concert. I remember singing 'Stormy Weather', a song that Will Talbot had suggested I should do because he thinks I have a blues voice, and we were all afraid it would rain, but I looked up at the clouds during the song, and they were starting to clear. By the end, I didn't want to leave the stage, but next up was the great Neil Diamond himself.

When he promoted the Aviva Stadium concert by appearing on 'The Late Late Show', Neil had spoken about forgetting words to songs and had joked that he was like a doddery old man. I can assure you that there was absolutely nothing doddery about him when he got onto the stage that night: he was magical, fantastic! And he was well able to neck a bottle of beer that somebody had bought him.

There was a group of nuns at the concert, from a hospice. One of the guys from the promoter's company had lost his beloved mother on the previous Thursday, God love him, and he had invited the nuns who had nursed her through her final days as special guests. I was asked if I would meet them? I was delighted to, of course. I found them waiting in the box where I was taken to watch Neil Diamond's performance. When I walked in, there was a fella standing with them. Who was it, only Gay Byrne! I said him, 'What are you doing here? I didn't invite you into my box.' He was roaring laughing and said, 'Watch out for these nuns, they're devils.' 'I know,' I said, 'the carry-on of them!' So, there we were, laughing together and slagging the nuns, who were great craic and a lovely bunch of women. Me and Gay Byrne, like old friends – my Mam must have been laughing to herself in Heaven!

A little while later, President Mary McAleese invited me up to her box. Up I go and who's there before me, only Gay Byrne! I sneaked up behind him and pinched him on the backside. 'Are you following me?' I asked him, making him laugh out loud. I said to the other Mary, 'Mary, I don't want you to go as President, but if you can't stay on, can you put him up for President?' pointing to Gay. He started saying, 'Oh you're just a big charmer. You'd charm the birds out of the trees!' Then everyone there was laughing and chanting, 'Gay for President! Gay for President!' He had a big red face on him. The funny thing is, Gay would later be asked to run for President, in the 2011 race, but decided it wasn't for him. I think he would have made a great Irish President.

It's gas though, meeting the likes of Neil Diamond, Gay Byrne and the President of Ireland inside sixty minutes or so. People wonder at me for not being knocked out by all of this. It's strange, but I just feel honoured instead of bewildered. I don't find that I get awestruck, as some might expect me to. This is my life now and I'm sort of just going with it. It's urging me on to do more and meet more people and ignore anyone who tells me there's barriers or limits to all this. Maybe it's my age or the fact that I'm happy in my own skin, but I feel very at home and comfortable talking to these people. I don't think that I'm better than them or that they're better than me, I just see them as people, just like me. When I walked into that room and met those powerful and famous people, I didn't feel any different from when I'd walk into Tesco: I was as delighted and interested to meet them as I would be to bump into someone on the street who says hello to me. When you're interested in people, everyone is fascinating, and I'm glad that's the way I see things.

By now, I felt like Will, my hard-working manager, was some sort of fairy godmother – whenever he called me, it was nearly always to deliver some wonderful bit of news. It was him who called me about the Queen and about Neil Diamond, and now he had reason to call me again, about a third incredible offer. He told me that I had been offered a starring role in the UK's touring production of *Grease, The Musical*, which had been booked into Dublin's fabulous new Grand Canal Theatre for August 2011. 'Thank you, Lord!' I said, letting out a little scream. After all the years of hard slog, this was a seriously charmed life I was suddenly living!

I had seen *Grease* when the movie was first released, in 1978, and I'd gone to see it over and over in our local picture house. John Travolta made me go weak at the knees, which was a big part of its appeal, but I also loved the music and the whole feel of it. When the stage show started, I dragged Betty's daughters, Diana, Brenda and Elaine, to see it six times each. I bought the soundtrack on vinyl when it was released as an album, and I still have it, then I got the movie on video and, later, on DVD.

I love *Grease, The Musical*. I love the fact that it's set in the 1950s, an era I'd love to have lived in, and I think we can all relate to the characters: the guy who is a hard man in front of his peers falling in love with a girl who is his total opposite, but she has seen his sensitive side. It's fair to say that it's one of my all-time favourite films and stage shows. The idea of actually being in it was almost too much for me – at this rate, I'd have to keep smelling salts by the phone to have to hand for Will's calls!

John Travolta's role, Danny Zuko, was filled by Danny Bayne, a gorgeous young man from England who had won ITV's reality TV show, 'Grease Is The Word'. Danny and the whole cast and production team made me feel part of their gang straight away. I was playing the character Teen Angel. The song I performed, 'Beauty School Dropout', is a great one to get your teeth into. The only other female who had played that part was a woman in South Africa, a large lady like myself, and I had watched her DVD to get a feel for the character. I found her big performance hugely inspiring.

After I got the role, I went over to see the show at a theatre in Bedford, Leeds. British Olympic champion figure skater Robin Cousins, also famous as a judge on 'Dancing On Ice', was playing Teen Angel in it and when I saw his performance I thought, Oh my God! How is a rookie like me going to do that! Then I was told, 'You're not going to be doing it like him, you're going to be doing it your way. 'What the heck is *my way*?' I thought. But I knew what they were saying: I could put my own personality into it.

The show was set to open at the Grand Canal Theatre on 9 August, but I didn't get to rehearse my part until the cast and the whole production arrived in town, and by then I had only two days to prepare for opening night. I know there's not much acting involved in my character, but I was still going to be interacting with people while singing, so there was a lot to remember for somebody who was doing it for the first time.

Then they sat me down to discuss what I would be wearing on stage. Ah, for feck's sake! A *white* suit! It might have looked fab on the late, great Irish singer Joe Dolan, but I'm a large lady and most bright colours just emphasise all your bits and pieces that stick out in the wrong places. Especially a bloody white suit. But when I tried it on, I thought, you know what, this is not about me as a person, it's all about the character I'm playing. I just had to get my head around that. The next big shock was the wig. Originally it was to be jet-black with a huge quiff, but then the wardrobe and make-up people thought it made me look too much of a diva for the part. 'What about a nice blonde wig, like Marilyn Monroe?' someone suggested. Out came the blonde wigs and when I tried them on I felt, yeah, I can become this character.

As I was being made up in my dressing room on opening night, I looked in the mirror and said loudly, 'You're starting to look like Marilyn Monroe on steroids.' Everyone laughed, but I was just trying to relieve my nerves. I was in a lather of sweat, worrying about falling flat on my face and forgetting my song on stage. My opening spot was on top of a big podium and I had to descend down a series of steps to the stage … while singing! As I took my place on the podium behind the curtain, my legs started to shake and I felt I was going to faint. Then I said a prayer that I recited before every performance: 'Jesus, please be with me and help me to remember the lyrics. Dear Lady, walk beside me as I walk down these stairs, don't let me fall. Mam and Dad, I know you're here, just help me to get through this and help me to entertain these people the way they should be entertained.'

The prayer didn't work that first night because I forgot the words to the song in the middle of the performance. But the first thing I remember from that night was the burst of applause, like a bomb exploding, when the curtain went up and a spotlight shone on me. The crowd just went crazy. I wasn't facing the audience at this stage, so I could only see 'Frenchie', the character I was performing with. I turned around and said, 'Céad míle fáilte, dear,' because it was home and I was Irish, and before I could open my mouth to sing the song, the place erupted with applause. It was like some big Hollywood movie star had just walked onto the stage and they just couldn't give that person enough applause.

Then I noticed all the smoke around me from the dry ice used to create the smoke effect. That wasn't there in the rehearsals, so now I really had to concentrate on the descent to the stage. I made it without falling on my arse, but then as I sang to 'Frenchie' my mind went blank and I couldn't remember the words of the song. Little Lauren Stroud, who played 'Frenchie', knew how nervous I'd been in rehearsals, so she was prepared for this moment and she stopped the disaster happening by mouthing the words to me. She gave me a look as if to say, don't panic, I'll get you through this. I could feel that coming from her and it gave me the confidence to go on and get through it and finish the song. God bless, Lauren, she's a beautiful kid and a great actress. The best part of it was that nobody in the audience noticed a thing. At the end, the crowd in the theatre that night gave me a standing ovation. They remained standing long after I left the stage. It had been a frightening and, yes, thrilling experience. I handed one of the backstage crew my mic ... and went straight outside for a cigarette.

The nerves would never leave me, but after that first night I didn't forget the words of the song and as the weeks went on, I had the courage and experience to put more of my own personality into the character of Teen Angel. One night, as I bent down doing a little shimmy, I heard my knees crack. 'Oh, there goes me arthritis,' I said into the mic and the audience went into fits of laughter. It had been a spontaneous remark, with me forgetting I was on stage in the middle of a performance, but from then on I kept that bit in the show and it got a laugh every night. As we headed into the final performances and the final night, on Saturday, 27 August, I didn't want it to end. I was improvising and ad-libbing more and more, and the *Grease* company was saying to me, 'Now we're seeing the real you. We're seeing what you can do once you've got that confidence in you.'

That whole experience of *Grease* has given me the itch to do more theatre. I'm definitely open to all offers, so I'm putting that out there now. Who knows, maybe my phone will ring and I'll hear Will's voice at the other end telling me that I'm going to be starring in *White Christmas*. That's another dream …

There has been one more incredible phone call from Will, would you believe, and just in time for me to include it in the book. I was over the moon to see my own album on the shelves earlier this year and thought nothing could top it, but right now my second, follow-up album is in the works. Universal Records signed me up to their label – which puts me in the company of performers like Lady Gaga, Rihanna, The Black Eyed Peas and Enrique Iglesias, if you don't mind! I'm busy selecting the songs and planning the sound and feel of the album, and I'm like a kid in a sweetshop about the whole thing. I absolutely love tracking down the right songs and piecing the running order together. I won't say too much about it just yet, but so far I've chosen beautiful, forgotten gems of songs that I think people will be very glad to hear resurrected. The album will be out for Christmas 2011, and it's just about the best present anyone could have given me. All in all, not bad going for the girl from Till 40, you'd have to say!

This is my life ...

If you had asked me two years ago, 'what is your life like?', I would have said it was wonderful in terms of my family, but a hard slog a lot of the time, with the daily grind of work and money worries lifted only by the moments spent singing songs on makeshift stages in local pubs. That doesn't sound like much, but it's what I did for years. I would have thought a person couldn't change so fundamentally after five whole decades of doing things one way, but they can – my life proves that.

It's hard for me to sum it all up, these past two life-altering years, because I'm still coming to terms with it myself. How did Mary Byrne checkout woman become … this? A woman who has shared a stage with some of the most talented, famous and powerful people in the world. A woman who is now constantly challenging herself with things that terrify the life out of her, and loving it. It's far from all this that I grew up, as everyone knows. I'm an ordinary person, but I've been given a fantastic opportunity. 'Given' isn't exactly right, though. I'm an ordinary person who, at the age of fifty, overcame every negative, self-hating bit of me to take a very big leap into a very big unknown. If I hadn't taken that first terrifying step, none of this would have happened. I don't have the words to describe how grateful and how proud I am that I found the courage to take that step.

If I had never gotten to live this life, I'd never have missed it, of course. It's too far off my radar for any of it to have occurred to me as a possibility.

Now that I am living it, though, I never, ever want it to end. I've worked hard and dreamed hard to get here, and I want to give myself over to it completely. In a funny way, maybe it's not so different from being the girl on Till 40. When I worked on the till, I had a very tiny sort of local fame – people sought me out to talk to me and have a laugh. They still do that, but now it's because what I've achieved has touched or inspired them, and they want to tell me that. I enjoy a warm kind of celebrity, where people see me as a sort of Auntie or Mammy. A little girl on Twitter wrote to me and said, 'Please Mary be my Twitter Auntie and follow me.' Little things like that mean an awful lot to me. Kids come up to me and all they want to do is hug me. I love the kind of relationship I have with people, and I'm glad God gave me the personality to have that kind of interaction, because it's beautiful.

So this is my life now: I'm still a working mother, but I'm not struggling so hard to pay the bills and I get to spend my days doing what I love: singing. I'm still a sister and a sister-in-law and a friend, and those roles are just as important to me as the ones I play on stage. The boxes for career and family are all coloured in, then, I'm happy to say. That leaves the relationship box, of course, and I have to say that it's rare I do an interview where I'm not asked if there's a man in my life. The honest answer is no. At least, not up to this moment, as I write these lines, but who knows what's in the future for me when it comes to love? I couldn't have imagined the rest, so maybe some unimaginable someone is out there for me.

My dream relationship would be to have a companion, someone who'd come travelling with me. He'd have his house and I'd have mine, and if other aspects came into it, like a bit of nookie, it would have to take place on neutral ground, not in my home and most certainly not in his. I don't know whether it's an age thing or whether it's simply because I've been living on my own for so long and I like my own company and routine, but I just wouldn't have any interest in living with a man anymore. I like my life the way it is, but that's not to say I wouldn't like to have a guy in my life. If it happens, well and good, but I won't lose sleep over it.

Having said that, I know only too well that life is full of surprises, so I'm not ruling out ever living with a man again. But it would have to be a long process of getting to know him, and I'd have to feel total trust in him before I'd even consider taking that step. I wouldn't be taken in easily because of all I've been through in the past, that's for sure. I think I used to give too much, too fast, but I won't be doing that again. The thing about Deborah's dad, Robbie, is that I really loved him and I tried so hard to convince myself it would work, even though my head knew it wasn't going to. After that, I gave myself too fast to other men, where I just hoped it would lead to something solid. I was searching for love, searching for that perfect relationship and I think I allowed myself to be used. It's only now I can see that's what I was looking for ... love. I was insecure and lacking in confidence and I must have felt that love would heal me. My brother, Willie, would often say to me, 'Sickness attracts sickness, alcoholism attracts alcoholism and drugs attract drugs. You see the same things in other people and think it's going to be compatible because they're into the same things you're into.' He's right. I would go after men who wouldn't be able to provide me with the emotional support I needed, and I'd sabotage the good relationships before they'd even get started, through my own insecurities.

I've known a few men since Deborah's father and some of them have been good guys. But with the good ones, I've been afraid to get too involved. Since Deborah was born, I kept to a policy of not bringing men into the house. She had been given, in my opinion, a hard start in life because of not having a father around, and I wasn't going to add to that. I wanted her to have a stable home and a mother who was going to be there for her. There was no way I was going to have different 'uncles' coming in every so often. I couldn't have let her get attached to people, only to have them disappear out of her life – I know how much that hurts. So I blew out lots of relationships because when they got serious I'd start thinking, well, if I bring him home and then he leaves, it will be too upsetting for Deborah.

The thing was, I always assumed they were going to leave me. I just didn't feel worthy of them, so I broke up with men who liked me because of how I felt about myself. I'm sure I broke a couple of hearts, too, through my low self-esteem. It wasn't that I led them on, like I'd been led on, but I ran away from them very early on, saying, 'No, this isn't happening!' That's probably the main reason why I've never had any long-term relationships, because deep down I believed I wasn't good enough for a strong, steady, honest and generous man. Am I ready now? Find me a strong, steady, honest and generous man, and I'd love to find out!

My life is fantastic now. I didn't think I'd ever say those words, but there you go. And when it comes right down to it, I'm not talking about wealth or fame when I say that, I'm talking about stuff that means far more to me. My life is fantastic because I've learned what it is to do your best and achieve something you've worked your guts out for – and that's an incredible feeling. It's fantastic because I've found out that being honest with people is the best way to be, whether that person is a Ballyfermot local or the Queen of England. I've stayed true to myself, and that's been the right thing to do.

My life is fantastic because I've opened myself up to new experiences and new people. I let go of the old fears about looking stupid or failing at things, and I've wholeheartedly given everything the best I could manage on the day. It feels like a kind of mad freedom to do that. As for the people, well, I'm so blessed with the new friends I've met – people like

Nigel and Yvie and Louis and Wagner and Katie, too many to mention, but all of them have given me warmth and respect and a new way of looking at things.

I'd never have felt I deserved the life I have now, sometimes I feel, Why me? Why did I get to have this brilliant adventure? It's a mix of things – work, ability, luck and passion. I know you hear all that self-help stuff about being the only one to hold yourself back, but you know what, now I think it's true. Every single one of us is entitled to happiness, we all deserve it and nobody is unworthy of it. It just takes a bit of belief.

Let me live. Let me live …

www.obrien.ie